CAVALIER
IN THE
WILDERNESS

Also By Ross Phares
(All Available from Pelican Publishing Co.)

Reverend Devil, A Biography of John A. Murrell
  (Pelican), 1941
Texas Tradition (Henry Holt), 1954
*Bible in Pocket, Gun in Hand: The Story of Frontier
  Religion* (Doubleday), 1964
The Governors of Texas (Pelican), 1976

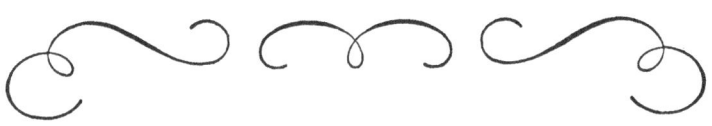

CAVALIER IN THE WILDERNESS

*The story of the explorer and trader
Louis Juchereau de St Denis*

By
ROSS PHARES

A FIREBIRD PRESS BOOK

PELICAN PUBLISHING COMPANY
Gretna 1998

Copyright © 1952
By Louisiana State University Press
Copyright © 1971 by Ross Phares
All rights reserved
ISBN (hard cover): 0-88289-128-6
ISBN (paperback): 0-88289-127-8
LCN: 76-1409

First Printing, March, 1952
Second Printing, October, 1968
Third Printing, June, 1976

Manufactured in the United States of America

Published by Pelican Publishing Company, Inc.
1000 Burmaster Street, Gretna, Louisiana 70053

To My Wife

Preface

FOR THE GREATER PART OF THE FIRST HALF of the eighteenth century, Louis Juchereau de St. Denis was the guiding force on the Louisiana-Texas frontier. It is probable that no other man exercised such a determining influence over so long a period in the early affairs of Louisiana and Texas. His rare talents served a vital and peculiar need for colonial France in a critical and most formative period.

Published accounts of St. Denis have been as inconsistent as the documents of his lifetime and by their very nature, as prejudiced. Interpretations of him have run the gamut from patriot to traitor, from saint to scoundrel. This was a period of heated rivalries. The French slanted their records according to their purposes and prejudices. The Spanish, with equally human weaknesses and zeal, did likewise. Furthermore, the commercial company which administered the affairs of the Louisiana colony was often at variance with the home government.

It was the author's plan, when this research was begun, to present the various sides of the picture in footnotes, along with references to the source materials. But it was soon realized that these annotations and references would run into a fair-sized volume. Footnotes, therefore, have been limited to the bare necessities of clarity. As this change in plan suggests, St. Denis, on first study of conflicting records, appeared to be a most puzzling and inconsistent character operating against an unintelligible background. However, after many years of research and study on the subject, the author sees him as a character of rather consistently fixed purposes and principles.

This work makes no claim for completeness. The ramifications of the many disputes about boundaries, diplomacy, politics, and trade become tiresome to the average reader. After reading as many varying accounts as were available, the author has set down what they indicate to him.

For those who wish to pursue the controversies further the bibliography will serve as a guide. The bibliography has gone through several stages of simplification. No attempt has been made to list all individual documents. Depositories are listed, and the general nature of the records wherein the interested scholar may locate these original sources is indicated.

Dates in the sources vary in many cases. When no definite conclusion could be reached from the documents the most logical date was chosen. Variations in the spelling of proper names are numerous in both primary and secondary sources. Incompetent clerks, many copyings, and translations are obvious reasons. Diplomats, then as now, pretended to be doing one thing while working at something else. Thus their instruments formed a perpetual source of confusion for both contemporary and future historians.

Some tradition has been included in the text, but it has been labeled as such.

Contents

		page
	Preface	vii
I	Wilderness Diplomat	1
II	Warpaths	23
III	Louisiana Becomes Commercial	35
IV	Road to Mexico	43
V	San Juan Bautista	49
VI	Prisoner	65
VII	Texas Re-established	92
VIII	Second Expedition to Mexico	111
IX	For Freedom and Property	125
X	Prosperity à la John Law	145
XI	War of 1719	152
XII	Aftermath of War	170
XIII	Tale of Two Cities	182
XIV	The Natchez War	194
XV	Boundaries	215
XVI	Contest for Control of the Indians	236
XVII	In the Day of Prosperity	249
XVIII	Last Days	257
	Bibliography	267
	Index	273

PREFACE

In a research involving nearly two decades and covering a wide area, names of many persons who have aided the author have, regrettably, been lost. However, the author wishes to acknowledge a debt of gratitude to these, and to those mentioned only by organizations: Biblioteca Nacional de Mexico; Library of Congress; Hill Memorial Library, Louisiana State University; New York Public Library; Northwestern State College, Natchitoches, Louisiana; Sabine Parish Library, Many, Louisiana; Shreve Memorial Library, Shreveport, Louisiana; The University of Texas Library.

Acknowledgments of indebtedness are due the late Mrs. Cammie Garrett Henry of Melrose Plantation for allowing the extensive use of her library and granting many other kindnesses; Miss Clara Mildred Smith, formerly on the faculty of Louisiana State Normal College, Natchitoches, Louisiana, for assisting with research among the Natchitoches Courthouse records; and Mrs. Franklin M. Armstrong, Librarian, East Texas Baptist College, Marshall, Texas, for reading the manuscript and offering many helpful suggestions.

Special acknowledgment is due Dr. Carlos E. Castañeda, of The University of Texas, for direction and invaluable suggestions to the author while he was doing research in the Latin-American Library and Archives of The University of Texas. Transcribed, catalogued Spanish records of The University of Texas archives and Dr. Castañeda's published historical works were important aids in this research.

List of Illustrations

	page
The French halt an Indian sacrifice	19
The wedding of St. Denis and Emanuelle	89
St. Denis in prison	139
Louis Juchereau de St. Denis	205
The burial of St. Denis	265

I

Wilderness Diplomat

THE RENOMMÉE, FRIGATE OF KING LOUIS XIV's navy, floated ghostlike through veils of fog toward the mysterious, broken shore line. The captain, Pierre Le Moyne, Sieur d'Iberville, called a junior officer to his side at starboard. The younger officer was the captain's cousin and uncle-in-law—a man who, like himself, bore a distinguished Canadian name—Louis Juchereau de St. Denis. The captain pointed a bold hand landward: "Louisiana!" he announced, with a ring in his voice. This was a magical word to Frenchmen, a will-o'-the-wisp name that had become alluring but not quite real.

Without waiting for comment, the captain continued to scan the shore line searching for a point called Deer Island, a name he himself had first written on the maps. Islands of gleaming, green-specked sand, reef-covered bars, and hazy timbered silhouettes on the distant mainland floated by.

Presently a wind-swept, water-beaten island loomed ahead—Deer Island. The ship steered northward around the island. Beyond was a bay, a river, and a lone outpost of colonial France.

Anchors dropped. Men rowed ashore. Iberville had returned to his colony. And on this seventh day of the year 1700, Iberville's cousin, Louis Juchereau de St. Denis, had found a new country and had been bewitched by it on sight; and the Louisiana colony unknowingly welcomed its strangest and most fabulous promoter and protector.

So overjoyed were the inhabitants of the outpost of Biloxi at seeing the relief ship that "all the guns and musketry of the fort" had been fired to salute the vessel. There were good reasons to be hilariously jubilant, for since Iberville had left them nearly nine months before they had seen evil times, indeed. What could a handful of men do against such a wilderness! Ragged, rheumatic, pallid men crowded around Iberville, tears from mingled joy and rage trickling through their shaggy, overgrown beards.

Iberville was disappointed at what he saw, but he could not tell these men so. Not now. They demanded to be heard first. They ranted about the cold and miserably damp winter, of an isolation that was maddening, of the eternal watch against the Indians, of the desperate struggle just to keep warm and partly fed, of reptiles and insects that plagued them endlessly, of the despondency of embittered, homesick men looking out constantly toward the sea for a relief ship.

Their story was enough to make Iberville wonder if he had oversold the king on the practicability of immediate colonization; if Louisiana was yet an unconquerable waste; if the simultaneous struggles against the swampland, wild natives, and jealous rivals were too much for France to meet.

But that night, under the warming influence of wine

and cheerful comradeship, men again talked great schemes with the throb of ambition in their voices. Iberville was one who could inspire as well as comfort. A veteran of many campaigns in His Majesty's navy, he was an erect, impressive individual with a sensitive, windmarked face, who knew both the culture of Paris and the savagery of the wild country. Men believed him instinctively. He told the assembly that he brought new hope and new blood. This colony would not die a-borning as some doubters were saying. This Louisiana, it would yet be conquered and made safe for France! It would become so strong that no army of Spaniards or Englishmen could ever take it! From the Gulf even to the mountains of Mexico they would spread the king's province and pour into the coffers of France quantities of gold such as the treasure-seeking Spaniards had never dreamed of. Furs and jewels the like of which the women of France had never seen before would be reaped from the country to the northward before the greedy English could get them.

It was all brave whistling in the wilderness darkness. But this boundless expanse of land was a place to inspire unlimited ambitions in strong men.

The tall, well-dressed St. Denis took both to wine and to talk slowly that evening. He listened and wondered. He was soon to meet many dreamers and men of action in this new world that was destined to go to the mightiest, and his own role was to be one of the most significant in determining who should control it.

Late that night one of the stories took a serious turn. Jean Baptiste Le Moyne, Sieur de Bienville, the brother of Iberville, who had been in command of the fort, told of meeting an English ship in the Mississippi River commanded by a Captain Barr.[1] The captain, it was understood, was seeking to establish a "republic." Bienville, who had an inferior command and realized that he could do nothing by force, had assumed a bold face and advised the English captain that he had made a mistake, that he was in a dependency of Canada and not in the Mississippi; besides, there was a large French colony located a short distance up the stream. The Mississippi, he explained, was farther on to the west. The duped English captain had then turned and sailed out of the Mississippi, heading westward.

The men laughed loudly at the joke Bienville had played on the English captain, but there was grim warning in the incident, and they all knew it. In the small hours of the morning plans were laid for an expedition to the Mississippi to establish a fort. The English might be much stronger next time, and they might not be so easily fooled.

There were good reasons for fearing England and hastening to forestall her without delay. With the end of King William's War in 1697 England had become free to colonize. A strong, ambitious rival with colonies so near gave stern warning to the French that their position was weak as well as precarious. Claims, discoveries, explorations, diplomacy, and tricky bluffs would not hold Louisiana against the land-hungry English or the gold-crazed Spaniards. Only possession would be adequate.

And so, before the sun rose, the fort was bustling with new life. Preparation for the expedition to the Mississippi had begun.

Numerous scouting excursions for routes were made

[1] This name is sometimes given as Banks.

before the main expedition started. Iberville selected sixty men for the expedition, including his two brothers, Bienville and Antoine Chateauguay, and St. Denis. Bienville was dispatched by way of the lakes and Bayou Manchac to secure Bayogoula guides and men and then meet Iberville's party on the Mississippi.

On February 1 the main expedition embarked on a small transport [2] "loaded with everything required for a settlement." [3] The chaplain of the expedition, Father Paul Du Ru, wrote a day-by-day diary, in which many vivid details of the historic journey have been preserved. "On leaving the Bay," Father Du Ru wrote, "we rowed in search of a breeze with the sloops towing us as much as they could. Finally we caught the breeze and we are moving by ourselves, but very slowly." Soon the breeze picked up, and the voyagers sailed westward along the coast into the spreading glow of a fiery sun that set in a cold sky beyond the mouth of the ever-important Mississippi. Darkness came on, and the chill winter evening invaded the ship's cabin, which was none too cheerful. The Jesuit missionary spoke of spiders and rats in the little cabin, which was only three feet high and about seven feet square. Five men were lodged in the cabin, but on a cold night the closeness was really an advantage.

On the second day they passed an island "full of wildcats [4] which the sailors of our transport hunt as game.

---

[2] Iberville had been sick and may have been delayed behind a portion of the party which historians have called the expedition. It is reasonable to believe that St. Denis left with Iberville on February 1, but it is possible that he may have gone across land with Bienville.

[3] Quotations used in connection with this journey are those of Father Du Ru unless otherwise indicated.

[4] Possibly, raccoons.

The animals are killed with clubs. They are very fat but rather tasteless."

At three o'clock on the morning of February 3, the party was aroused. The mouth of the Mississippi had been sighted. Blear-eyed men strained for a glimpse of it in the dim light. To Father Du Ru it looked dangerous and tricky, "entirely fenced in with trunks of trees, petrified and hard as rock," a place where one careless turn of the rudder would have meant disaster.

On the night of February 4, the camp of Bienville was sighted. Bienville came on board and announced that a location for a fort had been made. Later Bienville went ashore, taking with him some members of the party, including Father Du Ru. There in a bark-covered hut the men found an abundance of dried bear meat, venison, and an old Bayogoula Indian "more dried up than the meat."

The site selected for the fort was thought to be one of the most attractive in the region. Most important of all, the Indians assured the French that the place was not flooded during high water. The point was eighteen leagues above the mouth of the river, on the east bank, at a point where the river narrowed. "An edge of open forest, six hundred paces wide, extended along the river bank for about three leagues below them. Two leagues above was a forest of cypress . . . the very wood for pirogues. . . . Behind was an extended view of prairie land studded with clusters of trees." A group of workmen was set to work clearing the ground and making preparations for the erection of the fort.

But the laborers were slowed by a "hundred showers." When the thunder raged the old Bayogoula Indian had his own explanation. It was Ouga, the Great Chief, he told Father Du Ru, "who is firing cannon as we do." Apparently the Bayogoula had found some new expression for his religious beliefs after hearing French cannon fire.

The explorers found the climate of Louisiana most unpredictable. The wind changed to the south, bringing "clouds of mosquitos" and warmth for new violets. It was favorable weather for building. Hunters turned into carpenters and the party went without meat as a result, but the fort began to take shape.

On February 15 Henry de Tonti floated into camp with a party of Canadian traders. There was great rejoicing at the arrival of this seasoned veteran of the wilderness. De Tonti was a colorful character, already a legend among woodsmen. He was known to the Indians as the "Iron Hand," due to an iron hook which replaced a limb lost in battle and which, it is said, he wielded with special effect in hand-to-hand encounters with his foes. He had served in Canada and on the Gulf Coast as the lieutenant of another notable French explorer, René Robert Cavelier, Sieur de La Salle. Soldier, sailor, explorer, Indian conciliator, and fur trader, De Tonti was perhaps the best-informed man of his time on the mysteries of the western frontier.

That night the wind howled through the tall timber, and murky waves of the Mississippi slapped viciously at the river banks. Wet snow mixed with hail, and sleet beat down upon the men and smothered the fires. The men could not keep warm, but talk went on into the late hours of the night.

St. Denis, the tenderfoot, must have listened with amazement to the stories of De Tonti, tales of the great uncharted Mississippi Valley that stretched toward the

Canadian homeland, stories of strange Indian tribes, trade routes, mines, fur traffic, death and starvation of men too weak or unlucky for the wilds. Who could know what secrets this far-flung valley held in its wooded and cane-covered retreats! Such meetings around flickering camp fires stimulated adventurous souls and set men to dreaming of new worlds to conquer, new fortunes to be grasped, new romantic lives to be lived.

St. Denis wondered why Louisiana should have waited nearly two centuries after discovery to be colonized, why it should be among the last strips of land on the continent to be possessed. Was it because of its mystical, treacherous-looking swamps, its tricky, half-hidden coast line, its entangling bayous and lakes that explorers and colonizers had turned back? Was the climate considered too unhealthy, the Indians too dangerous, the land too poor? Had France been too weak, too busy, or too interested elsewhere to seize this territorial prize? Men voiced apologies and speculations without conclusions, and then reaffirmed their faith in their own courage and in the power of France; England and Spain be damned!

To St. Denis this new land was a playground for brave and romantic hearts. Just what resolutions he may have made as the Frenchmen and Canadians sipped sparingly on their limited wine in the late hours of that stormy night cannot be known. But the dark magic of the wilderness had possessed him. Explorers, colonizers, politicians, men of fortune were to come and go, but St. Denis had planted his feet and soul firmly upon the rich black soil of Louisiana. Except for brief periods he was never to leave it again.

When the wind became favorable for ascending the river, St. Denis was sent with a sloop to prepare the way for a visit to the Bayogoula tribe. This was an important mission, for it was essential to the security of the fort to have friendly natives for neighbors, who would serve as a buffer against the English and the hostile savages. From the very beginning of his life in Louisiana St. Denis was the chief "advance man" or scout. Strange, that almost at once he should become the chief diplomat, conciliator, bargainer, and suave contact man in general, but such was his role. His influence was almost uncanny from the very beginning. He had an instinctive understanding of the Indians, such perhaps as no other man in the Southwest ever possessed. He early realized that the man who controlled the Indians would control the wilderness. And in this realization lay his greatest power and success and claim to fame.

In spite of stormy weather the main party sailed up toward the village of the Bayogoulas. Rain slashed down like perpendicular rivers; the wind whipped the fires so furiously that it was impossible to cook enough food. The men ate half-cooked sagamité dipped from simmering kettles with spoons of biscuits. The river was rising, and the treacherous currents and floating deadwood made small-boat traveling hazardous. One of the Canadians injured his arm in an accident, and it had to be amputated with a saw made out of a big knife.

But at times the sun would break through the low rain clouds and penetrate the swampy mist. Then it would be noted that "there was always a fine hedge of green cane and occasionally willows standing out" along the river's edge, against a background of more cane and tall trees that struggled to rise above the swamps. Myriads of wild ducks and other fowls rose from the water's edge, their wet wings flinging sparkling sprays into the sunlight. There were parakeets "by the thousands," birds of strange noises and grotesquely gorgeous hues. They enlivened the drab, rain-drenched forest.

As Iberville and his men approached the village of the Bayogoulas, French beards were trimmed and fresh linen put on. It was understood that St. Denis would have the population prepared for the dignity of the occasion.

The landing place was lined with the natives. A bizarre welcome to the French it was; for the Indians were decked in their best feathers and beads and were singing the calumet, their song of peace, at the top of their voices. In the lead canoe, especially decorated with bright flags, came Bienville, who had gone ahead with St. Denis.

It was an impressive and successful meeting. St. Denis, the master of ceremonies, had arranged matters well. There was something of the stage director in St. Denis. He became famous for such Indian maneuvers.

Like other natives of this section, the Bayogoulas were a religious folk, worshiping their own favorite gods. Even those too poor to own their homes contributed to the building of temples. Their temples were built of thatch and covered with cane. Inside burned the lamps of eternal fire, among many rows of packages piled one on the other. These were the bones of the dead chiefs carefully wrapped in palm mats.

Entertainment of the best quality was in order for the guests. Father Du Ru, impressed by the Bayogoulas, gave considerable space in his diary to their customs: "In the evening there were ball games. The men play in pairs; one of them has a ball in his hand and throws it ahead. Both of them run as fast as they can, throwing a big stick at the ball, and as well as I could make out, the one whose stick is closest to the ball wins the play. Then the one who wins throws the ball the next time. This is a rather strenuous game; nevertheless, it is played by both the old and young. The women have a game also. They separate into two parties between the large posts in the square. Somebody throws a little ball in the center, and the one who seizes it first tries her best to run around the post on her side three times, but she is prevented by the women of the opposite party, who seize her if they can. When she can no longer resist them, she throws the ball to her people, who make a similar effort to run around the post. Sometimes the ball falls into the hands of the other side, which then tries the same maneuver. The games are very long and ordinarily when they are over the women plunge into the water to refresh themselves."

After the games, dances were begun. "The singers appeared first and went to sit on the mat in the midst of the square. The leader of the band beat the measure on a small drum of deer skin. . . . The men wear skins and red linen cloth. The women have on the dresses of bark . . . with a fringe about their waists of the same material, [falling] down like the nets which one puts on our horses in summer to protect them from flies. The nets reach down to the knees and cover them effectively. Each man carries something in his right hand: a hatchet, an umbrella, a knife, . . . and the women have in both hands large bunches of fine white feathers. The singers have very soft voices and the dancers very beautiful cadence. The women are of a surprising modesty. They dance opposite their men, their bodies a little bent, their eyes cast down, . . . marking the cadence admirably well with their bunches of feathers, so that it is only their hands that move. Flutes and drums set the measure. These are played by handsome young people with their legs decorated with small gourds filled with stones with which they make the cadence. There is one thing prettier than anything else I ever saw before; this is the bizarre color with which they paint their faces."

After the dance came the banquet royal. All the delicacies of the tribe were spread in abundance.

At last the great exhausting day of festivities drew to an end. It had been an elaborate reception abounding in good manners, entertainment, and food. But the Bayogoulas knew no limit to hospitality. The French were asked if all had eaten enough, and if a woman was wanted for each man. It is recorded that Iberville answered by showing them his hand, saying that the skin of the Frenchman was white and should not be blended with that of the Indian, which was red and swarthy.

Colonial alliances, it appeared, were off to a good start.

But alarm as well as gaiety was in store for the French at the Bayogoula village. They were told that the English were arming the Chickasaw. That could be for no other purpose than setting this powerful tribe on the French. This reminded them anew that all the arts of diplomacy, duplicity, and battle common to the winning of empires could be expected in this territorial contest.

It was Iberville's first plan, upon hearing of the English design, to instruct De Tonti, on his return to Illinois, to entrap the English leaders into coming among the Tonikan Indians of Louisiana by promising profitable trading, and then to arrest the English and hand them over to a detail of French Canadians. However, it was learned that the English were too numerous for this stratagem to prove successful. The best that could be done at the time, then, was to try to unite all the Indians south of the Chickasaw in a pro-French confederacy, and possibly to arm them.

There were obstacles to this plan at the beginning. Bad medicine was brewing between the Bayogoulas and the neighboring Houmas. However, obstacles or no obstacles, it was expedient that an Indian alliance be accomplished if possible. The first step in such a plan was to settle local controversies, to make allies out of neighboring enemies. The nearness of the two tribes to the proposed French fort made it exigent to bring the Indians to terms. For if the Bayogoulas lived near the French as allies, the Houmas would regard both French and Bayogoulas as enemies unless an understanding was reached.

Again St. Denis was sent ahead to begin the twofold diplomatic work of starting a friendship between the French and the Houmas and suggesting that they come to terms with their enemy, the Bayogoulas.

On March 5 the main party reached the village of the Houmas. The travelers found evil times upon the tribe. Attacks by the Bayogoulas and an epidemic of the flux had laid them low. But they rose up as best they could to meet the occasion, and a few lean warriors stood at the landing bravely singing the calumet.

Whether because of the devastating raids of the Bayogoulas, the weakening effects of the flux, or the diplomacy of St. Denis, a treaty was arranged between the two tribes without delay. It was a victory for the plagued, bedridden Houmas as well as for the French.

However, for a time, this important diplomatic victory hung by a delicate thread. In this nation the white men learned the vital lesson that winning friendship and keeping it are two very different things, that Indian diplomacy was not so simple as they would like to believe.

Iberville, in the course of the final negotiation, committed a most offensive blunder. The Houmas demanded that the Bayogoulas come to them to smoke the pipe of peace, bringing presents to ransom the Bayogoula prisoners according to the customs of the day. This was done as ordered. It was observed that the Indians conducted intertribal relations with dignity and honor and according to a form of "international" law. Thus far, all had been well. But Iberville was either too cautious or too skeptical, or as the Indians might have explained it, "too European." He arranged an escort for the Bayogoulas on the return trip, just to be sure that they would arrive with their scalps intact, and that the work of peacemaking would not have to be done all over again.

The Houmas were greatly offended; they let the white men know that they considered their honor doubted and insisted that in the future reliance should be placed upon their word. It was a tense moment that the French did not forget.

While the diplomatic tribunal was in session, Father Du Ru had time to look about the Houmas' village. He found it in a miserable condition. Great numbers had recently died, and the village was in full mourning. "The women bewail their dead day and night." The Great Chief had been among the victims and had been lying in state for over two months. As soon as all the flesh had dropped from his bones, they would be removed to the temple and there stored with his former possessions. The widows of the Great Chief spent some of their time spinning bark and weaving at the looms, but most of their days were occupied in mourning. Among other ceremonies, they drank ritualistically in honor of their dead. They would swallow as much as three or four pots of water and then strain horribly to spew it up. When it was not found easy to emit the liquid, they put herbs in the water to provoke vomiting. In spite of their gruesome rituals, however, the observing chaplain found them a people not without enchantment. "The women charm us by their modesty. . . . They speak softly."

It was Iberville's intention to secure guides from the Houmas and journey up the Red River to the Caddodaquois nation as soon as possible. For it was reported that Spaniards from Mexico had pushed eastward as far as that river, and the proposed alliance should be arranged as rapidly as possible. But a disappointment was in store for the Frenchmen. The Indians told them that up the river a great log raft had been formed by a mass of tangled logs, which clogged the Red River from bank to bank for miles and made passage by boat impossible. The only other way they knew to reach the Caddodaquois was to ascend the Mississippi to the village of the "Big" Tensas, and from there proceed overland to the west, beyond the village of the Natchez Indians.

The expedition set out. Pulling against the gray swirling current of the swollen river was a strenuous task, but by March 12 the French reached the Natchez nation.

The approach to the Natchez villages was an inspiring sight. Situated upon a high, picturesque bluff, beautifully landscaped with magnificent trees, the place looked like a strange fairyland. The peach and plum trees were in bloom, and in the March wind the waving patches of white and pink gave animation and delicate color to the landscape.

The French were met by the brother of the chief. He was an impressive man of fine build, with a long face, sharp eyes, an imperious aquiline nose, a chestnut complexion, and the "air of an ancient emperor." He brought the regrets of his brother, who, at the time, was another hard-hit victim of the flux.

The officials, in time, were presented to the chief, who received them with dignity lying on a cot in his home. His domicile was different from those of the lesser chiefs; only he and his women slept in it. There was one bed in it, an especially elaborate piece of furniture colorfully decorated. It was explained that this was the bed used for death only and that the chief was expected to use it soon. In spite of his critical condition gifts were exchanged and friendship acknowledged.

The Natchez were found to possess a superior culture and highly developed social, religious, and political systems. They were a fine-looking people. The women were known for their grace and beauty. They dressed in white linen robes which extended from their shoulders to their ankles.

The dress of the girls was different from that of the women, "for they are clad only in a species of skirt, fastened around the waist. . . . The skirts of the girls are sewed with fine white thread and only cover their nakedness from the waist down to the knees. They are fastened with two strings, with tassels at the end of each. The front is ornamented with fringe. The garment is worn by the girls until the period of nubility, when they assume a woman's garment. They are very courteous and obliging, and fond of the French. . . . [The women's] heads are enveloped in long, black hair, which falls gracefully around their waists, and in many instances to their ankles."

St. Denis was a favorite among the Natchez. His

stately bearing and graceful manners impressed the Indians. He possessed the knack of anticipating their thoughts, and his understanding of their nature and customs was soon to become legendary. St. Denis, in turn, was charmed by this gentle race, who lived life simply and beautifully in their picturesque fairyland.

If there had been a prophet to foretell the future, this meeting of the French and the Natchez would have been grim instead of gay. For this was the first act in an ironic drama. This same winsome St. Denis, who charmed and was charmed by this noble race, was the man who one day would blot their ancient culture from the face of the earth. That the Natchez nation was a military power strong enough to threaten the existence of a European colony was a fact that dawned only later upon the French colonizers. Strange dramas were in the making during the gambles of these formative years when the seed of the Louisiana colony was sprouting.

From the Natchez the French journeyed up the river about thirty-five miles to the Tensas tribe. On the second day there they witnessed a frightful spectacle. During an electrical storm, lightning struck the local temple. In mad confusion the Indians assembled around the flaming structure "howling like devils possessed," tearing out their hair, elevating their hands to heaven and invoking their Great Spirit to come down and extinguish the flames. They took up mud and besmeared their faces. When these ceremonies did not bring an end to the fire, the fathers and mothers brought out their children and, after strangling them, tossed them into the flame. On orders from Iberville to stop this mass murder, the French seized the infants by force, but not before over two hundred had been prepared for the sacrifice and seventeen had perished.

While at this village Iberville developed some trouble with his knee and was unable to walk. He was forced to give up the prospective Red River expedition. It was left to St. Denis and Bienville.

On March 22, St. Denis and Bienville set out with twenty-one Canadians, six Tensas and one Ouachita for the Red River country and the nation of the Caddodaquois.

Only hardy, brave men would have attempted such a journey at that season, but it was considered extremely urgent. Though no established boundaries for Louisiana existed, the French spoke of the alleged activities of the Spaniards in the Red River section as "encroachments" and a threat. With the Spaniards established so near, both on the east in Florida and on the west in Mexico, and with the English bearing down from the north, this was neither the time nor the place for fair-weather explorers.

The country had been overflowed; trails, where there were any, had been washed or covered from sight; slashing rains soaked everything. The entire first day was spent marching in a country which was knee-deep in water.

On the morning of the twenty-third the party crossed a river in a pirogue which they had been able, with rare good fortune, to borrow from some Indians. More often the men swam or waded the streams, pushing their baggage before them on improvised rafts, and firing their guns to frighten the alligators away.

After two days the Tensas deserted. They did not like walking naked through cold water. Bienville himself

The fathers and mothers brought out their children . . . and tossed them into the flame.

lamented upon the disadvantages of wading for a man of medium height in such circumstances, and he envied the tall St. Denis.

On the twenty-seventh two men came down with the flux, but the expedition had to proceed. A comrade was left to care for them, and the explorers plunged on farther into the boggy forest.

Next day they arrived at a small village of the Ouachitas, where they secured a "Nachito" to guide them to the Natchitoches village. Three days later they camped on the soggy edge of a marsh. Provisions were low, and three men had been walking with a burning fever for two days. But the following day the full crew was wading in water up to the armpits while torrents of rain beat down upon them. No game had been found, and rations were now reduced to two small sagamités a day. That night they could find no large trees to strip for bark for temporary cabins, so the men curled themselves upon the sodden ground and slept with the rain washing over their exhausted bodies.

The rain was still gushing down next morning. They came to a canebrake and had to fight the sharp wet blades from their faces. The entire day of May 5 was spent crossing a swamp. During the day seven men were seized with chills and were obliged to climb up into the trees and remain there until they recovered.

Bienville wrote in his journal: "This is good work for tempering the fires of youth. . . . We never stop singing and laughing, to show our guides that fatigue does not trouble us, and that we are different men from the Spaniards."

On the sixth, near the Red River, they came to the Natchitoches nation. The peace pipe was smoked, and presents were exchanged. Upon the success of such small tribunal meetings in the flooded wilderness depended the permanency of Louisiana and the French colonial empire. Here, along the Red River, was an enchanting bit of country populated by an amiable, industrious people who would become important in the life of St. Denis and the colony.

The party, after securing a guide from the Natchitoches chief, headed out over a tedious country of bogs, swamps, and a network of log-jammed streams. They passed through the village of the Nakasas on the bank of the Red River, and on the twentieth arrived at the Yataches. It had been expected that the long-sought Caddodaquois would be found only a two-day journey from here, but due to the strong current of the river the French were told that ten days and nights would be required.

There were some Caddodaquois visiting at the village, and they told the French of a Spanish settlement five and a half leagues to the west of their village, "where there are white, black, and mulatto men, women, and children engaged in cultivating the land." The Indians said that the Spaniards often came to the Caddodaquois on horseback to the number of thirty or forty, but they never slept there. Asked if the Spaniards had mines, they replied that the white men raised corn and had money like the pieces the Frenchmen showed them and that they staked it on cards, some of them stamping their feet and tearing the cards to pieces when they lost. They could not speak definitely about the mines.

So much time had been lost because of the flooded country, and the time designated to meet Iberville was so near, that the French decided to return without further investigation. On the return trip they discovered that war had broken out among their neighboring allies. The Bayogoulas had gone on the warpath and massacred their neighbors, the Mongoulachas, and filled their empty cabins with an importation of Colapissas and Sioux.

When the party at last reached Biloxi they reported, "The rumors are true!" The Spaniards were very near on the west, almost to the Red River.

II

Warpaths

BACK IN BILOXI THE COUNTRYMEN OF ST. Denis and Bienville had stories to exchange, some of them with amusing aspects, but all with grave warnings. The most humorous of them all was about the visit of Governor Andres De la Riola of Pensacola, which had occurred before Iberville's return.

The Spanish governor had sailed up to the French post aboard a frigate of twenty-four cannon accompanied by two smaller vessels, his flags waving boldly in the Gulf breeze and his guns glaring brazenly. With the air of a conqueror, he majestically informed the French commander, one M. Sauvole, that he had come to drive the French away.

Possibly the Spanish governor could have wiped the place out easily enough. But His Excellency seldom had the opportunity in this boresome wilderness to be both a diplomat and an admiral. Further, he found the Frenchmen not so easily impressed as he had expected. So he tampered with the art of diplomacy and rephrased his demands. He explained that he was acting in pursuance of the orders of the viceroy of Mexico—that it was supposed that the establishment was merely some trading community.

"Some trading community?" the Frenchmen echoed, in a tone suggesting a slur on the governor's intelligence. Surely His Excellency could not be so meagerly informed!

Time was required to discuss the threat of the Spaniards, and the French officers in the interim made the best of the situation. The miserable crew put up a bold, gay front. The unwelcome visitors were showered with honors and regaled with a generosity that both delighted and disappointed them. No such signs of weakness, dissatisfaction, or misery as the Spanish might be accustomed to at Pensacola were seen at Biloxi. The visit lasted four days, and it was a continuous fiesta. The garrison was kept in gala uniforms and on true holiday rations. Traces of sickness and privation were cautiously hidden. Corn was banished from sight, while the carefully guarded stores of wine and flour were lavishly drawn upon. Laughter rang out from the highest to the lowest rank, while the hunger-pinched little garrison took on a sparkle and magnificence fitting a royal post of imposing splendor.

Good wine and French delicacies seemingly tempered the governor's gun talk into polite diplomatic phrases. "Finding the community to be a representative of a crowned head rather than a trading community," the Spanish functionary took leave, but not before he had delivered a formal written protest against the establishment, which he stated the French had made in a possession of the king of Spain contrary to the good understanding which existed between the two crowns. He instructed the French to make no further settlements on that coast until he had communicated with His Spanish

Majesty, which he proposed to do directly. He then sailed away as pompously as he had arrived.

The French, it turned out, were destined to play host again to the Spanish, still with a touch of humor. Seven days after the Spaniards left, someone standing on the beach before the fort sighted an open boat at sea. The Frenchmen gathered around and watched it float slowly in to shore, and then saw three wretched creatures fall out onto the sand. They were His Excellency, Governor De la Riola, and two of his officers. They had returned, this time without any trace of their previous pomp and dignity—indeed, without even their shirts.

The three Spaniards told a horrible story of storm and shipwreck. For five days now they had labored on the tossing sea, almost without food and constantly plagued by swarms of huge mosquitoes. All ships had been wrecked on the Chandeleur Islands. Everything, even to the wardrobes of the officers, had been lost.

Again the Biloxians were "equal to the requirements of the honor of France." Messengers were dispatched to Pensacola with news of the disaster, and boats were sent to rescue the crews perishing on the sandbars of the Chandeleur Islands and bring them to Biloxi. Food, drink, and clothes were prepared again, and De la Riola was equipped from the wardrobe of Iberville. The Spanish governor insisted upon departing at once, to relieve his host of the burden of his men and equipage. But he was given to understand that he did the French an injustice if he supposed he inconvenienced them in the least, and was so strongly urged to remain until he and his men were completely rested that he consented. When he returned to Pensacola, part of his crew were transported in French boats, and all had been provided with three weeks' refreshment.

Thus was the game of diplomacy played in the wilderness; thus were wars made, delayed, or avoided.

The Biloxians told with mocking gestures of the visit of the pompous Spaniards; yet they laughed with suppressed fears, for other visitors had appeared at the post. Two French traders had come in from the northern woods, bringing confirmation of a rumor that the English were stirring up the Indians to the northeast of them. That this meant the Chickasaws might march against them immediately could not be concluded, but no unnecessary chances could be taken. So the post was put in the best state of defense its meager resources would allow, while men hoped tensely for the best.

When St. Denis and Bienville gave their report, it was only bad news to exchange for bad. First, there was their report of the massacre of the Mongoulachas by the Bayogoulas. This was particularly alarming in view of the reports from the Chickasaw territory. Indian alliances were clearly not to be taken too seriously.

The report about the Spaniards to the west was equally disquieting. Iberville wanted to know in what force the Spaniards were there, whether they had mines, what the extent was of their control over the Indians, what their designs were. No one could answer these questions.

For the peace and security of the colony, answers to such vital questions were necessary—immediately.

Spring had come to the Gulf Coast; the rains had slackened; the cold winds had ceased. It was a favorable time for action. On May 28, Iberville sailed for France.

Sauvole was left in command at Biloxi; Bienville took command of the new Fort St. John on the Mississippi; and the more important job of explorer-ambassador was designated to St. Denis. Almost any mediocre administrator might command a small garrison, but to promote trade and peace among the Indian tribes and to maintain an alliance among them strong enough to fend off the English and the Spanish were tasks for one gifted of the gods.

On May 29 St. Denis set out with twenty-five men to continue the exploration of the Red River country. His instructions were as bold as they were general. He was to push as far westward—consequently, as close to Mexico—as possible, in search of gold and silver mines, and in the name of the king of France to take possession of any he discovered; to conciliate any hostile Indians on the route; and to make maps of the country.

How far St. Denis traveled into the country beyond the Red River—territory which the French at that time were calling Louisiana—is not known, nor is there much definite record of what he did. But this was the beginning of several expeditions during which St. Denis learned the geography of the country, the language and customs of the natives, and their system of trade, government, and religion; made friends and customers of them; and in so doing became the best informed and most powerful man of his age in this territory.

In 1701 Bienville became governor of the colony. And in the following year the French established another fort farther east on the Gulf Coast, called Louis de la Mobile, in a location considered better suited for farming and for controlling the Indians of that section. It soon became the colonial capital. St. Denis was apparently in command of Fort St. John, the new fort on the Mississippi, which he was using as a base for his expeditions.

The military situation during this period was an international conflict on a rather crude level. The English of Carolina played the Indians against both the Spanish of Florida and the French of Louisiana, and the French and the Spanish in turn pitted the Indians against the English and each other.

When the War of the Spanish Succession broke out in 1702, the undercover war in America flared out into the open. The southern English colonies received a fleet from their government; and the French and Spanish, now technically allies, became wildly alarmed.

The English lighted the torch of war among the northern tribes, and bloody destruction spread rampant. The missionaries and their attendants were usually the first victims. In village after village they awoke to find their sheep turned into wolves. The proselyting English had converted them with a more appealing gospel.

In the matter of trickiness, the Indians needed little encouragement or advice from the whites. In late 1702 some chiefs of the Alabama tribe came to Mobile and said they had large supplies of corn. Bienville, then in great need of grain, immediately dispatched five men with them to make purchases.

Near the Alabama village the Frenchmen were requested to wait until the morrow to see the chief of the nation. While they lay sleeping that night their arms were stolen and a party of Alabamas pounced upon them and hacked them to death with tomahawks—all except one man who, though wounded in the shoulder with a hatchet, swam a river, bound up his wound with pine resin, and finally reached Mobile.

Revenge was the order of the day. Bienville determined upon immediate "satisfaction," a task which he little suspected would consume nearly a decade of war with the Alabamas, to the delight of the English.

Bienville sent to Fort St. John, it seems, for St. Denis. He and De Tonti were placed in joint command of an expedition of revenge against the Alabamas.

Bienville instigated and directed this war; St. Denis acted merely as a soldier under orders. The campaign furnished St. Denis his first real taste of Indian warfare in Louisiana, and from its tragic, foolhardy blunders he profited in later years.

Word of the Alabama treachery was sent to the Mobilians and other allied Indian tribes, and many warriors answered the call to fight with the French. War preparations began in Indian fashion, with a war dance and elaborate feasting. Bienville stated that the Indians and the French appeared to be one nation. But events soon proved that he had much to learn about Indians.

After days of delay the march finally started, with natives as guides. When eighteen days of traveling had passed, it was discovered that the army was little, if any, nearer to the enemy than when it set out. The Indians would not begin the journey in the morning until two hours after sunrise, forcing the French to march during the heat of the day. The French, unused to the exposure, heat, and exertion, began to drag behind and even to die. Finally the remaining French discovered what they should have known in the beginning: the Indians were friends and allies of the Alabamas. To chastise them, however, would only have replaced a passive, with an active, enemy, and apparently the French decided upon a "strategic withdrawal." By retreating in a straight line the army reached the fort in four days.

News of the French retreat, it was assumed, would reach the Alabamas. A surprise attack was therefore planned.

The French rested a few days, replenished their supplies, and, this time, with only Canadians added to their group, slipped out at night by water.

Near the scene of the original massacre the army sighted a party of Alabamas on a hunt with their families. Bienville, eager for revenge, was for attacking at once. But his companions prevailed upon him to make a surprise attack at night.

So throughout the rest of the day and into the night the invaders waited silently in hiding places. When the Indians settled for the night the French began to advance through a matted canebreak. Someone stepped on a dry twig. The war cry rose in the crisp air. A gun went off in the darkness. A Frenchman slumped over, dead in his tracks. The old men, women, and children broke from the Indian camp and scampered into the forest. The warriors retreated slowly, firing as they backed toward the cover of the forest. The Frenchmen pushed on through the darkness, firing blindly. A few moments later not a live Indian could be seen; they had all escaped except four. As to casualties, the combatants split honors.

For all practical purposes the campaign was a miserable failure. But Bienville was playing the fierce fighter and showing the iron hand in his control of the Indians. Upon his return to Mobile he opened a market for Alabama scalps, offering a gun and five pounds of powder with balls for each scalp brought to him.

Although the French did not yet trust the Chickasaw implicitly, they, along with the Choctaws, were encouraged to join the scalping. Both of these nations were ambitious for rearmament on a modern scale. And the collecting of Alabama scalps was considered a rather sporting way to arm, as well as to test their new implements. Soon Bienville had a large collection of these trophies.

To avenge the deaths of four Frenchmen who had been killed by outlaw Indians, perhaps without the sanction of the tribe, the French governor started a war that lasted for almost ten years and cost hundreds of lives. French and English animosities flourished at only the small expense of guns and ammunition supplied to the savages. Bienville's bullheadedness, first and last, cost the colony much in blood and reverses. His saving grace was that he later learned to depend upon St. Denis' judgment and tactics.

During this period it seems that each race, white or red, held against the entire nation any transgression of individuals of the other race. To attempt to have the individual culprit brought to justice and made responsible without condemning the whole clan apparently appeared to most leaders impossible or a sign of weakness.

St. Denis learned the folly of such nearsighted judgments, a lesson that contributed much toward making him one of the most noted Indian manipulators of his age. The Alabama war was a practical but expensive course in New-World military tactics.

After the Alabama campaign St. Denis returned to Fort St. John on the Mississippi to take up his command. He found a discouraging task before him. Food was scarce; the colonists had depended too much upon the

Indians for corn. Gardens had been planted, but dozens of black snakes from the swamp had eaten the lettuce and other vegetables to the roots. High water crept up from the river until it was knee-deep outside the cabin doors. Mosquitoes descended upon the colonists in dark whining clouds, so thick at times that "men could not be distinguished at ten paces." The water supply was inadequate. Then, the Tensas had defeated the neighboring Bayogoulas in battle and burned their village to the ground. The fact that the two tribes nearest their fort were engaged in a war to the death posed a serious problem for the French. And to further complicate matters, the Bayogoulas who had been fortunate enough to escape the Tensas flocked to the fort for protection, becoming an added charge. Despite the shortage of supplies, St. Denis provided a place for the Bayogoulas to erect new cabins and gave them what provisions he could spare. Taking care of friendly Indians was a policy he never abandoned.

St. Denis observed that the colonists depended too much upon the mother country for provisions. He set out to overcome this weakness, but only by ingenious pioneering was he able to discover which crops could be raised locally and thus keep the post going.

The year 1704 began auspiciously. On January 24 the *Pelican* arrived bringing provisions and "other articles for the colony," including two nuns in charge of twenty-three young women. The bachelor colony gave them a gay and attentive reception. Courting started immediately, and before the end of the month all the girls were married.

The meager records of the time are silent as to the

spring and summer of that year, but they show that September was an evil month. De Tonti and thirty new troops which had arrived that month died. Half the crew of the *Pelican* died, and men from the garrison had to be used to sail the ship back home.

In December Governor Bienville's scalp-collecting campaign took a weird turn. The chiefs of the Tonikan tribe came to the governor soliciting the return of one Father Davion to their village. He had abandoned them upon the death of a Father Foucault, killed there by the Koroas and Yazoos, supposedly at the instigation of the English. How Father Davion escaped is not known. Bienville told the chiefs that he would not agree to their request until the blood of Father Foucault had been avenged. If they wished to have their missionary back they must attack the Koroas and Yazoos, and bring him all the English that might be found among them. To encourage the enterprise he promised to send St. Denis with a detachment of troops to assist them.

The Indians were delighted. Preparation for the expedition was made, and the Tonikans set out for the Mississippi to meet St. Denis. But St. Denis did not approve of such gruesome tactics. He refused to have any part in the plan. And without his support Bienville could do nothing.

Until 1707 St. Denis' time was spent commanding the fort on the Mississippi and making exploring and trading trips into the Texas country. According to his own accounts he lived for extended periods among the Tejas [1]

---

[1] "Tejas" originally applied to the tribes in the region which is now East Texas, then to the province of Texas. The transition to the modern "Texas" was slow, and an exact date for the change in name is difficult to assign.

Indians, and in the year 1705 extended his journeys as far southwest as the Rio Grande.[2] During the year 1707 the fort was abandoned. However, St. Denis maintained headquarters in that region, under orders of Bienville, to exercise control over the tribes there. At some time between this date and 1711 he resigned his commission and settled on Bayou St. John near Lake Pontchartrain to engage in private trade. During this time he moved part of his favorite Natchitoches tribe over to settle around him. Later he relieved Bienville as commandant of Biloxi.

The abandonment of Fort St. John was only one of the many signs of French reverses in the struggle for colonial survival.

[2] An account of the extended trip into Texas in 1705 is based mainly upon St. Denis' own statement, made at the presidio of San Juan on the Rio Grande. But St. Denis had a way of confusing his own record. He was a diplomat and soldier, and he usually wrote only under the pressure of urgent necessity, to fit a purpose. In explaining his actions to the commandant at the Rio Grande when he visited there in 1714, he said that in this year he had been among the Tejas Indians. The route of his trip had been from Mobile to the Choctaws and, after a visit with them, to the Natchez. From the Natchez he traveled forty leagues in a southwesterly direction to the Nachitos; after a short stay with this tribe he went to visit the Tejas Indians, and from there he proceeded "over the same route as in 1714 to San Juan Bautista on the Rio Grande."

III

Louisiana Becomes Commercial

THE SECOND DECADE OF THE EIGHTEENTH century opened gloomily, indeed, for Louisiana. The first years of settlement had proved miserable and unprofitable. As a royal colony Louisiana showed no promise. It was a drain on the royal treasury at a time when the treasury could stand no drain.

Costly wars and extravagant expenditures of the court of Louis XIV had brought France to the very verge of bankruptcy. Louis was not a man who concerned himself greatly with the future. He set about to rid himself of this expensive wilderness possession.

Louisiana might have reverted to the Indians, or passed to the Spanish or the English or to whoever was strong or patient enough to possess it, except that Louis had one practical thought on the subject. He decided that it would be well to have Louisiana remain attached to France—perhaps through a private speculator. If the enterprise turned out a success the king of France would not be without benefits. If it was a failure, well. . . .

The court of Louis XIV drew many ambitious adventurers with money to risk and the disposition to risk it. Louis began to look them over judiciously.

Among the prosperous dandies was one Antoine Crozat, a man who liked to earn money and to spend it, who was jealous of social and business distinction and possessed with the vanity of an empire builder. Louis favored this courtier with the opinion that his great wealth and business experience might be more extensively utilized for the benefit of himself and the glory of France.

With the braggadocio of a horse trader Louis pointed out to Crozat the great possibilities of this potential empire across the sea, filled with mines, precious jewels, and unlimited furs. True, all these prizes had not been found, but think what the right man with capital might do.

One account states that Crozat had a daughter, Marie Anne, who was set upon marrying nobility. But this ambition could not be realized because Crozat came from peasant stock. After Louis made his proposition it dawned upon someone in the Crozat household that there might yet be a way. The daughter might be made a princess, if the father first became a prince. Louis was offering a domain across the sea vaster than the landed possessions of royalty itself. Here a master of men and finance might build a principality over which he would reign. Then noble blood would come seeking an alliance with his house.

Whether it was to marry off a royal-minded daughter, to gain wealth and position, or both, Antoine Crozat became the charter owner of the colony of Louisiana for a period of fifteen years, for what profit he could draw out of the monopoly of its trade. The grant included all the territory south of the country of the Illinois and between the English of Carolina and Mexico.[1] Thus Louisiana became a commercial colony.

---

[1] This was one of the first attempts to define the boundaries of Louisiana. And vague as the limits were, they were probably as definite as the French wished to make them.

Louis now relaxed in the hope that the troublesome Louisiana problem was solved.

Regardless of what may have been the policy concerning Louisiana up to this time, there was not the least question about it now. Louisiana had a mission, simple and understandable. Like any other investment or business, the enterprise was expected to pay dividends. The chief sources of revenue, Crozat was informed, should come from the development of mines (which he was told existed in fabulous numbers), trade with the Indians, and trade with the Spanish. Very little was said about the last source, though it was given more thought, perhaps, than both the others.

Odd circumstances produced odd men of the hour during this period. Crozat needed a manager, or a governor, with a background giving him unquestionable understanding of the purpose of his task. It so happened that at that time Antoine de la Mothe, Sieur Cadillac, who had already served twenty years on the frontiers of New France, was at the French capital. He had established the post of Detroit and served as a captain of a company with some distinction. But he had reached no high military position nor had he become rich. Disappointed on both scores, he was in a receptive mood for any get-rich-quick proposition, especially one which carried with it an impressive title.

On May 13, 1713, Governor Cadillac arrived in Louisiana, bitter about his failures but eager to make up for lost time. He had no illusions about his duties. Simply, his task was to keep this colony on a businesslike basis, or neither he nor his associates would have a job. His instructions stated, in part, that he was "to establish posts in the direction of the country of the Illinois, to search diligently for mines, to cultivate friendly relations with the Indians to the west, and to establish trade relations with Mexico."

One of Cadillac's first moves was to approach the Spanish concerning trade. Without delay he loaded with merchandise the ship which had brought him to Louisiana, and dispatched it to Vera Cruz to exchange the French goods for cattle and other necessities. There the ship was not allowed to approach nearer than the roadstead. The viceroy sent word to the ship's commander to keep his goods out of Mexico. He warned further that reciprocal trade between the two countries was out of the question, and that the ports of New Spain were closed to all foreign commerce.

So the first venture of the commercial colony turned out to be a disappointing failure because the most profitable source of income was to have come from trade with the Spanish. Crozat's enterprise definitely was off to a bad start.

Other possible sources of revenue were no more productive. The glamorous talk of rich mines diminished as the governor came closer to their expected location. And instead of trapping furs for the markets of Paris the Indians were busily scalping their neighbors, who sometimes were French trappers. In many instances, the Indians preferred to trade scalps rather than corn for French merchandise.

Cadillac was in a quandary, facing as he did what appeared to be prompt bankruptcy and final failure for himself and France.

But Louisiana was an unpredictable land of ironic and surprising answers to the apparently unsolvable. At this desperate time, when it seemed that one of the richest merchants of Europe would be broken and an empire lost for France, a letter from a Spanish missionary furnished the stimulus that may have saved Louisiana. It was an amazing but understandable epistle written by the missionary priest Father Francisco Hidalgo, addressed to the governor of Louisiana. It was two years old when it reached the governor.

Father Hidalgo was a zealous missionary who had brought the faith to the Indians of the Tejas in 1694. The Spanish administration had since abandoned the section of their eastern province in which this tribe was located, and the missionaries had been forced to leave the natives again to their pagan gods. The Spanish government was showing no more signs of vigor. Father Hidalgo had waited "on the outskirts of Coahuila" for an opportunity to return. But all his requests for re-establishing a mission among the Tejas came to nought. The priest was getting old. The great passion of his life was to see the Indians of this section Christianized before he died. Despairing of ever being able to stimulate the Spanish officials to go back to his beloved neophytes, he decided to write to the governor of Louisiana, inquiring about the welfare of the Tejas and deftly asking for French co-operation in establishing a mission for the Indians.[2]

Father Hidalgo may have been more clever and less treasonable than his action indicates. If the French became interested in making establishments in Texas, Spain would, in turn, find jealous purpose in re-establishing the country, and the priest might again join his flock under the banner of his native Spain. The Louisiana-Texas frontier was a place without precedents.

[2] To make certain that the letter would reach its goal, Father Hidalgo made three copies, which he sent by different routes. The letter was dated January 17, 1711.

Cadillac recognized his opportunity. He would be glad to help the missionaries rebuild their churches. It was as good a way as any to establish contact and, subsequently, trade.

Ever since the landing of La Salle on the Texas coast, Frenchmen from time to time had prepared memorials to the crown insisting that the country of the Tejas belonged to France and should be settled. Suggestions had been made to the king that the Mississippi be used as the base for the conquest of Mexico. The archives of France held reams of papers bearing the claims of France to this country.

But Crozat's company had a more pressing concern than that of boundaries, diplomacy, military conquest, or politics. Trade was needed—business which would bring in cash for the stockholders.

A decision for action was more easily reached than executed. Contacting the Spanish would be a delicate undertaking, indeed. The route was long and unmapped, the Indians were not always friendly, the Spanish were jealous and suspicious, and the campaign would take the French into a country claimed by a rival enemy.

The governor realized that such an expedition would require a leader of unusual qualities. He should of necessity be not only a man of courage, resourcefulness, and experience but a diplomat, linguist, and businessman endowed with a hardy physique and a tactful manner capable of dealing with both the Indians and the Spaniards under any circumstances.

Again, the unusual circumstances produced the unusual man. In all New France the governor knew of but one man who possessed all these qualifications.

A messenger was sent to Biloxi to bring its commandant, Louis Juchereau de St. Denis, to Mobile. When St. Denis arrived, Governor Cadillac informed him of the projected plan and explained that by virtue of his thirteen years' residence and extensive travels in the country, his friendship with the Indian tribes, his knowledge of the western routes, and his familiarity with the Indian dialects and the Spanish language, he was admirably suited for the undertaking.

St. Denis needed little persuasion. The expedition promised adventure, danger, difficulty, and profit. Here was a challenge of the first degree. That was enough.

A passport was prepared for St. Denis bearing the date September 12, 1713, and setting forth the object of the expedition: "The Sieur de St. Denis is to take twenty-four men and as many Indians as necessary and with them go in search of the mission of Father Francisco Hidalgo in response to his letter of January 17, 1711, and there to purchase horses and cattle for the province of Louisiana." The passport left much more unsaid than said. But no one was better able to understand what was left unsaid than Louis de St. Denis.

Arranging the details of the expedition caused two or three weeks' delay. Because of the vague nature of the enterprise and the subsequent complications, the true particulars are not known. One source states that St. Denis entered into a contract with Cadillac "by which he agreed to take ten thousand livres worth of merchandise from the public store, to transport it across Texas to Mexico, and to endeavor there to dispose of it." Cadillac evidently made a contract with each of the traders in the name of the company, by which he advanced them a certain amount of merchandise, the value of which they were to repay in silver upon their return. It is recorded that the expedition was delayed because of the governor's desire to make an advantageous bargain for himself. His object was to have the traders assign to him a tenth of the proceeds of whatever trade they might carry on. A deadlock resulted until some practical wit pointed out to the traders that since His Excellency had no means of checking the amount, it might be whatever they chose to give him. To what extent the enterprise was a company affair and how much a private deal among the individuals concerned cannot be determined. It is hardly reasonable to assume that the traders were in the adventure purely for the sport of it.

In late September, St. Denis and his party set out from Mobile. On that early fall day, when the first cool breezes stimulated action involving the valuable merchandise which rested securely in the canoes, no one could suspect that the delays and annoyances they had experienced with the French officials were insignificant, indeed, compared to troubles to come when they met the Spaniards.

IV

Road to Mexico

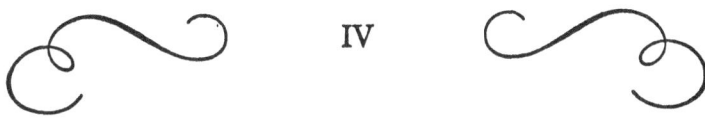

THE TRADING PARTY STOPPED AT BILOXI TO
reorganize and to secure Indian guides; thence it
proceeded to the Mississippi and on to the mouth
of the Red River.

The travelers found the Red River valley an impressive country. Floating on the clay-red river in their slim canoes, they watched a panorama of flat land, luxuriant in fruit and game and fowl, unfold in "endless wonder."

The year was nearly ended when they reached Grand Ecore—titanic, majestic cliffs towering above the river —the point at which the hill country on the west pushed through the flat valley to the river's edge.

In the vicinity of this ancient landmark the French met again the friendly Natchitoches Indians, now living on an island formed by the separation of the river into two branches. In dramatic fashion St. Denis assembled the Indians. He addressed them not as a stranger but as a friend and benefactor. He distributed presents, including grain and corn for planting, which he explained would be needed by the French who had come to live among them. The Natchitoches had nothing to fear from hostile tribes now, he told them. The French would see to that. This was bold, presumptuous talk, but both races wanted to believe it, and for that reason many of their members doubtless did.

This was a cheerful, history-making reunion. Simple logic dictated a settlement here. First and foremost was the advantage the French would derive from friendly, co-operative natives; secondly, this point was at the foot of the great raft, at which river transportation became impossible, and, coincidentally, this was the nearest point on a water route to the Spanish settlement of Mexico.

On the site of this meeting rose the first permanent settlement in the territory later known as the Louisiana Purchase. The "metropolis," called Natchitoches, began in simple frontier fashion. The French leader distributed axes and other tools among the Indians, who cleared grounds and constructed houses of logs for the traders and their merchandise.

As soon as two storehouses were completed St. Denis stored part of the merchandise, left ten men as a guard, added thirty Natchitoches to his contingent, and set out for Mexico.

The route followed by the traders, according to legend, was an old trail made by the buffalo on their winter migration from the plains to the river bottoms of Louisiana.

Beyond Natchitoches St. Denis found a country vastly different from the coast and river regions he had come to know so well. Sharp, irregular hills twisted incessantly, giving the topography the likeness of a great sheet of paper that had been crumpled and then spread out loosely. The trail curved around these hills. Here were vast highland forests of pine peppered with oak and hickory, and along the streams growth was luxuriant. Game was unlimited. It was too late for fruit, so the travelers subsisted mainly upon corn and wild meat.

The first notable stream they reached was the Sabine,

a quiet, grey-colored river that bordered the hilly red lands. The men passed through the red country without incident and after twenty-two days reached the Asinai nation.

They found horses and cattle in plenty here. A thriving trade began immediately. French guns, knives, beads, and cloth were exchanged for livestock and buffalo hides.

The Asinai tribesmen were a colorful group, different in many respects from the natives of the Mississippi and Red River valleys. One Penicault, the chronicler of the expedition, noted, for example, distinctive characteristics of their warfare: "They are all mounted on horseback, with quivers fastened behind, filled with arrows. They carry a bow and a small shield made of buffalo-hide, which is held in the left hand and is intended to protect them from the arrows of their enemies. They have no other curb or bridle for their horses than a piece of hair rope; their stirrups are made of the same material, which are fastened to deerskin three or four inches in thickness, thus forming their saddle."

St. Denis wrote of this nation, "Their lands are all cultivated and there are no fruit in the world richer . . . nor more wonderful grapes of various kinds and colors in such quantities. The bunches are as large as twenty-eight and thirty pound shot. There are also such extensive fields of such excellent flax that all the fleets of Europe could be supplied with cordage."

The Asinai was a large nation of the Tejas group, and trading was so extensive, it appears, that St. Denis returned to Louisiana at least once to obtain additional supplies and to report on his activities. Evidently, a considerable traffic was conducted between the tribe and the Natchitoches storehouses.

Fortunately for the French, several of the women

spoke Spanish, and through them St. Denis was able quickly to learn the Indian dialect.

Profitable as this trade was, the chief purpose of the mission was not being accomplished. After several gainful and pleasant weeks, St. Denis decided to push on farther toward the Spanish settlements. He justified his extended trip in a letter to Governor Cadillac on the grounds that Father Hidalgo had not been found among the Tejas. The report contained a flattering evaluation of the love of the Indians for the missionary and their desire for his early return. There could be but one course —to search farther for the good priest. If St. Denis failed to mention that more profitable customers might be found farther to the southwest, the Louisiana governor would not construe that he had abandoned his merchandise.

The head of the Asinai nation, Chief Bernardino, and twenty-five of his braves accompanied St. Denis on his advance. This group more than made up in numbers for the several Frenchmen left at the Asinai to carry on trade. St. Denis now had only three of his countrymen with him—Penicault, the historian, a former ship's carpenter; Pierre Largen; and Medar Jalot.

Of the three, Jalot was the most colorful. Seemingly, he was all things to all men—valet to St. Denis, surgeon to the French wounded in battle, temperamental chef on expeditions, fellow warrior with the French soldiers, diplomat for his country, historian for posterity, philosopher to those needing comfort in the wilderness— and, by no means least, a grumbling, prankish lover. As a valet he was a devoted servant and may have been responsible, in part, for his master's reputation for immaculate grooming; as a surgeon he manifested a particular fondness for arrow wounds, which he declared to be the "nicest and genteelest of all injuries"; as a chef his chief interest was breaking the monotonous diet of dried corn and wild meat with green salads prepared from vegetables and fruits found along the route; as a historian he left some amusing, enlightening, and even baffling accounts of his travels; as a philosopher he was a sustaining force —a wit, part priest and part clown, with a mind as versatile as his hand; and as a lover he both complained at, and encouraged, St. Denis' love-making while he himself carried on in Jacques-like fashion courtships with the wenches along the border.

The expedition marched across the gently rolling Tejas country until it came to the vicinity of the Colorado River. Here the monotonous scenery changed abruptly. Canyons with colored banks broke through among the hills of olive-green mesquite, dotted with towering moss-draped oaks. Ripened berries glistened in the morning dew like scattered jewels; and multicolored wild flowers were a brilliant carpet under the horses' hoofs. Across the winding, rust-colored river spread an endless expanse of rolling green hills. It was a setting to lift the hearts of weary travelers.

But all was not beauty for long. A war party of "two hundred hostile Indians" swooped down upon the travelers from the hills with the "furiosity of demons." Had it not been for St. Denis' experience on the frontier and his understanding of Indian warfare, the attack might have become a massacre, and the future history of Texas might have changed on this spot. Instead, the French commander so stationed his men with such speed that his meager forces won a decisive victory.

At this point twenty-one Asinai Indians, including Chief Bernardino, turned back. One Indian, however, had no choice in the matter of continuing the journey. He was the victim of a "particularly interesting arrow wound," which so fascinated Jalot that he insisted on carrying the patient along, regardless of inconvenience, for observation.

The party in time came to a village of friendly Indians on a branch of the San Antonio River. St. Denis, impressed by the attractiveness and advantages of the spot, stated that surely one day it would become the location of a presidio. His conjecture was prophetic. He was standing upon the future site of San Antonio.

The diminished caravan plodded slowly onward through a shimmering world of cactus, sand, and mesquite, until the Rio Grande was sighted. The long journey in search of the Spanish was almost ended; across the stream was the presidio of San Juan Bautista, the northern outpost of the Spanish.

But was the end of the journey to be the beginning of a more hazardous adventure? Every Frenchman wondered. Before them bristled the fort of a rival nation of jealous, emotional, unpredictable people—a nation which had already sent Governor Cadillac's loaded ships from its harbors with the stern warning that the ports of New Spain were closed to all foreign trade.

Armed only with a letter from a priest and a questionable passport, supported only by three Frenchmen and a half-dozen ragged Indians, and equipped with his embarrassing merchandise, St. Denis marched upon the Spanish garrison.

V

San Juan Bautista

THE PRESIDIO OF SAN JUAN BAUTISTA, known also as Presidio del Norte, had served for fourteen years as an outpost of colonial Spain. It guarded a mission, "regulated" Indian affairs, strove to make the population partially self-supporting, and sent out long reports of its activities to Mexico City and Spain. Its existence, in the main, had been uneventful. Men in the service went dully about the king's business from day to day as if tomorrow would always be the same as yesterday.

But events of July 19, 1714, jarred San Juan Bautista from its complacent slumber into a state of panic. From that day on, the tempo of life on the Rio Grande was never the same. The Spanish would thereafter be obliged to watch a rival, guard a border, and prevent—or promote—smuggling.

First, the Indians brought word that an army of palefaces was marching from the northeast. They said the palefaces had defeated a group of Indians, identified by some sources as Comanches and by others as Apaches. That alone was a feat to inspire Indian talk. Exaggerated speculations flew wildly through the settlement. Invasion —massacre—change of sovereign! The threats were ominous.

Later that same day a soldier looking out from a tower at the edge of the square spied the invaders approaching from the direction of the Rio Grande. This was no army, but only a handful of men. He adjusted his glasses again and swept the desert toward the Rio Grande with them. An advance party, he concluded.

The commandant, Captain Diego Ramón, was a man capable of meeting such emergencies. The occasion called for coolness. A commandant must know when to be a soldier and when to be a diplomat. He alerted his command and waited.

One slight blunder by the "invader" that July day in 1714 might have changed the history of the Southwest. And a lesser diplomat might never have survived the ordeal. St. Denis did not overlook the psychological effect of arriving with as small a retinue as possible. On the other hand, he knew that this was not the time nor the place for timidity. Only a dauntless, nonchalant air could win for him admission to this foreign citadel. So, dressed immaculately in fresh and beautifully tailored linen, he strode boldly onward toward the Spanish post as if he were spreading the map of France with every step.

Before the guards could properly challenge him he announced in good Spanish that he wished to see their commandant. Automatically, they honored his wish.

Inside the commandant's quarters St. Denis' forceful Spanish and polished manners gave the impression at the very outset that he was not a man to be dealt with lightly. He presented his passport to the astonished officer with the dignity of a true diplomat. He told him of Father Hidalgo's letter to the governor of Louisiana and commented upon the priest's anxiety about the Tejas Indians.

He spoke of his own coming as if nothing more logical could have been expected.

Don Diego was courteous, but he could not believe this; this was no missionary expedition. St. Denis shifted the approach. This first talk, he indicated, was introductory conversation and related only part of his purpose. He explained that he had set out from Louisiana to purchase grain and cattle, greatly needed at Mobile, from the missions thought to exist among the Tejas Indians. Upon finding the missions abandoned and learning from the natives that the Spanish settlements were not far away, he had continued his march to the Rio Grande in search of his supplies.

Don Diego was bewildered. This poised, fearless Frenchman before him spoke of the affair as casually as of the flavor of his wine. Did he not know that the frontiers of New Spain were closed to all foreign trade? Less than two years before, the viceroy had issued strict orders to all frontier commanders urging extreme diligence in preventing the introduction of foreign merchandise and the entrance of foreigners under any pretext. The commandant had the order before him. He read the mandate to St. Denis.

There could be but one course to take. He must follow his orders and arrest these intruders, pending instructions from higher authority.

If rules must be rules, Don Diego knew how to make the best of them. The arrest was made with characteristic Spanish courtesy. And no prisoner could have been lodged in a more desirable prison—the home of his apprehender, the Spanish commandant.

If St. Denis was a prisoner, he was also a distinguished

guest. His bearing commanded polite attention. That evening he proved to be a charming, engrossing dinner-table wit; and both he and his news-hungry hosts made the most of their time. St. Denis had been in many strange lands and had known many breathtaking experiences with the Indians. He was an engrossing storyteller and could make a pun in Spanish as well as in French; and besides his true Parisian charm he exhibited a sense of humor that was equal to the most delicate situations. The meeting was refreshing for cultured minds too long dulled by the isolated monotony of the frontier wilderness.

Seemingly, San Juan Bautista offered little to hamper either the spirit or movement of its French captive. Of course, he must remain at the presidio. But San Jaun Bautista was in reality an object of his mission for which he had traversed hundreds of miles of wilderness. On the other hand, why should the Spaniards worry themselves about guarding him so closely? If he should run away they would be rid of him, and thus their objectives, for all practical purposes, accomplished.

The next day after his arrival, St. Denis wrote a letter to Father Hidalgo expressing regret at not finding him. Also, the priest of the local mission wrote to Hidalgo speaking of the work of St. Denis among the Tejas Indians, with the joyful announcement that the man from Louisiana had opened the way for work among the Indians of the Tejas. And the commandant himself wrote to Father Hidalgo, who was farther in the interior, giving the story of the Frenchman's arrival. For a prisoner St. Denis had made quite an impression.

San Juan Bautista was not a bad place to while away

some time, especially after a long wilderness journey. The presidio, situated a mere two leagues below the Rio Grande, was not an imposing municipality by European standards, but on the desert frontier it was an oasis. Around the plaza stood the quarters and offices of the officials and soldiers, the workshop, and the supply houses. On one side of the plaza quarters for the Indians were arranged in parallel lines; there was a large workshop where baskets were woven, and a granary. From the square the little city of adobe fanned out abruptly into patches of grain and pastures, and beyond these was the neverending sand-gray desert. An irrigation ditch had been dug leading from the head waters of the Santa Rita some twenty leagues away, encouraging the desert to flower. A small lake had been constructed in which the Indians fished and also washed their clothes. And an imposing mission was situated on the hill *muy suave* a short league from the presidio.

St. Denis' staff—Jalot, Penicault, and Largen—were comfortably quartered and were extended the hospitality of the post. The aesthetic Frenchmen found much to feast their senses on in this quaint outpost of Old Spain. What a contrast this balmy, dry desert garden was to their foggy, low-lying Gulf Coast, with the damp, vine-choked woods crowding to the edge of the sea. Here was a touch of civilization, and here were white women, the society of which the French colonists had not had an opportunity to enjoy in a decade and a half. This was a realm which by contrast and color was exciting. In the sun-bleached adobe cottages of the peons, strings of bright red peppers dangled against white and cream-tinted walls, and every window displayed at least one pot of brilliant flowers, patterns of vivid scarlet, yellow, and deep violet, framed by window facings of gleaming white. Brilliant hues were everywhere—in the gay skirts and gaudy jackets of the peons; in the mystifying patterns of Indian blankets; in the uniforms of the officers and soldiers; in the magnificent braided coats and laced trousers of the gentlemen. All this color splashed against a panoramic background that was neither the white of bleached sand, nor ivory, nor the yellow or rose of baked adobe; but a strong, fascinating blend of all, created out of the desert earth.

Days passed into weeks, and no reply came from higher authority. The alarming incident of the Frenchmen's arrival turned into a prolonged *fiesta*.

The Ramóns knew the art of entertaining. In true Spanish fashion they let time pass lightly. And the Frenchmen quickly caught the spirit of this Spanish land. Here at San Juan Bautista were fresh, crisp linens to sleep between; silver to drink from; delicious, highly seasoned food cooked by skilled, patient women; leisurely, clever conversations with men of state; and occasions for polite small talk with women of breeding. Refreshing entertainment in good taste did much to relieve the anxiety over the outcome of the commandant's letter.

The Ramóns were of an old, cultured Spanish family. Several members of the family later came to be more or less noted in the history of the Southwest, among them two sons of Don Diego, Alferez Domingo and Diego, and a grandson, a third Diego, son of Domingo. But the most glamorous, and indirectly perhaps the most important historically, was a sheltered, seventeen-year-old girl, the daughter of the second Diego—Emanuelle Sanche de Navarro.[1] Beautiful, charming, clever, energetic, member of an old distinguished family of Spain, and a favorite grandchild of the commandant of one of Spain's most important outposts, she was possibly as well equipped as any female of that age and nation to play a historic role.

Descriptions of Emanuelle are fragmentary. That she was beautiful the references consistently record—"the most beautiful girl in all the northern provinces of Mexico." It is legend that there were mother-of-pearl tints in her complexion, which were ravishingly distinctive in a country of predominantly darker skin. The way in which she seized opportunities for self-assertion quickly proved that she was a woman of quiet dignity and fiery action as well as a compelling beauty.

When St. Denis saw Emanuelle he was charmed by her exotic loveliness. The stage was set for a romance: charming handsome strangers meeting in a strange situation under unusual, dangerous circumstances; time enough for adventurous, amorous people to spend it dreaming and making love—or seeking the opportunity to make love; and hanging above all anxiety and suspense, suggesting the possibility of any event on the morrow.

The official household became increasingly concerned as they saw the acquaintance between Emanuelle and their foreign "guest" take a turn that indicated something more than an acquaintance. Who was this Louis Juchereau de St. Denis who had appeared so suddenly at their presidio and then at their home; who first threatened their official positions and now their family circle?

---

[1] This name has been subjected to many versions and translations. The one used is that which appears most consistently in the French records at Natchitoches and apparently that preferred by Emanuelle. The French influence is obvious.

It was Jalot who let the most stimulating and interesting information leak out informally. He was enjoying himself in his own way with the maids about the place; and what better and more exciting subject was there to talk about than his wonderful master, the hero of many marvelous, hair-raising adventures. Skill in the art of the press agent was not the least of Jalot's accomplishments. He knew how to be reserved and modest in such an agonizing fashion as to make the Spaniards call for more information about this spectacular man, and how to hint about dangers in such a way that his master's enemies would be impressed. If he embroidered the facts somewhat it is hardly more than could be expected. The bare facts alone made an engrossing story. Jalot told just enough of his hero's youth to suggest that his love of danger and adventure was greater even than his love of woman. Jalot knew just how much to tell, and his reticence made for intriguing conversation around the washing stones and ovens as well as in the patios. There had been a duel. Oh, it was really nothing; he had merely mentioned it in passing. But the suggestion had been made that the man was a dangerous swordsman whose honor was not to be trifled with. And the St. Denis family? Were they pleased with Louis? *Oui,* they were adventurers and fighters, too. It was their desire that he settle in Canada, made comfortable and loved by a home girl liked and recommended by the family. The family had dispatched letters to Louisiana asking this unsettled, roving son about his plans and referring to the girl near Beauport. Ah, so there was a rival! Such intelligence could not be without effect upon Emanuelle.

Whether or not St. Denis sought or encouraged Jalot's aid in furthering his suit or even sanctioned his patio and stable chatter is not known. Quite possibly he did, for the men were close friends, more than master and valet. Jalot may have been one of those rare males who are matchmakers; more likely, however, idle time and the love of talk accounted for most of Jalot's part in the affair, for he had a romance or so of his own in progress.

It was from the more international-minded and scholarly priests that the Ramóns officially learned more of this dashing, mysterious Frenchman who had his eye, presumably, on both the province of Texas and their prettiest relative. The Spanish missionaries always promoted St. Denis, even more than did those of French Louisiana, many of whom saw St. Denis as a worldly minded man, his soul set more on an earthly fortune than on saving heathen souls. The religious of Texas and Mexico accepted St. Denis from the beginning as a great benefactor and friend interested in their welfare and the promotion of their work. And their first reciprocal aid was to speak respectfully of him and his family as people of honor and distinction. St. Denis' family, they told the Ramóns, was well known in Canada and France.

Louis Juchereau de St. Denis belonged to the Juchereau Duchesnay family. His grandfather, Jean Juchereau, Sieur de Maur, was born in Ferte-Vidame, near Chartres, France, where the Juchereaus were prominent. Several of the men of this generation had become prominent jurists. The name was closely associated with the affairs of that part of France.

His generation lived during a restless period in France, and there was a restless, adventure-seeking strain in the Juchereau Duchesnays. Other than of war and the rumors of war, the exciting talk of the time was of New France

—more specifically, a place called Canada. Reports were that almost anything might be accomplished in this boundless land which offered her rich resources to the brave and hardy. In 1632 Noel Juchereau, Sieur des Chatelets, brother of Jean, migrated to Canada. He wrote back that the country was as wonderful as reported. In 1634 Jean Juchereau packed what belongings shipping would permit, and with his wife—nee Marie Langlois—and four children set sail for this promising New France.

In 1635 the brothers Jean and Noel received a "concession" for a plot of land on the bank of a river. In 1650 Jean Juchereau took possession of fifty arpents near Quebec on the St. Lawrence granted to him by Governor de Montmagny. The property became known as *La seigneurie de Maur*. The Sieur de Maur so distinguished himself in the service of Canada, serving as a member of the council, among other positions of responsibility, that in 1667 Governor Alexandre de Prouville de Tracy asked for letters of nobility for him. His wife died in 1661; and on February 7, 1672, Jean followed her, leaving their four children—Jean, Nicolas, Noel, and Genevieve—to make names for themselves in their own way in this rugged land of their father's adoption.

Jean's second son, Nicolas Juchereau de St. Denis, father of Louis, married Marie-Thérèse Giffard, daughter of Robert Giffard and Marie Renouard, and settled down to his land. But few of the St. Denises were destined to commonplace lives. Nicolas' life was eventful and varied —fighting in the armies of Canada, serving in the council, clearing and cultivating his rugged acres, and providing for his large family of thirteen against the long, cold Canadian winters. To protect his family and neighbors against the Indians he formed and led a militia against the Iroquois, and later against other hostile tribes. In this service he fought with one De Courcelles, and as a result of his good leadership and bravery he was given a command for life. He defended his colony so well that King Louis XIV sent him a long letter praising his courage and thanking him for his service. In October, 1690, when Sir William Phipps and his boats were threatening Quebec, Nicolas Juchereau de St. Denis, Sieur de Beauport, was well past sixty, but with the vigor of a youthful veteran he fought for three days with his people in the defense. The battle brought him his final wound and supreme honor—a broken arm on the battlefield, and documents from Louis XIV praising his bravery and granting him letters of nobility. But he had little time to enjoy his nobility; he died the year the distinction was granted, 1692.

Louis Juchereau de St. Denis was the eleventh of a family of twelve children born to Nicolas Juchereau. He was born September 17, 1676, at Beauport, or possibly in the nearby city of Quebec. Louis' opportunities for education and advancement were above the average among the Canadian colonists, and he took the best advantage of them. In his early youth he was sent to Paris, possibly to the Royal College of Paris, to be educated further and to absorb some of the culture and atmosphere of that city.

Tales abound of exciting escapades of the young St. Denis in the gay, pleasure-loving capital. There are stories of love affairs and duels—legends, perhaps, invented to match the later accomplishments of the noted mature man. All the days of his life Louis Juchereau de St. Denis inspired legends.

It was easy enough for the Ramóns to believe the glowing accounts of their uninvited but captivating guest. Who but a most courageous one would push through a wilderness of disputed enemy country, fighting savages and beasts, to peddle linen and fine laces from Paris; and who else would dare to make love to the granddaughter of the highest frontier official in his very home? On a frontier where men lived by their wits, and where even existence at times depended upon personal bravery, courage was often rated above patriotism. To the romantic Emanuelle the man was soon glorified above the rank of an enemy invader—at least, of an ordinary invader.

The commandant's family was duly impressed though obviously disturbed. This Frenchman might bring down official wrath upon them all if they appeared too friendly toward him; they might lose their jobs—and fortunes—because of the friendship. But by the time the probability of complications was foreseen, events were taking a more natural and uncontrollable course. Emanuelle was smiling at the courtly St. Denis and often having "secret" talks with him. To make the matter more serious Emanuelle had a mind of her own and a temper to back it up.

The commandant was sorely troubled. Not only did it appear that he could not control the course of events on the frontier but that he could not control his own household.

St. Denis, who seemed capable of making capital of almost anything, turned what appeared to be a serious business reverse into a subject for distracting, stimulating talk. Realizing that this ruling family liked him and that they must reckon him a prospective in-law, whether they liked the idea or not, he took advantage of his gains and began to talk of fortunes that might be made by trade between the Spanish and the French. The Ramóns, he had come to believe, as summer wore into fall and fall into winter, were practical-minded people. Subtly and indirectly the thought was transmitted to the Ramóns that perhaps he would be a profitable connection. It was suggested that Spain in the near future might relax her stringent trade laws, and then with an entree into French Louisiana they would be strategically situated to become rich, perhaps, in intercolonial commerce. St. Denis might become the commandant on the other side of the frontier, even as Captain Ramón was commander on the Spanish side. And then, if this French commandant should be an in-law . . . ah, that would be a convenience worth thinking about.

The most serious complication which gave the Ramóns sleepless nights, according to one historian, was the fact that Emanuelle was the sweetheart—probably the fiancée—of Don Gaspardo Anya, the governor of Coahuila. This the Ramóns could not overlook. If they should become in-laws of the governor, their immediate superior, favors and promotions would be in order. On the other hand, if they sanctioned St. Denis' suit and let the encroaching foreigner steal the governor's *novia*, their official heads might come off. There were a number of factors to discourage Don Diego from playing the spy for the governor's political favors, however. In the first place, Emanuelle is said to have spoken of His Excellency as a fat widower better suited for complaining of his gout than for making love. She was not happy over the prospects of marrying him, even to become the first lady of Coahuila. Or Don Diego, after being influenced by St. Denis' salesmanship for a while and hearing of the great advantages of trade with Louisiana, may have felt that the brighter future lay in that direction. It was an old European custom to give daughters in marriage with an eye to the fortunes of the entire family. The Ramóns had a grave and far-reaching choice to face. They realized the gamble involved. But fate was to settle the matter. For in the first place, it was soon seen that Emanuelle was apt to make her own decision: she was in love with the Frenchman from Louisiana. And a fiery, determined, seventeen-year-old Spanish girl in love was not an easy force to control. In the second place, official forces from higher up were due for a say in the matter.

On February 15, 1715, St. Denis "secretly" dispatched letters to the governor of Louisiana at Mobile to inform him of what had happened since his arrival at San Juan Bautista. It is not clear just how the messages were dispatched. St. Denis explained in one letter that the Spanish commandant had been exceedingly kind, that he could escape with ease but preferred to stay. By way of giving a clue for his lack of desire to escape he wrote: ". . . seeing a good fortune before my eyes and wishing to put my name in repute, I rejoice at all that may happen, for I fear nothing from these people or from Mexico." When St. Denis spoke of fortune he knew what the governor would be thinking about, and what he would like most to hear. He let his superior know that although his surroundings were rather pleasant, he was keeping his mind on his business. He wrote about "the silver mines sixty-one leagues from here [Boca de Leonez], . . . where there are rich merchants who have many 'piastres' and 'lingots.' " He stated that the merchants and miners were delighted at the prospect of trade and had promised him that if he wanted unmarked silver they would trade every year. Apparently there was some news too good or too secret to put onto paper, for he continued, "You will pardon me if I do not write more fully to inform you of what happened here; the carriers that I will send from here in secret will tell you the better part of it." Notwithstanding the proper slant and the optimism of the messages there was a hint of discouragement or suspicion in one of the final epistles, which concluded with a practical appeal to the governor: "After the risks I have run," he wrote, "and the services which I have rendered to the public, I flatter myself that you will serve as my patron, and that you will procure me some employment at Mobile." Was the prolonged suspense wearing heavily upon the Frenchman? Or were his rivals in Mobile unofficially undermining him during the long wait and was he beginning to hear of it?

The Louisiana governor apparently was well informed about what was going on, whether from St. Denis' letters or from the carriers; for the next year he wrote, referring to a letter from St. Denis, "St. Denis writes that he will be [in San Juan Bautista] until the end of the month. It is believed that he will amuse himself and that his trip will be longer since he is waiting to marry a Spanish girl."

Long after the February letters were dispatched the wait continued. Winter passed into an early spring on the southerly Rio Grande, and the desert began to bloom again into a vista of green and yellow and blue. Warm breezes floated in from the Gulf of Mexico. Such days, doubtless, caused Penicault later to write that he left San Juan Bautista with the greatest reluctance, "for the Spanish damsels of that village were very agreeable to us, and were themselves vexed at our departure." It had been a rather delightful imprisonment for captive and captor.

But it was a short Rio Grande spring for St. Denis. The long-awaited answer finally arrived during the last days of March, or possibly the first of April. And a stern answer it was: an officer and twenty-five armed men came riding in from the provincial capital of Coahuila under orders of the governor to bring the captured French peddler to him for examination and justice. Hurried farewells were secretly exchanged, and St. Denis, in chains, was put astride a horse and, heavily guarded, escorted away hurriedly toward the provincial capital.

VI

Prisoner

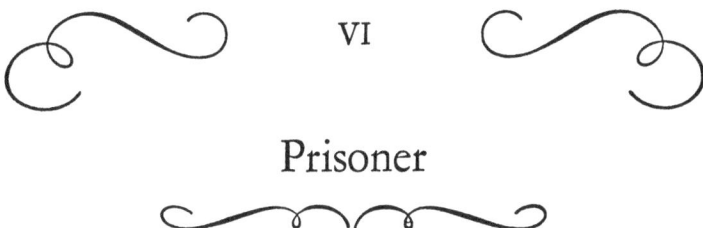

THE GUARD CONDUCTED ST. DENIS FIRST TO Monclova, the capital of Coahuila, if we are to believe one of the strongest traditions of northern Mexico.[1] The governor's reception was courteous enough. The Spaniards could be polite even while bowing one off to the gallows. Nonetheless, St. Denis was locked in prison with Jalot, who had insisted upon accompanying him.

After a few days Don Gaspardo descended into St. Denis' cell and offered him freedom if he would renounce his claim to the *señorita* of San Juan Bautista. This solution the governor evidently considered as easy as it was generous, for what else could the prisoner look forward to except execution or imprisonment. It was logical for the amorous governor to reason that if he could frighten his prisoner forever from the boundaries of Spain both his personal purpose and that of his government would be accomplished. But to his consternation the proposal was flatly rejected.

The account further relates that the governor dis-

---

[1] The accounts of St. Denis' imprisonment in Monclova are so varied and contradictory that it must, in the main, be labeled a tradition. The story of the journey from the Rio Grande to Mexico City is so hazy and shows such evidence of coloring that it is impossible completely to resurrect it.

patched a message to Emanuelle saying that if she did not consent to marry him he would take matters in his own hands, and her lawbreaking lover would be put to death immediately.

It is also recorded that Emanuelle sent word to higher authority that a Frenchman, a presumed spy, was held unjustly and cruelly by the governor of Coahuila, who had concealed the knowledge from his superiors. It seems likely that Emanuelle exerted some influence in having St. Denis brought to a quicker justice than was common in colonial Spain at that time. He was, at any rate, brought to Mexico City. And when he arrived in the capital, or shortly thereafter, her uncle, Domingo Ramón, was there, obviously to plead the cause of St. Denis.

However, it seems hardly possible that the jealous Coahuilan governor could have done more than delay St. Denis and otherwise make him uncomfortable, without risk to himself. For the Frenchmen's presence in the northern provinces had been known in Mexico City since shortly after their departure from Mobile, thanks to the talent for spying on the part of His Excellency, the governor of Pensacola. Their capture had been hoped for in the capital, if not expected.

The delay in Coahuila was not too extended, for by June 21 St. Denis was in Mexico City. His arrival created no surprise, but the more his journey through Spanish territory was discussed the more sensational it began to sound. His expedition had penetrated deep into Mexico, and he had brought quantities of goods.

St. Denis' calmness and poise bewildered the Spanish. He assumed the position that he had expected the Spaniards to be overjoyed at the prospect of trade; he had never expected that he might not return safely and the richer to his base at Mobile with the thanks of the Spanish. He boasted that his imprisonment at the Rio Grande had been voluntary and enjoyable, that he could have escaped, but he wished to marry the granddaughter of the commandant. Such a bold, international-minded character was something more than the unimaginative officials were prepared for. More astonishing still, they were soon to learn that this man's composure was not to be broken by chains and prison walls.

Before their long-sought prisoner finally arrived, the Spaniards had done much talking and writing on the subject. Upon the first warning received from the Pensacola governor, even before word had come of St. Denis' adventures at San Juan Bautista, the fiscal of Mexico City had recommended that active steps be taken to prevent any *entrada*. After long waiting and planning the Spaniards were well prepared to deal with St. Denis, or so they thought.

The viceroy had written Cadillac that he had been apprised of the intentions of the French and had warned him against entering any territory that belonged to the King of Spain. For many months Cadillac was without news from St. Denis, and in the interim additional protestations and warnings were received from the viceroy. Most alarming of all, Cadillac heard that the matter had been reported to the Spanish court. This had a personal touch, and he feared that it might give him trouble at home. For the leaders of the home government often were at variance about practical policies in the colonies, a nerve-racking variance for colonial officials. News had come from Vera Cruz by way of Pensacola that "St.

Denis and some other Frenchmen had been apprehended by eight hundred Spanish cavalrymen, who conducted them to Mexico in irons." St. Denis evidently was still at the Rio Grande when this report was received, but the story no doubt was deliberate, to convince the French governor that he should not try to send goods into Spanish territory. The premature dispatches, however, gave an ominous flavor to the real ones which followed.

Most distressing of all, the report came that the viceroy planned to send St. Denis to the gallows, or at least to Spain in irons. This report so disturbed Cadillac that he sent an appeal to the French minister to intercede at the court of Spain to have St. Denis and his companions released.

With the presumptuous Frenchman safely in their hands in the Mexican capital, the Spaniards felt that the threat of invasion could now be disposed of without delay. They were in a superb mood to give some stern and lasting lessons to all overambitious French traders.

After a time, St. Denis was brought from his cell to appear for questioning before the viceroy, Fernando de Alencastre, Noroña y Silva, Duke of Linares. St. Denis' answers were direct and consistent and were given with amazing calmness. He consistently asserted that he had been sent by the governor of Louisiana to locate Father Hidalgo and to secure some horses and cattle greatly needed by the people of Louisiana, for which they were willing to pay in silver or merchandise. He had not found Father Hidalgo among the Tejas as he had expected, and upon being told by the Indians that the priest was at the Rio Grande, he had continued his march to that place.

The viceroy was disconcerted. Such an involved, aggressive act could not be explained so lightly. No Spanish colonial report could be made properly from this meager story. The Spaniards were not accustomed to such simple and direct explanations. Not satisfied with St. Denis' reply, the viceroy ordered him to make a formal statement in writing, giving all the details connected with the expedition, so that it might be submitted to the fiscal together with his passport and a map of the country over which he had traveled.

All information concerning Texas since 1688 which was then in the office of the viceroy was turned over to the fiscal, Joseph Antonio de Espinosa Ocampo y Cornejo, that he might formulate therefrom a dictum embodying his opinion and recommendations on the matter to be laid before a *junta de guerra*.

St. Denis in his "declaration" again proved himself a master diplomat in his manner of relating the incidents of his journey. He stated that he was captain of Fort St. John, located on a small stream of that name which ran from the Mississippi River to Lake Pontchartrain. He had been called to Mobile by Governor Cadillac, and there he had been given the commission or patent now in possession of the viceroy. He had left Mobile with twenty-four French Canadians; twenty-one of these returned to Mobile from the Asinai. He had finally reached the presidio of San Juan Bautista on the Rio Grande a year and nine months, more or less, after his departure.[2] He described in detail the different stages of his journey and the physical characteristics of the country visited, most of them routine details which could not prejudice his cause.

[2] Indications are that an error was written into the original declaration. Either the time should have been described as "a year or nine months," or the period given was supposed to represent the time spent between Mobile and Mexico City, instead of between Mobile and the Rio Grande.

He emphasized at some length the natural affection which the Indians held for the Spaniards, and their great desire to have the priests return and establish missions among them. Never for a paragraph did he let the officials forget that he had come into the country by invitation of a Spaniard, and that the lost souls of the natives were at the bottom of it all. St. Denis pictured in glowing terms the fertility of the Tejas country, the richness of its fruit, the abundance of its flax, and the admirable qualities of the Tejas Indians. If the writer was a master at choosing his topics and phrases, he was a past master at the art of omission. He neglected to account for the "year and nine months" that it took him to make the trip. The matters of the two storehouses built at the village of the Natchitoches, the lively trade carried on with the Asinai during the long stop there, and his hurried visit back to Louisiana before continuing the journey escaped his memory. In view of the evidence piled up against him he made a remarkable effort to have it appear that the journey had been continuous and that nothing had happened during the entire trip prejudicial in any manner to the interests of the Spaniards. So cleverly did St. Denis conceal his omissions that few questions were raised.

The prosecutors were in such a hurry for St. Denis' official declaration that it was sent to the fiscal the day on which it was written, June 22, 1715.

The fiscal immediately drew up a dictum. He pointed out, as he had done before, that the introduction of merchandise into the provinces caused a great part of the silver from the rich mines to be diverted, with grave detriment to Spain; that the French, having learned the route to the Rio Grande, could "with impunity" introduce their merchandise in violation of the orders of the

Spanish king and with much detriment to the trade of the northern provinces. The map submitted by St. Denis, he noted, showed a more accurate knowledge of the country between the Tejas and the Rio Grande than that acquired by the Spaniards since the first *entrada* of the missionaries. The French had laid out a road to Coahuila, and it would be but a matter of a short time until they discovered the mines of Mexico. Their knowledge of the country would make illicit trade easy. In short, the commerce of the north was threatened with destruction, the mines were liable to immediate discovery, and Spanish possession of the province of Tejas was in imminent danger. The fiscal made two recommendations. The governors of the northern provinces must be reminded at once of their orders to prohibit Frenchmen from Spanish territory and instructed to put these orders into execution or face the most severe penalty; and missions must be established upon the eastern frontier without delay.

The fiscal further recommended that His Excellency issue the corresponding orders at the earliest possible moment for Father Antonio de San Buenaventura Olivares, Father Hidalgo, and one other religious, escorted by twenty or twenty-five soldiers, to proceed to the province of the Tejas without delay to establish a mission. "By this means, similar incursions will be prevented, and what is more and more important, these Indians will obtain instruction in our holy Catholic faith and the spiritual welfare of their souls, to which the zeal of His Most Christian and Catholic Majesty is so inclined."

What a spiritual revival St. Denis' arrival in Mexico City set off. Even before a recommendation was made for the disposal of St. Denis' case, specific and detailed plans were in motion to assemble the savages of Texas for attention to their immortal souls. For years the missionaries had prayed that the Spanish officials would be turned toward these heathen natives. And for years their supplications had gone unanswered until Father Hidalgo mixed a little scheming with prayer.

The viceroy considered the case so serious that he convoked a junta general as soon as the fiscal's dictum was received.

The day of the assembly, August 22, was an important day in Mexico. All the members of the royal *audiencia,* the alcaldes of the criminal court, the officers of the treasury, and other high dignitaries were present.

The report of the fiscal was read. Deliberation was brief. There was but one course to take. The junta unanimously agreed that the recommendations should be put into effect at once.

There was a question of finance, but this was an emergency. The fiscal, "fully aware of the depleted condition of the royal treasury," urged that all means, including funds for the military escort, be provided for the founding of a mission.

The assembly made numerous general recommendations to the viceroy, which he immediately formulated into colonial policy. The missionaries and soldiers were to be impressed with the supreme importance of doing their duty in civilizing the natives along the lines of Spanish allegiance; the incursion of the French would thus be prevented by this Indian buffer province and the introduction of French merchandise would be avoided. The missions would act as observation posts, and thus the strength of the French could be ascertained. The frontier officials were to be reminded that the French were not to be allowed to enter the province under any of the pretexts at which they were so adept, such as their urgent need for horses, cattle, grain, food, or supplies of any kind, even if they offered to pay cash for them. Only with the expressed consent of the king of Spain were Frenchmen to enter the province.

If stern policies and laws could have been enforced, the Spaniards had enough to keep the French forever where the Spaniards thought they should be kept. And if the viceroy had followed up his first threat and sent St. Denis to Spain or otherwise rid the country of him for good, his and his successors' laws for the frontier might have meant something. But that had been his plan before the viceroy had become acquainted with his distinguished prisoner; the failure to understand St. Denis was the undoing of many of Spain's most stringent statutes and fondest hopes.

For St. Denis gained his freedom. Just how is not definitely known. Doubtless the Spaniards came to regret it too much even to write about it, and St. Denis wrote little about himself. But the bare fact of his emergence from the position of prized captive into that of a visitor in favor with the viceroy suggests a miraculous story.

First, there is a legend which relates that St. Denis was released from prison through the intercession of a French officer whom he had known in Paris and who now had risen to high rank in the Spanish service. Many young Frenchmen had entered the service of Spain during this period, and the fact that St. Denis was well known in social and military circles of the French capital gives the story strength. Also, the Ramóns, especially Don Domingo, may have exerted some influence.

But viewing the episode in the light of later happenings, the greatest factors probably were the man's suave diplomacy (a politician's logic, which can turn adverse criticism and circumstances to advantage), his ability to laugh off what could not be explained and to make a joke of serious adversities, his cleverness at phrase-making that left no answer for opponents, and his keenness in anticipating his antagonist.

As long as St. Denis lived, he was a thorn in the flesh of the Spaniards. He outwitted them at every turn, tearing their resolutions and laws into shreds; making a mockery of their tedious, tyrannical policies; going and coming almost invariably when and where he pleased; being always polite, cunning, charming, unpredictable, the supreme puzzle to his opponents; letting both his power and generosity be known, and withal creating in his adversaries a strange blend of fear, love, and respect.

The Spaniards never found a way to outscheme St. Denis. Prisoner, diplomat, commander, trader, citizen—it was all the same. Title or position made little difference. The Spaniards in future years recognized and reconciled themselves to the fact that as long as he remained in the Southwest most of the happenings on the frontier would be influenced by his wishes. To the Spanish he never became "commandant," "Indian agent," "friend," or even "foe," but simply "St. Denis." His name became title and rank within itself. The triumph of St. Denis in Mexico City was one of those strange quirks of history that result from the magnetic personality of an individual.

From the dank prison of criminals, St. Denis was invited to the festivities of the viceregal palace, and there he was banqueted and courted. Spanish gentlemen were talking about the noble bearing, learning, and culture of this charming Frenchman and what a power the man might become. It appears that the Spaniards of influence considered that they now had this power under their control.

Banquets at the viceregal palace amazed even St. Denis, who knew the extravagant wonders of Paris. Here in the gorgeous halls of Montezuma, where the barbaric splendor of the Aztec emperors had been preserved, the Duke of Linares strove to add the gaiety of Versailles and the pompous pageantry of Spain. The dazzling result was a grandeur of both the Old and New Worlds. Not only the elaborate chandeliers but even the massive andirons in the banquet chamber were of silver. The utensils were deeply carved and embossed with magnificent designs. Walls were alive with paintings and ornamented with mirrors which multiplied and reflected the exotic beauty of the scene. According to the custom of the day the viceroy and attendants were dressed in the most elaborate and colorful costumes. Uniforms glittered with ribbons and royal decorations. Magnificence knew no limit. And St. Denis, thanks to the dutiful and meticulous Medar Jalot, had enough of an elaborate wardrobe so as not to be outshone by any of them.

In the glittering banquet halls St. Denis met the elite of New Spain—noblemen, soldiers, perfectly groomed magistrates, subtle diplomats, and smiling, bejeweled ladies. Over superb food and wine there was talk of Spain, Europe, and the New World. Afterward, there were smokes and subtle jokes for the men, and for those who chose, conversation with the ladies. These affairs were always very gay, very beautiful, very formal; but in these mirrored halls much of the shaping of the New

World was done—such shaping, that is, as the kings entrusted to colonials.

Sometimes St. Denis met the duke and they talked only of business and the affairs of state. The viceroy suggested that St. Denis would make a valuable man in the service of Spain, as were so many of his countrymen. And Spain offered such wonderful opportunities for men of his ability and accomplishments. The duke had heard that the Frenchman had his eye on a prominent and very beautiful Mexican *señorita,* that he desired to marry into one of the distinguished families of Mexico. Perhaps his guest's plan already was to enter the service of Spain? St. Denis was noted for his ability to carry on agreeable delicate conversations without committing himself. The Spaniards never learned Don Louis' secret. Possibly no one ever understood the man's inner secret power. He could give encouraging, agreeable impressions, but they were all very ambiguous. To feel that one knew St. Denis was only to fool oneself. One by one the Spaniards were to learn this, usually too late. And so weeks passed while there was talk of a possible change of allegiance and of arrangements, expeditions, possibilities of position, fortune, distinctions, new countries, and new people. St. Denis listened a great deal, talked a great deal, but said little.

It is quite possible that St. Denis never asked for anything while in Mexico. Though he was taken there as a prisoner, the Spaniards apparently played into his hands with no more encouragement than a mere hint. On one subject only St. Denis declared himself in no uncertain terms. Spain should settle the land of the Tejas, he announced, for here were wonderful possibilities—rich lands, Indian trade, and natives without benefit of the church. The Spaniards never completely saw through the man's motives. Many of the officials reasoned that he simply wished to marry a Spanish girl and become a citizen of Spain. For did he not talk of the advantages that would come to Spain from settling a country claimed by France? St. Denis puzzled as well as delighted Mexico City.

There were many conversations with the viceroy. Then the viceroy made a proposal that startled many people, but perhaps not St. Denis. If St. Denis did not wish to become a Spanish subject, perhaps he would at least lead a Spanish expedition back to the Tejas to found a mission. The viceroy had now worked into the very hands of his previous prisoner. Though he had, the calm, dignified Frenchman probably did not commit himself about his true intentions and still asked no favors of His Excellency. Anyway, he accepted the proposal.

Even if St. Denis had not helped promote the plan to resettle the Tejas country, he was the type of man who would have used the *entrada* to his advantage. It is possible that the idea of inciting the Spanish to move into East Texas was a long-range plan conceived by St. Denis before he reached the Rio Grande or even left the Natchitoches. He came into Spanish territory with one objective, to open up trade. His career was to prove that if he could not do a thing one way he would contrive to do it another. He had been told that Louisiana could not exist without trade, and, with good reasons, he believed it. The company could not weather many seasons without commerce—and where else could it come from if not from the Spaniards. Better than anyone else St. Denis knew the dangers and expense involved in trading over such a distant route as that from Natchitoches to the Rio Grande. There were many disadvantages to this wide separation of prospective customers. Losses from various sources were sure to occur. Convoying traffic over this hazardous distance might absorb all profits and run the company deeply into debt, or even out of business. Now if it was well and profitable to have the Spaniards for customers, it should be still more convenient and profitable to have them near the company storehouses. St. Denis held no youthful illusions about merchandising. With true business instinct, he knew the needs of the organization he served. He sensed the fundamental principles of economics: to increase one's traffic one should increase one's customers; the more prosperity the customers enjoy the more they can buy; and the shorter the haul the greater the margin of profit.

St. Denis did not belong to the diplomatic corps. He was not sent to Mexico to conquer or explore (any such activities were purely incidental) but rather to represent a commercial company which would stand or fall upon the trend of trade. Antoine Crozat, the proprietor, knew what was necessary to keep his associates and relatives, Governor Cadillac, and himself with a job or in business. Crozat was doing the one natural thing that any executive would do—he was pushing business, striving for dividends.

Some romancers have "explained" that St. Denis, at the time of his "inexplicable" decisions, was a man madly in love; a desperate pleasure-seeker, long confined and love-starved; and an adventurous fortune hunter whose lust for finery and wealth would drive him to desperate measures. They contend that with these great passions gnawing at him, he was hardly a man with a clear head.

Some have ventured the suggestion that he betrayed his country for love. But the man must be viewed in the light of his time and his instructions and, in particular, of the needs and demands of his immediate superiors. That policies, administrations, and needs of national governments conflicted and changed in time is not to be credited to St. Denis. He held only a small piece of destiny in his hands. That rulers should change their minds, often contradicting themselves and their agencies, and in the doing sometimes burst empires, fortunes, and reputations into pieces was beyond the power of any mortal to anticipate.

Evidently much political bargaining was carried on behind the scenes in Mexico City before and during the preparation for the reoccupation of the East Texas missions.

St. Denis accepted the position as *conductor de viveres* for the expedition to the Tejas. As guide he was allotted the same salary as the Spanish officer in command of the expedition "for such a period of time as his services were required," and he was even paid one half of his annual salary in advance.

The selection of the Spanish officer in charge gives rise to some interesting conjectures. The junta left the designation of the Spanish commander to the viceroy, with the admonition that he "exercise all care in choosing a man of ability, skill, and experience and one in whom are found the qualities and virtues necessary to aid in founding a mission, in congregating the Indians, in introducing our holy faith, and in procuring the spiritual welfare of their souls."

Now where could the viceroy find a man to meet the exacting requirements laid down by the junta? It hardly seems a coincidence that the man who "met" these requirements and in whom the viceroy recognized the required "ability, skill, and experience" was the one man in all Mexico whom St. Denis would have most desired to head the expedition: Alferez Domingo Ramón of San Juan Bautista, who was then in Mexico City.

Just when, how, or why Domingo Ramón came to Mexico City at this time is not definitely known. Possibly Emanuelle urged her uncle off to the capital in double haste to try to save her lover. Or perhaps Don Domingo, knowing St. Denis as he did, probably calculated that profitable dealings would ensue, that the Frenchman not only could take care of himself but others as well. Had he not done so in his first encounter in Mexico at the Rio Grande? Anyway, he was at the capital early enough to take advantage of the opportunities afforded by the new venture.

Just who helped whom is something to guess at. It is logical to assume that one of the Ramóns could have helped the Frenchman in his still-precarious situation. Don Domingo could give account of the man's good conduct during his stay at San Juan Bautista. He could say that St. Denis expected to marry his niece, that this was a good indication that he might become a Spanish subject. He may have whispered to the viceroy that he might convert St. Denis to the Spanish cause. It is possible that he had influential friends in the capital and that he used them in St. Denis' behalf. But the conjecture that Ramón acted on the belief that St. Denis might help him is equally probable. For St. Denis had made himself recognized at San Juan Bautista as a master diplomat, equipped with the best assets of the trade. It seems that at this early date Don Domingo Ramón had decided to hitch his wagon to St. Denis' star.

On September 30 Ramón and St. Denis received their official appointments. Ramón was promoted to the rank of captain. Preparations for the expedition had at this time been under way for more than a month. Apparently, after a long period of complacency in the capital, everyone was enthusiastically helping in the preparations.

As early as September 4 Ramón presented a long inventory of the goods which were considered necessary to outfit the twenty-five men of the expedition. Ramón estimated the cost of the goods at 5,000 pesos, plus 6,500 pesos for horses, 11,250 pesos for the salary of the soldiers, and 2,277 pesos for the cost of gifts for the Indians. In addition to the military equipment and accessories a number of interesting articles appeared on the list: one dozen pairs of ladies' silk hose, twelve bolts of assorted laces, eighteen bolts of various kinds of ribbon, four dozen men's and ladies' shoes, and eighteen pairs of silk hose for men. Items listed for the Indians included blankets, tobacco, blue- and red-woolen cloth, butcher knives, beads of various colors, medals, ribbons, and hats. Materials recommended for the mission indicated that the labor of the religious was not to be limited to spiritual vineyards, but that there would be much strenuous secular effort as well. Hoes, tillers, axes, hacksaws, hammers, chisels, cooking pots of various sizes, hand bars, yokes for oxen, and various kinds of seeds were included on the list.

One wonders what part St. Denis had in making the inventory. He was a man who always asked for more than he actually needed; and he may have been responsible for the fact that Don Domingo's list looked padded—at least to the factor, Ignacio José de Miranda, who cut this budget considerably. The factor approved 5,121 pesos for the soldiers instead of the requested 11,250 pesos, and 910 pesos for the Indians instead of 2,277 pesos. In years to come St. Denis was to teach the Spanish the folly of cutting down on this last item. He never discouraged spiritual aid for the Indians, but practical observer that he was, he never overlooked the effect that a few bright beads and colored cloth could have in gaining their political allegiances. What could be done with Indians the idealistic Spanish missionaries never seem to have learned.

On September 9, the viceroy ordered that instead of one mission there would be four. The expedition was growing in importance and in scope.

Both groups, the military and the religious, were happy, frightened, and ambitious over the reoccupation; but there was rivalry, as always, between the factions. For example, Father Juan Lopez Aguado, Guardian of the College of La Santa Cruz of Querétaro, made a special trip to Mexico City to see that the religious were not slighted in any way.

Father Aguado recommended that "everything being carried by Captain Domingo Ramón for the cultivation of the land be placed in charge of the religious, that in this manner they may be preserved and increased. . . . That in each of the missions that may be founded, two soldiers be placed to protect the religious, and that these be independent of the governor. That the soldiers not be allowed to undertake trips on private business, out of regard for the serious evils experienced in the missions founded heretofore." Many missionaries blamed the military for the failure of the first colonial venture in East Texas. As yet they had discovered no way to keep business and religion separated. Father Hidalgo, who possessed an exceptional practical slant, understood the necessity of combining the two.

The purpose of this expedition was in the point of view. To the missionaries it was a great spiritual campaign to save the souls of the Indians; to the officials at Mexico City it was an emergency campaign to save the vast territory of Texas for Spain; to St. Denis and the Ramóns it was primarily a commercial venture.

By November, the second inventories had been made, cut, and finally approved; reports and reports of reports written, rewritten, and at last accepted; finances scrapped from various departments, and excuses and justifications written about them. Purchases had been made, but in most cases too few; some soldiers had been recruited. But withal the Spanish colonial red tape had been cut. The day for which Father Hidalgo had prayed, dreamed, and schemed was dawning.

Domingo Ramón left Mexico City shortly after his appointment to go north to Saltillo to recruit mounted soldiers and collect livestock for the *entrada*. Don Domingo had done well for himself that summer and fall. He had come to Mexico an *alférez*, corresponding to the rank of ensign or second lieutenant; he left a captain, heading one of the most important expeditions ever to set out from the Mexican capital.

The force and supplies recommended for the expedition were small by modern standards, but at that time and place they were considered elaborate. Much time elapsed before Captain Ramón was prepared to move toward San Juan Bautista and East Texas.

St. Denis and Medar Jalot are not mentioned in Captain Ramón's diary before he reached the Rio Grande, and no records have been found of their activities in the capital after plans for the expedition were completed. So it is assumed that they had left earlier in the fall for San Juan Bautista.

There was much to prompt St. Denis to rush up to the Rio Grande. He was a man in love, and he was duly impatient; and the status of a considerable personal, as well as a company, investment was in doubt. Though he had had his moments of glory in the glamorous capital, he had been a prisoner for a long time, and he was not so unassuming as to trust all the Spaniards. He realized what the change to an unfriendly viceroy could yet do to him. Now, after so many long months of hardships, hair-trigger diplomacy, labor, and suspense, possession of the woman he loved, along with undisputed freedom and possible fortune, was in sight. These were reflections to hurry the steps of any man.

The reunion of St. Denis and Emanuelle at San Juan Bautista must have been one of great happiness. Both had waited long under nerve-racking and heart-rending suspense. During the endless days when their future hung so delicately in the balance, to be shifted by the whim of any one of many men, they had suffered the agony of separated lovers.

Like most long-parted lovers, they wanted to make up for every lost moment. They wanted to be married at once. But according to a long-accepted legend, a crisis arose.

Parenthetically, the legend gives the impression that

Diego Ramón, Emanuelle's grandfather, was not entirely in favor of the marriage. His was not a serious objection; it was perhaps akin to the age-old parental concern over impressionistic girls who tend to fall in love with the first dashing knight who comes along. Whether Grandfather Ramón was dubious of the lovers' sincerity or whether he was just stubborn or skeptical is not clear.

However, Diego Ramón had little time to reflect upon the proper course of events for the reunited lovers. San Juan Bautista was not the peaceful, orderly place it had been in the summer of 1714. A more serious and far-reaching problem faced the commandant than marrying off, or preventing the marriage of, a lovesick granddaughter. Not only the Ramón household but the entire mission and presidio were in gloom and despair. The Indians stationed around San Juan Bautista had deserted to the last man to escape Spanish despotism. Inasmuch as the chief function of the presidio was the conciliation and control of the frontier Indians, their departure meant abandonment of the mission, reduction of the presidio to uselessness, and for the commandant, loss of face and doubtless recall for misconduct or negligence.

The Frenchmen during their stay at San Juan Bautista had boasted of their leader's power over the natives, and St. Denis himself had referred to it with not too much modesty. When St. Denis reappeared, someone at the presidio recalled this talk, and the frustrated commandant was reminded of these boasts. And so, in desperation, he conceived the idea that this would be an excellent time to see what this highly recommended Frenchman could really do.

St. Denis could hardly have failed to volunteer to help. All wedding plans stopped. The fate of the post, and according to the belief of some observers, the fate of St. Denis' suit, hung upon the success of the Frenchman's mission.

St. Denis set out in pursuit of the Indians, possibly accompanied by Jalot. The natives formed a large caravan, and, moving with their women and children and all their effects, they traveled slowly, leaving a plain trail.

St. Denis had not gone far before he discovered the moving train of Indians from the top of a hill. Approaching within sight of the caravan, he raised his white handkerchief upon the point of his sword and hastened toward them. Apparently the chiefs hastily assembled in a powwow. At least, they halted long enough for St. Denis to catch up with them. When he reached them they formed a dense circle around him and waited for him to speak.

The account of his discourse with these Indians may not be wholly true in detail, but it is typical of St. Denis' insight into Indian character and his simple, direct reasoning with them. Although it may not be a word-for-word account, it appears to be entirely typical in spirit and method. St. Denis addressed the throng in Spanish, a language the Indians understood well:

> My friends, I am sent by the governor of the Presidio . . . to tell you that he pleads guilty to his red children; he confesses that you have been long laboring under grievances which he neglected to redress, and that you have been frequently oppressed by those whom it was his duty to keep in the straight path of rectitude. This is a frank avowal, as you see. With regard to the governor himself, you know that he has always been kind and upright, and that, personally and intentionally, he has never wronged any one of you: the old chief has been too weak with his own people—that is all you can say against him. But now, he pledges his faith

that no Spaniard shall be allowed to set his foot in your villages without your express consent, and that every sort of protection which you may claim shall be extended over your tribe. Do not, therefore, be obstinate, my friends, and do not keep shut the gates of your hearts, when the pale-faced chief, with his gray hairs, knocks for admittance, but let the words of repentance fall upon your souls, like a refreshing dew, and revive your drooping attachment for him. Do not give up your hereditary hunting-grounds, the cemeteries of your forefathers, and your ancestral villages, with rash precipitancy. Whither are you going? Your native soil does not stick to your feet, and it is the only soil which is always pleasant; and the wheat which grows upon it, is the only grain which will give you tasteful bread; and the sun which shines upon it, is the only sun whose rays do not scorch; and the refreshing showers which fall upon its bosom would elsewhere be impure and brackish water. You do not know what bitter weeds grow in the path of the stranger! You do not know how heavily the air he breathes weighs on his lungs in distant lands! And what distant lands will you be permitted to occupy, without fighting desperate battles with the nations upon whose territory you will have trespassed? When you will be no longer protected by the Spaniards, how will you resist the incessant attacks of the ferocious Comanches, who carry so far and wide their predatory expeditions? Thus, my friends, the evils you are running to are certain, and behind them, lie concealed in ambush still greater ones, which the keenest eye among you can not detect. But what have you to fear, if you return to your deserted villages? There, it is true, you will meet some old evils, but you are accustomed to them. That is one advantage; and, besides, you are given the assurance that to many of them a remedy will be applied. Why not make the experiment, and see how it will work? But if you persist in going away, and if you fare for the worse, your situation will be irretrievable. On the other hand, if you return, as I advise you, should the governor of the Presidio not keep his word, and should you not be satisfied, it will always be time enough to resume your desperate enterprise of emigration.[3]

When St. Denis had finished, there was a short powwow among the chiefs. Then they announced that they would follow him back.

At the approach of the returning tribes, the presidio of San Juan Bautista burst into a great demonstration of welcome. The Ramóns must have felt that they had been given a new lease on their professional lives. Commandant Ramón immediately proclaimed that the soldiers were not to visit or molest in any way the living quarters of the Indians, under penalty of death. The matter was successfully settled.

The entire Ramón household was duly impressed as well as grateful. One might have expected the sound of wedding bells immediately. Domingo Ramón's arrival from the south with the expedition was expected momentarily; then St. Denis would be off on the march into the wilderness again. Time was precious. But time was never a thing to bother the conventional Spanish. This was an eighteenth-century, Spanish, Catholic community. No circumstances could prevent an important wedding from coming off with proper ceremony.

The Ramón women had their say. There were many, many arrangements to be made—clothes, clothes, clothes, gifts, and fine foods and wines for banquets; and there must be plenty of time to plan and chatter if the momentous occasion was to be enjoyed and celebrated by everyone to its fullest.

After preliminary formalities, the marriage articles

[3] Charles A. Gayarré, *History of Louisiana* (New Orleans, 1903), I, 180–81.

. . . the first international wedding of note on the Franco-Spanish frontier.

were signed. At last a definite start had been made. St. Denis felt that under the pressure of circumstances some of the elaborate etiquette could be dispensed with; and Emanuelle, who enjoyed it, was restless, because she was afraid that the settling of a vast country and the saving of lost souls would not be delayed for the formalities of an elaborate wedding—even if the participants were important people.

And then, as if too much time had not already been lost, a relative was sent down to Monclova to buy dresses and other wedding accessories. St. Denis sent Jalot along to make purchases in his behalf. The shopping tour consumed a month. When they returned to San Juan Bautista with their purchases there were fittings and still more final arrangements. But before the end of a week preparations for the ceremony were at last completed.

San Juan Bautista was a riot of color and gaiety. Never before had the frontier witnessed such an impressive occasion; the pomp and ritual of old Spain blossomed. The entire population turned out, and Indians and Spaniards together lined the bridal path in phalanxes as the procession wound its way from the commandant's house up the gentle hill to the chapel. No detail of dress which the frontier could afford had been overlooked. To each of the soldiers St. Denis had given three piasters and a cockade of yellow ribbon for his hat. Soldiers as well as civilians were decked in gala attire.

At the altar seven priests officiated before an overflowing chapel.

The wedding festivities lasted three days. The soldiers feasted to their heart's content and did much firing of their musketry. During the celebration it was all play and no work at the presidio. This was a social affair the frontier was not likely to forget soon. If not the most important, the marriage was at least one of the most important international marriages that had taken place on the continent up to that time. It was the first international wedding of note on the Franco-Spanish frontier. Its far-reaching consequences were yet to be known.

VII

Texas Re-established

DOMINGO RAMÓN'S DELAYS IN SALTILLO added precious days to St. Denis' honeymoon. Just when the wedding took place is not certain;[1] it was probably during the last two months of 1715 or the first few days of 1716. At best, there was little time for the groom to make up for the long years in the forest solitude, especially since he would be off again as soon as Domingo arrived.

Life was different at San Juan Bautista now. Previously, St. Denis had been a prisoner with many risks to be faced before anything could be settled. But now he and his bride could relax and enjoy themselves without the bother of chaperones or the fear of a summons. It was the cool, dry season so suitable for *fiestas*. St. Denis and Emanuelle made the most of their numbered days, even as they looked often to the southward scanning the desert for a messenger or a procession they did not want to see.

Despite the suspense and business distractions, these were proud and happy days for St. Denis. For the most beautiful girl in Mexico was his bride. Further, he

---

[1] St. Denis was in Mexico City as late as September 7, for on that date he wrote a letter to Governor Cadillac. One writer recorded the date as early as October 26, the same date which one document gives as the time of his departure from the Mexican capital. Logic would place the marriage date much later than October 26.

had been successful in arranging Spanish trade for the Louisiana Company, even if the Spanish officials in Mexico City either did not know or did not believe it yet.

St. Denis' honeymoon did not take his mind completely from the fine art of trade. He had brought a great deal of merchandise to the Rio Grande, and though it had been technically confiscated it is hardly to be supposed that, with his connection with the commanding family, all was appropriated by the Spanish government. Penicault and Largen may have disposed of some merchandise. They reputedly left San Juan a month after St. Denis was carried into the interior, but exactly what happened to the goods is still unknown.

It was February 17, 1716, before Domingo Ramón decided that his force was strong enough to leave Saltillo, and even then he was not adequately prepared. The priests held the train up for ten days while they collected alms at Saltillo; and finally, he had to wait for more horses—he was always short of horses. This campaign to reach the Tejas before the French called for more haste than the Spanish were accustomed to, or could understand.

But the march crept on, with a tempo typically eighteenth-century Spanish, plagued always with its petty and dramatic troubles; delayed by frequent, long religious ceremonies, desertions, deaths, births, fun-making. The light-hearted Spaniard could mix his troubles with his fun so that his life appeared strangely frivolous and dramatic at the same moment. He could laugh at misfortunes through a veil of tears, but he refused to be hurried. *Mañana* would always take care of itself.

Most of the last half of March passed while the party was stopped—awaiting more horses, celebrating religious holidays, looking for watering holes in barren country, waiting for a woman in labor to give birth to a baby, searching for a small boy hopelessly lost in the woods, "hunting lost mules and wild horses." There seemed no end to the delays.

On April 17, exactly two months after the expedition left Saltillo, it crossed Amole Creek and came within a day's march of San Juan Bautista.

The next day, Commandant Diego Ramón, accompanied by his officers and men, met his son Domingo's expedition two leagues out from San Juan Bautista. It was a long-awaited occasion, and each party must have tried to outdo the other. Commandant Ramón drew his men up in line on either side of the road, and when the procession came in sight the soldiers fired a roaring salute. Domingo Ramón, in true Spanish fashion, returned the compliments.

It was not entirely a military ceremony. The religious also had their ceremonious greetings. Father Espinosa, president of the missions of the Rio Grande, turned out, accompanied by three religious, to salute the party.

The presidio staged a colorful spontaneous welcome. Gay banners and lace handkerchiefs waved from everywhere. The *fiesta*-dressed male population lined the streets. And the travelers, equal to the occasion, paraded through the town in their most impressive formations.

The expedition had reached the last Spanish outpost. Ahead lay contested, unmapped territory.

No time was lost at San Juan Bautista. The day after its arrival the ensemble was busy assembling provisions and supplies preparatory to crossing the Rio Grande, and on the following morning it pushed on. By dusk that day the equipment and supplies, including more than a thousand head of goats and sheep, had been floated across the river.

But once across the Rio Grande the inevitable delays began again. More livestock had to be rounded up and brought across. Then two days were spent celebrating the marriage of a soldier and the daughter of one of the settlers traveling with the expedition. Finally, there was further waiting for the missionaries to catch up; one of them had fallen ill and two friars and two soldiers had been left to attend him. Doubtless the French guide did little to hurry the undertaking so long as it lingered near San Juan Bautista.

At last, on April 27 the expedition was ready to march into the Tejas country. It had now entered the "wilderness." Long dreams, prayers, and schemes were materializing.

That day the long train passed in review before Captain Ramón, and he listed all the persons on the expedition. What a strange, colorful, motley crew he reviewed: at the head of the column marched the dignified and resolute Father Espinosa, followed by seven other priests and two lay brothers.[2] Near Father Espinosa marched the ardent and zealous Father Hidalgo. Twenty-three years had passed since he had seen his beloved neophytes of the Tejas. His hair had turned white during the waiting, but his faith, his energy, or his prayers had never slackened, or his sense of humor dulled; his body appeared as unbending and unbroken as his spirit, for it was noted that he walked erectly and that his countenance glowed.

[2] Two other priests joined the party later, before it reached the Tejas country.

Before him at last was his promised land, and as long as he could utter a prayer he would remember the Frenchman who had crossed the Red River, the Rio Grande, and the mountains of Mexico and made this day possible.

Behind the religious marched the military. This position in the ranks was arranged to demonstrate the relative position of the two departments. The soldiers were coming along to lend support and protection to the missionaries. Had it not been a missionary who brought St. Denis into Spanish territory, and thus furnished the stimulus for this expedition? No wonder there was a glow on Father Hidalgo's face.

Twenty-five mounted soldiers were counted and listed, not including Commander Domingo Ramón. The list of the military included the second Diego Ramón, father-in-law of St. Denis, with the rank of *alférez,* and another Diego Ramón, son of Captain Domingo, with the same name and rank as his uncle.

Captain Ramón listed three Frenchmen with the civilians: "Captain Don Luis de St. Denis, *Cabo Comboyador,* Juan Medar [Jalot], and Pedro Largen." One wonders about Largen. Did he fail to leave San Juan Bautista after St. Denis' departure, as reported, or is his presence an indication that there had been continued visits between the French and Spanish all the time?

The civilians formed a varied group. The list included two retired military men—an ex-ensign and an ex-sergeant—with their families, seven married women and one betrothed woman, two mule drivers, ten helpers to drive the stock and conduct the freight, one Negro, two Indian guides, three Indian goat drivers, one boy six years old, and a girl four years old. In all, the traveling population amounted to between 75 and 80 persons.

Captain Ramón listed 64 oxen, 490 horses and mules, and more than 1,000 goats and sheep. A final check was made of the great assortment of luggage, supplies, gifts for the Indians, and equipment for the missions. There was not as much of anything as Ramón had asked for. But he was determined to do his best with what he had.

Much of the morning passed before Captain Ramón completed his inspection and brought his roster up to date. But at last the expedition was across the Rio Grande on the march toward the long-anticipated land of the Tejas.

Up in front now rode Captain Ramón; and by his side, St. Denis, guide, scout, interpreter, advance agent; behind them or along the ranks, the two Diego Ramóns; then the missionaries with their coarse, drab robes rippling in the late May breeze, silent, determined, with a visionary gleam in their zealous eyes; finally, the procession of pack animals, drivers, soldiers, civilians, and livestock. A monstrous, rumbling blend of sounds echoed dully across the low-lying hills as the motley pageant wormed its way onward—cows lowing, goats bleating, stock drivers yelling at their animals, cavalrymen shouting their commands, and the never-ending thump of leathered and hoofed feet beating upon the dark Tejas soil.

The group was varied indeed, with purposes equally as varied: the missionaries, the wholly unselfish segment, coming with thoughts only of converting and teaching the savages, their reward one to the spirit only; the soldiers, some coming along purely for the excitement of a new adventure or a fight, or just for a full stomach and adequate clothes or the simple hope of finding a more comfortable place to exist; civilians (whose different purposes may have equaled their number), some hoping to settle in a more advantageous country and rear a family, some to be on hand if mines were discovered or profitable trade developed; the helpers, in the main, coming as simple, discouraged fortune-seekers; the Ramóns, hoping for promotions, perhaps, contraband trade, or, more altruistically, for legalized trade, expansion of Spain's dominion, or conversion of the natives. Domingo Ramón's diary indicated a conscientious interest in the mission work as well as a true religious nature. Missionary work and smuggling were almost inseparable enterprises along the frontier during the middle eighteenth century. Whatever their motives, there is little doubt that the Ramóns were under the spell of their new French in-law.

It was as if Texas was coming into being that winter and spring, as if a part of old Mexico was flowing out of its tall mountains onto the rolling hills toward the Sabine and Red rivers—a mere trickle of a stream, in time to become a river and then a sea, deep, vast, and permanent.

St. Denis' purpose appears to have been clear-cut and logical. However, the expedition set off endless speculations about his motives.[3] He was to be accused, among other things, of letting Spain rather than France get possession of the Tejas country. But in view of the commercial situation there appears no ground for concluding that he ever knowingly gave Spain what he considered an advantage at the expense of France. Once he allowed the Spaniards to come as close as he thought the Louisiana

---

[3] It has been claimed that he led the Spanish expedition into contested territory to get himself out of prison in Mexico. Various facts contradict this probable motive; once out of prison he might have escaped or ridden quietly out of the capital without difficulty. And time was to prove that he was never too afraid of the Spanish to go near them, whether to fight, visit, or trade.

colony needed them for their trade, that was as near as they could ever come, try as they might.

St. Denis kept his superiors well informed concerning his actions and plans;[4] and there is no indication that he was ever censured for his actions by them. Cadillac in one of his letters referred to statements about the Spanish made by St. Denis in his communications from Mexico: "He is certain that they will be maintained [along our frontier] only if it is agreeable to us. It will be easy to destroy [the mission] or take it from them." Just how his agent proposed to keep the Spanish near enough to be profitable to the Louisiana Company and no nearer, how he would "destroy" them if desirable, were questions not clear in the governor's mind but apparently not a source of particular worry to him. Possibly he did not believe that St. Denis or anyone else could maintain such a delicate balance. But trade was a requisite for survival. Due partly, perhaps, to St. Denis' diplomacy and partly to coincidence, the trade was maintained and the Spanish-French boundaries were respected as long as St. Denis lived.

[4] While at the Rio Grande as a prisoner St. Denis had been able to correspond with his governor to a surprising extent. In Mexico City he appears to have kept Governor Cadillac well informed about what was happening. On September 7, 1715, he had written him that the viceroy was preparing to send a party to establish a mission among the Tejas. (Only two days later the viceroy was to authorize the three additional missions.) He recommended that a brigantine be sent to occupy the Bay of Espiritu Santo, San Luis, or San Bernardo, with two purposes: ". . . first, in order to control all the natives between Mobile and the said bay, and second to make certain of having a depot easily accessible by sea or land wherein to keep our merchandise, near to Coahuila and Nuevo Reyno de Leon." It is claimed also that St. Denis wrote Governor Cadillac that it would be necessary for the king of France to demand that the boundary of Louisiana be fixed at the Rio Grande. Contradictory as it may appear, it is probable that St. Denis did make such a recommendation. He obviously felt that he could handle the Spaniards in the Tejas country.

This first, hopeful day beyond the Rio Grande was plagued to the very end. The country was without water, and men and stock alike suffered. Only three leagues were covered. That night, just as the missionaries were completing the evening services, a terrible storm arose. Ramón recorded in his diary that "nearly all our supplies which were piled on the ground were blown down." The main pole of one of the tents was crushed under the impact of the fury, and for a while it seemed that everything would be twisted loose and swept away by the raging wind. One cavalryman was picked up, horse and all, and hurled through the air a considerable distance. The horses and other stock stampeded in the confusion. The missionaries fell on their knees and prayed to the Mother of Sorrows and all their patron saints for deliverance. There were moments when it appeared that the expedition would end after only one day in the northern country.

But after a time the wind and rain subsided, the stampeded stock was rounded up, and the supplies were found to be more scattered than spoiled. The religious held a service of thanksgiving because all the stock had been found and the losses were slight. The padres offered explanations for the seemingly unnatural phenomenon of the storm by suggesting that it was a battle with the devil to keep them from their work—"the infernal furies had instigated it!"

The next day St. Denis returned to San Juan Bautista for a few hours. Father Espinosa related that it was "for an Indian." One wonders if this was an explanation or an excuse. It is not surprising to find if such a trip was necessary, St. Denis was the man to make it. A last visit with his pretty bride was a privilege no one would have denied him.

There were times when only the most faithful and optimistic could believe that all the omens were not against the undertaking. On the third day some Pacuache Indians stole twenty horses. The scarcity of horses made this a calamitous loss. So Lorenzo García, the ex-sergeant, was sent out in pursuit of the Indians. He tracked them down, recovered the horses, and captured four Indian thieves. García must have been a brave and efficient man, as well as a rough one with Indians. For when Ramón saw the captives he was so moved by their frightened condition that he decided they had received punishment enough. Instead of hanging them, as he had said he would if they were ever caught again stealing horses, he gave them tobacco and set them free.

Father Espinosa kept a diary and preserved many interesting details of the journey. Though he devoted much space to accounts of religious ceremonies, mishaps, and routine details, he gave ample evidence of having enjoyed much of the beauty and adventure of the travels. While the captain worried about lost horses and outlaw Indians he observed the landscape. "We passed a few low hills without trees," he wrote, and described "sandy brooks . . . several marshes with mesquite and Indian fig trees, whose fruit was not ripe." He reported on the weather, speaking of "depressing heat." On May 1 the father found the scenery more beautiful. Even Ramón took time to record in his diary that the party passed over "a beautiful country, a land covered with a variety of flowers with admirable fragrance."

The following day the Nueces River was reached, but the river was so low that it was necessary to deepen one of the small pools to permit the animals to drink. Despite the dryness and "scorching sun" Father Espinosa found the Nueces River attractive with its "abundance of ash trees, walnut, mulberry and others of various kinds. . . . We were hailed by mosquitoes playing their trumpets who entertained us both day and night."

May 3 was Sunday, so the procession halted to celebrate the feast of the Finding of the Holy Cross. Seven masses were said; a considerable number received communion; and a large procession was formed, in which a cross, made and blessed for the purpose, was carried with great solemnity.

May 4 was both an amusing and a near-tragic day. Commander Ramón came near losing his life, or so he recorded. The incident all started as some innocent fun inspired by "one of the Frenchmen," who attempted to show his skill at picking a hat from the ground while riding. His act must have been most challenging. Apparently, most of the Spaniards contested; for there were five severe falls—including that of the commander—while they were trying to imitate or outdo the Frenchman.

It appears that this showing-off and frolicking took place out of sight of the priests, as they did not record such frivolities. Father Espinosa told of the accidents but attributed the mishaps to "land so rough and swampy."

The Ramóns apparently were not just hangers-on or family appointees taking advantage of their situation. None, seemingly, shirked his duties, though it is not entirely clear what these duties were. For instance, the next day after the reckless sports events, there was "no little amusement and surprise" in camp when "Diego Ramón" (it is not certain which one) told how he had captured Joseph del Toro, a runaway soldier. He had left the caravan in search of the fugitive, accompanied by an Indian. When the runaway soldier was discovered hidden in the top of a tree Diego told the Indian in a loud voice that he was going to shoot into the tree, whereupon the Indian associate, as prearranged, begged him, "in God's name," not to shoot the soldier. Before the dialogue progressed far the fugitive tumbled out of the tree. This was considered a great joke, and the story spread rapidly throughout the camp.

May 5 marked another wedding. Anna Guerra, a mestiza, and Lorenzo Mercado, a Spanish soldier, were joined in wedlock, as Captain Ramón had promised they might be, "provided the proper practices were observed before the marriage ceremony." Now that the banns had been published and the "proper practices" observed, the wedding came off with "due solemnity" and fireworks; the Spaniards were never in too big a hurry to find an occasion for a *fiesta*. It is probable that this marriage between Spaniards was the first to take place between the Rio Grande and the San Antonio.

When the party again took up the march it was, according to Captain Ramón, "near the foot of some hills extending down to beautiful canyons with oak trees and many strange and unknown flowers of rare fragrance, among them a great deal of marjoram." Father Espinosa recorded simply that their path was adorned by "flowers praising their creator."

For a whole week the beauty and the strangeness of the country were the subjects of the diarists. This new land beyond the Rio Grande was presenting flowers, trees, fruit, and vines in a quantity and beauty that the Spaniards had never seen before. There were pecan groves, beautiful lakes, "clusters of mesquite, woodlands of oak and poplars, . . . thickets of brambles and briars." A grapevine "almost a yard in circumference" was found. There were bubbling springs and hills of "small stones." Ramón also commented on the "loose dirt" and "good pasturage," the "fishing," the "frost" and "intense heat." The weather must have been as varied as the landscape.

May 13 was a bad day. When the horses were started across the Medina River they swam over to a high bank. The lead horses, unable to climb the bank, turned or fell back; and soon the whole drove was milling in the deep part of the river. Before they could be rescued, eighty-three were drowned. This was a near-disaster. There was "grievous discouragement among the weaker hearts." To prevent discouragement Ramón paid the owners of the horses out of his own pocket—or so his diary says. Yet, he writes further, "all of them said that if all the animals had been drowned they would have continued on such a blessed journey. Perhaps the devil had done this to hinder the conflict about to be made against him. To crush him a High Mass was said the following day."

The next day was well suited to lift their spirits. The party reached the San Pedro Spring and the San Antonio River, one of the beauty spots of the entire journey. Father Espinosa declared the scene a most desirable place for a mission. He found the river "surrounded by tall nopals, strawberry vines, and genuine fan palms, flax, wild hemp, abundance of maiden hair fern, many medicinal herbs. . . . waters are clear, crystal and sweet."

On the seventeenth, according to Espinosa, St. Denis and Jalot "went ahead [eastward] to look for the Tejas who were to come and meet us."

May 27 was a red-letter day of sport and feasting.

Captain Ramón and most of his party had their first sight and taste of buffalo. The occasion inspired an interesting description of the beast in his diary: "The animal at first sight is beautiful, but on closer observation is ugly. It is larger than an ox, with hoofs very much the same; and the horns although very black are much shorter and curved. The buffalo neck up to the forehead is ill shaped. The bison has long hair which obstructs its view. For that reason it runs against the wind. The animal is very malodorous, does not hear well and sees less on account of the mane of hair.... It has a tail like a hog. It runs very fast, and a horse must be very quick to catch it. The bison has more meat than two steers, and is very wholesome and good."

Father Espinosa's diary entry for the following day relates that "some of the men ate too much meat and had stomach ache."

The next day the expedition delayed while the men recovered, the missionaries said seven masses, and the buffalo meat dried.

The period from June 3 to June 12 was the proverbial dark hours before dawn. The party had reached a literal wilderness. The timber was no longer sparse or even in groves. The undergrowth had thickened, and vines grew rampant with new foliage that made a matted, blinding wall. A labyrinth of winding streams laced with willows and briars brought disheartening confusion. There was no grazing ground. Men and animals wandered bewildered in the denseness.

In the thick of it St. Denis rejoined the main body. He must have told a tale of extreme hardship, for Father Espinosa wrote: "Learning of the hardships [St. Denis] underwent we gave thanks to God that we had not traveled through the forest where he came, because our way was the most clear."

It is significant that it was the missionaries who wrote most of St. Denis. There is not the least indication of enmity between St. Denis and Captain Ramón; but because of St. Denis' overshadowing personality, thorough knowledge of the country, and uncanny anticipation of Indian action and thought, the Spanish leader might easily have been a little jealous. If he was, he did not record deeds in his own diary of another man who may have stolen the show.

Even though lost, St. Denis could swagger about like a man master of all he surveyed. Ramón was the plodder —capable, but feeling his way in unfamiliar country with a new job and new responsibilities that weighed upon him. It would seem that responsibility did not worry St. Denis. His was the soldier's outlook—self-confident, relying upon his training and experience, his efficiency and best effort.

On June 12 the travelers came upon a delegation of Indians of various nations. This is assumed to be a meeting prearranged by St. Denis on the advance mission he had undertaken with Jalot. One of the head chiefs knew Captain Ramón through unusual circumstances. He had many years ago "led thieving expeditions to the presidio on the Rio Grande" and in the course of events came in contact with Ramón. The *entrada* was guided to the Indian village where they pitched camp "about a rifle's shot from the village." There were feasting, religious ceremonies, and, at long last, trading. The meeting was considered a diplomatic as well as business success.

When the Brazos was reached there was plenty of help from the Indians in getting the equipment across the swollen stream. The main obstacle was an alligator which frightened the natives from their work. But Captain Ramón was equal to the occasion: "I relieved the anxiety by shooting the alligator through the eye, as this is the only vulnerable spot. The Indians were greatly impressed with my marksmanship."

By the time of the Brazos crossing St. Denis, accompanied by young Diego, the son of Captain Ramón, had set out ahead of the main party to inform the Tejas of the approach of the expedition. A few days later Diego Ramón returned and announced that St. Denis was assembling all the Asinai to greet the Spaniards. St. Denis was once again acting in his most fascinating role—one in which he was unsurpassed—that of master of ceremonies and spokesman for the Indians. The fact that St. Denis went ahead of the main expedition indicates that his influence among the Tejas was greater than that of the Spaniards. That he was able to assemble them so quickly and rehearse them in the proper ceremonies for greeting the Spaniards showed his great power among them.

Making the proper impression on the Indians was one of the most delicate and important functions of the campaign. For upon their friendship, or lack of it, the "occupation" would stand or fall. Many of the tribesmen wished to see the Spaniards return, but the sentiment was far from unanimous. When Diego Ramón reported that the Indians had rallied around St. Denis and were preparing to welcome the *entrada*, the Spaniards were happy as well as relieved. This welcome did not ensure success, but it indicated a good start. If St. Denis thought he was using the Spanish to the advantage of himself and France, the Spanish likewise felt that they were using the

Frenchman to the profit of Spain and the Church. It is yet an interesting speculation as to who used whom to the best advantage.

It was on June 27, according to Father Espinosa, that the long-awaited event took place. St. Denis, with the Indians, met the expedition. The priest watched the proceedings with deep joy. "News was brought of the approach of Don Luis with the Indians," he wrote, "and we got ready to receive them. They came in file behind Don Luis, and were received in the following manner. We arranged the soldiers in two files placing our captain in the center with the Religious, and in this order we went to greet and embrace them, our hearts overflowing with joy. In order to enter befittingly, the Indians left their horses behind with their bows and arrows and firearms. . . . There was a general salute on our part, and in the meantime we went to the place prepared for the reception."

Captain Ramón also wrote a description of the meeting: "I marched in the center accompanied by the Religious, and carried the banner. St. Denis fell on his knees to venerate the token. In succession he embraced me and all the Religious. He [was] followed by all the captains and the other people." This was St. Denis setting the proper example, teaching many fundamental, all-important lessons in a few simple gestures. The Indians might, in time, grow tired of the Spaniards, but they would never forget the solemn, colorful formalities of this reception led by the Great White Father from the east, who knew so well the proper way of doing things, and whom the forest men could follow with such confidence.

At the place of reception the pipe of peace was smoked, gifts distributed, and salutes fired. Through St. Denis, Captain Ramón addressed them, saying that the Spaniards had come to look after the welfare of their souls and to bring them to a recognition of the authority of King Philip V, who, by the hands of the Duke of Linares, viceroy of New Spain, had sent them these gifts as a token of his love.

Similar ceremonies followed during the next days while the work of establishing the four missions began. The missions were established along or near the road by which the French had made their "incursions" into the Tejas country, and thus were intended to guard against further "trespasses." Spain now had settlements as far east as the present Nacogdoches County.[5]

Father Hidalgo was befittingly appointed pastor of the first re-established mission. Five years and five months had passed since he had written the famous letter that stimulated this expedition, but now his great day had arrived.

Various estimates of this expedition have been made: it was merely a romantic escapade of a young and daring adventurer, who had won a Spanish bride; a great missionary revival; the permanent laying-out of a great thoroughfare, the San Antonio Road, through Texas; a life-saving commercial arrangement for France. The real significance of the expedition is that it led to the firm establishment of the Spanish in Texas and gave strength to their claim to the land east of the Rio Grande

[5] These missions were Neustro Padre San Francisco de los Tejas, on the Neches River; La Purísima Concepción, on the Angelina River, nine leagues north of the first mission; Nuestra Señora de Guadalupe, on the present site of the city of Nacogdoches; and San José, near the northern boundary of Nacogdoches County.

by fact of actual possession. It decided, in a great measure, that Texas should be Spanish and not French and that the eventual boundary between the United States and Mexico should be the Sabine and not the Rio Grande.

VIII

Second Expedition to Mexico

BY EARLY SEPTEMBER ST. DENIS WAS BACK IN Mobile, telling of his narrow escapes, his beautiful wife, the vast, promising country to the west, and the great advantages of trade with the Spaniards, and introducing his father-in-law, a soldier of the Spanish army now turned horse trader.

Despite hardships, reverses, and the official enmity of the Spanish, St. Denis had much to show for his efforts. He had brought customers near by; he had married into an influential Spanish family; he gave evidence that he could handle both the Indians and the Spaniards on their own grounds. The governor was "charmed" at his success, and the bored soldiers and monotony-cursed civilians of the isolated little post were wide-eyed with admiration.

While Don Diego went about his profitable business of horse dealing, St. Denis and Governor Cadillac and his aides talked over the possibilities of another trading expedition into Spanish territory.

The tone of their talk was that of gamblers and speculators sobered by a common understanding of the risks of their proposed enterprise. It was as if St. Denis had plunged into the wilderness and tweaked the whiskers of the great lion of the mountains of Mexico. If the lion had been curried gently with apparent favors until he appeared friendly or asleep, a little tramping on Spanish soil under the weight of bundled French merchandise might awaken him into a destructive, dangerous mood; at the very least, he might be roused into a roaring protest that would be heard far enough to bring political or commercial ruin to them all.

Governor Cadillac was not a man without understanding or imagination. He was caught between the variant policies of the company and the home government—a situation which demanded, in effect, that he promote a highly hazardous trade to support his company at his own risk, without official government sanction. Fundamentally, the company had to make a profit, and the only apparent means at the moment was through Spanish trade. If another commercial invasion of Mexico should cause a serious international incident and goods and men should be lost—well, that would be unfortunate. But St. Denis suggested that he could handle the situation. The governor wanted to believe him and needed to believe him; in the end urgency tipped the balance, requiring him to believe him. The men decided upon another expedition.

Just what kind of an arrangement was made is not clear. One account states simply that St. Denis proposed to some Canadians that they join him in a trading expedition into Spanish territory. Goods were to come from Crozat's stores. How many men entered into the co-partnership cannot be said, because before the venture was over the weakhearted had scattered and were trying to avoid having their names connected with the affair. It is evident that St. Denis had some partners, for the amount of merchandise involved has been placed at be-

SECOND EXPEDITION TO MEXICO

tween 43,200 and 89,214 livres. One account has it that the above-listed persons took 69,214 livres worth of merchandise belonging to the India Company, and 20,000 livres which were paid for by the traders. Apparently the enterprise was partly private and partly a company venture, but the whole story cannot be known. The matter, first and last, possibly inspired as much recorded lying as any one incident that occurred on the Franco-Spanish frontier.

St. Denis and his party left Mobile in October and arrived at Natchitoches on November 25. Here St. Denis purchased some horses and then continued, with his father-in-law, to the Spanish missions clustered in the area of present-day Nacogdoches, Texas. They arrived in time for a Christmas family reunion.

But it was not a happy Christmas at the missions. Hard times had befallen the Spanish settlements. A severe winter had set in with cold northers and flooding rains; malaria had sickened and killed many; soldiers had deserted; because of swollen rivers, hostile Indians, lack of funds, and the great distance to their base, supplies were critically short; some of the tribes refused to be congregated and continued to be idolators, much to the consternation of the religious, who could not destroy the Indians' idols without a larger garrison for protection.

But the spirit of the missionaries had not been dampened. They had failed to gain many converts, but this only made them eager to seek other fields. However, adverse circumstances had deleted their power or understanding for expansion. Some looked upon St. Denis' reappearance as an instrument of answered prayer. Strange that this foreigner repeatedly should be such an inspiration and help to the missionary colonizers.

With the help of St. Denis, who had a knack for getting work out of the Indians that the Spanish never achieved, the religious began the construction of two additional missions.[1] St. Denis helped in other practical ways. He made three trips back to Natchitoches to buy maize for the six missions. If he was carrying on trading activities in the meantime, the missionaries loved him none the less for them. They saw more clearly than the soldiers how dependent they were upon him for control of the Indians, which meant, among other things, the keeping of their scalps intact.

St. Denis remained among the Tejas until March, 1717, when he left part of his goods in the care of four associates and a servant and set out for the Rio Grande. Accompanying him were his father-in-law and Alférez Francisco Hernandez, by whom Captain Domingo Ramón sent dispatches to Don Martin de Alarcón, the newly appointed governor of "Coahuila and the Province of the Tejas." Captain Ramón also very thoughtfully sent along his mule train to be placed at the disposal of the new governor. If his nephew-in-law should happen to load the mules with some merchandise it was not supposed that it would harm either the mules or the family relationships. Supposedly these were army mules; and so while Spanish officials were protesting against the menace

---

[1] This is based upon St. Denis' declaration in 1717. The missions referred to were possibly Dolores de los Ais, and San Miguel de Linares among the Adaes Indians. The account of the founding of these missions is open to debate. It is possible that Ramón established them in 1716; St. Denis may have helped him at the time. The more probable date is the spring of 1717. It is probable that plans were made at this time but that nothing of a permanent nature was built. The beginning and finishing dates may have been far apart, thus causing confusion in reference to them. Though some construction and religious activities may have already been underway, there seems reason to believe that St. Denis helped in some way with building or improving the missions.

of French encroachers, it appears that St. Denis was quietly smuggling his goods—or at least part of them—into the heart of Mexico on the backs of mules belonging to His Majesty, King Philip V.

Between the Colorado and Onion Creek the party was attacked by a band of seventy Apaches. A strange tale was told about this encounter. The Indians were covered with buffalo hides, which made them somewhat the harder to overcome, said St. Denis. The savages were at first driven off; however, they later made a surprise attack from the rear and succeeded in driving off fifteen loaded mules and twenty-seven other animals before they were put to flight. In view of the lengthy arguments that later came up over the amount of this cargo, one wonders if the reported loss might not have been greatly exaggerated to help Grandfather Ramón explain the unexpectedly small amount of goods that supposedly arrived and were shortly to be confiscated at San Juan Bautista. Such an Indian raid could have served as a most convenient explanation. And explanations as to how the cargo had dwindled were at a premium before the matter was quieted.

Somewhere north of the Rio Grande St. Denis left the main party and hastened on to San Juan Bautista. A messenger had apparently contacted him with exhilarating news. The cumbersome mule caravan moved much too slowly for a man traveling to see his young wife and his first-born.

It had been nearly a year since Emanuelle had told her husband good-by after a brief honeymoon. Life had been comparatively dull for her since the memorable weeks filled with the strange and spectacular activities of her lover and husband. Her life, in a great measure, was to be a series of waitings for her restless, traveling mate.

It was a joyous reunion. St. Denis thought Emanuelle more beautiful than ever. And the baby was named after her father. St. Denis was expansive in his pride. "Luisa Margarita"[2] was a typically Spanish name, but the French father had been remembered in the supreme manner, and he was intrigued to find his name made both Spanish and feminine.

If St. Denis or Emanuelle thought he could now settle down to peaceful home life and unhampered trade, the pleasant illusion did not last long. Trouble began almost at once, as soon as St. Denis' merchandise caught up with him at San Juan Bautista. St. Denis' *entrada* and the approximate amount of his goods were no secret in Mexico by the time he arrived on the Rio Grande. The jealous and alert Spaniards at Pensacola had rather accurate information as to what he had planned and done since his departure from Mobile. The Frenchman's delay on the eastern frontier had allowed the news to precede him to the interior of Mexico. Captain Gregorio Salinas Varona of Pensacola had early informed the viceroy that St. Denis had left Mobile for the Rio Grande with 30,000 pesos' worth of merchandise. And without doubt some eager patriot from East Texas reported how many mule loads of merchandise left there. For many months embarrassing information continued to reach the Rio Grande and be scattered over Mexico.

---

[2] There is some inconsistency in the records as to which of St. Denis' children was born first and how many were born at San Juan Bautista. One report has it that it was Marie Rose, but logic does not favor this. Luisa was the only one of five girls who did not bear the name Marie. And Luisa Margarita acted as godmother at two baptisms in May, 1729; if she had been the fourth-born, she would have been rather young to serve as godmother at a ceremonious baptism.

One account suggests that at one time the affair of the merchandise was pretty well settled, but that when St. Denis rushed on ahead, management fell into less competent hands. This source states that "it seems a disagreement occurred among the members [of the party] as to the price which should be paid [certain] Spanish officials as hush money. And in the squabble the secret as to the ownership of the goods leaked out." This might indicate that the goods were to be brought in as property of a Spaniard. Whatever the scheme, too much fuss had been made about it for St. Denis or the Ramóns to hush it up or ever get it under control. Probably St. Denis would have appeared far enough ahead of the gossip about him to have smoothed matters over before official wrath came down upon him, had not some slip occurred. So much ado was made about the matter from one quarter or another that before the end of April Grandfather Ramón had to seize the goods to save his own political career. Captain Ramón, according to the custom of the day, wrote long letters and reports in which he affirmed that he was taking stern measures to prevent entrance of French merchandise, what the measures were, and so on, sounding very official and proper, though somewhat ambiguous. One gains the impression that he was minimizing something, or, perhaps, everything.

The confiscated goods consisted of seven mule loads made up of thirteen bundles and a box. Long discussions echoed in the Ramón household. But Grandfather Ramón stood firm, or as firm as he reasoned official necessity demanded. Mexico City already had wind of the matter, and it must have been quite a foul wind, from what the befuddled commandant could hear. There were enemies and spies in their midst, and they included at least one prominent priest. Who could say how many there were? Illicit trade was Spain's pet bugaboo at that period. This was tedious business, and no one could know this better than the elderly Ramón, whose chief assignment was to prevent such trade.

Indications are that St. Denis advised his grandfather-in-law that he would handle the matter differently. St. Denis knew from experience the endless delays and red tape involved in resolving problems by Spanish reports. Accordingly, when Commandant Ramón told him—as seems to have been the case—that he was free to expedite settlement, St. Denis was just the man to do so. He promptly decided upon a course of action in which he could act alone.

Within a few days after his arrival he was off again over the long, tortuous mountain route toward Mexico City. The Ramón men may have thought his decision foolhardy. Or perhaps they hoped that by some stroke of luck or diplomatic genius this Frenchman might clear his goods and free the traders of suspicion at the same time. Anyway, there was no stopping St. Denis despite the damning facts that he had broken one of the basic laws of New Spain, evidence of which violation was securely in the hands of the Spanish officials; that every governor and Spanish official of importance had repeatedly been ordered to enforce the law to the letter; and that they had been warned to be on the lookout for just such encroachers. The man should logically have been running in the opposite direction.

St. Denis apparently stopped at Querétaro to enlist the aid of Father Joseph Diez. The priest, guardian of the College of Querétaro, was a man of high position and influence. If St. Denis' personality and importance were not already strongly felt among the churchmen in this section, his visit was most effective, for Father Diez wrote a strong appeal to the viceroy in the Frenchman's behalf. The missionaries recognized more clearly than any other group St. Denis' influence with, and control over, the Indians and seemingly had a better understanding of the importance of this factor of colonization.

St. Denis arrived in Mexico City about the middle of June. He was courteously received by the viceroy, Baltasar de Zúñiga, the Marquis of Valero. But his reception was not as cordial as his meeting two years before with the Duke of Linares, who had since been replaced with the charge of being "lenient toward the French."

The politics which had brought the new viceroy into office gave him much to ponder when he reflected on his pleasant appointment, and the same politics must have robbed St. Denis' talk of much of its glamor. The marquis appointed the auditor general to hear St. Denis' petition. Once St. Denis had the auditor general's ear, he poured his best arguments into it. He berated the actions of Commandant Diego Ramón in seizing his merchandise. He lamented that he had been compelled to sell his arms, his saddle, his horses, and part of his clothing to supply his needs. He reviewed the services he had rendered Spain, modestly, of course, but with a vividness intended to impress the auditor with their scope and worth. He wanted only to go back to the Rio Grande and live in peace with his wife and child. Could a humble man ask any less?

The auditor was duly impressed. And he immediately penned an opinion to the viceroy reviewing St. Denis' record of service in Texas, relating that he had become a Spanish subject, and, in view of all this, recommending that the release of his goods was justifiable. There was a final recommendation, intended to free the viceroy of suspicion if the Frenchman resumed illicit trading: St. Denis should be warned not to import more merchandise from Mobile or elsewhere upon any pretext.

But before the viceroy could act upon these recommendations, the picture began to change. When St. Denis reached Mexico City dispatches about him, and encroaching Frenchmen in general, had begun to trickle into the capital. His early arrival and prompt and vigorous action had netted him an advantage. But just as the viceroy decided to release his goods the trickle became a flood.

Reports from the Spanish at Pensacola grew more damning, including in them the name of St. Denis' in-laws. The Frenchman's first trip, they said, had opened up a route by which merchants of Louisiana had undertaken to supply merchandise to the greater part of New Spain. St. Denis' relation by marriage to Captain Domingo Ramón, officer in charge in East Texas, and to Diego Ramón, commandant on the Rio Grande, gave him convenient stopping places for his trading trips. Details were furnished about the latest expedition that must have surprised even St. Denis.

St. Denis might have overcome these damaging reports from Pensacola; but before he could secure the necessary order for the release of his goods and get out of the city, reports arrived from the vicinity of the Rio Grande corroborating the intelligence.

The most troublesome flies in the ointment were a newly appointed, headstrong, overambitious governor, Don Martin de Alarcón, and a jealous, disappointed priest, Antonio de San Buenaventura Olivares. Such people are always sources of turmoil and confusion. It was a bad combination to have against anyone—saint, scoundrel, or drone. St. Denis had proved that he could deal with viceroys, fiscals, auditors general, commandants, high-ranking missionaries, and warring Indians, but this was a new and dangerous combination.

Don Martin de Alarcón had been appointed governor of Coahuila and Texas on December 7, 1716. His first important duty was to investigate the accusations against St. Denis. In June, 1717, he was in Saltillo enthusiastically scouting for information. He was going to show his caliber by accomplishing a task at which viceroys and others had failed. He wanted to make an impression on the viceroy; doubtless even the king would hear about him. The ruler of such a vast and promising territory as his should show his mettle, and soon. First, it appears, he had only St. Denis as a target, but before he had finished he had implicated the entire Ramón clan and prominent religious reported to be in league with the French.

His first inspiration, apparently, was a letter from Father Olivares, whose missionary career had been climaxed in the Espinosa-Olivares-Aguirre expedition of 1709. Though the expedition had not reached the Tejas Indians, as it had set out to do, it was credited with paving the way for the expedition of 1716. At least, Father Olivares thought it had opened up the way for later and greater work, so he naturally wanted to be a part of the next expedition to the Tejas. The desire had become a consuming ambition. According to one historian, Father Hidalgo had "besought St. Denis to prevent Olivares from going on the expedition on account of his turbulent and jealous disposition." Olivares had been left behind, and he considered himself shamefully snubbed.

Now his day for retribution had come. The Ramóns were under fire; St. Denis' goods had been captured; and St. Denis himself was in Mexico, where he might soon be in prison again if the proper evidence and pressure could be brought to bear.

Father Olivares' letter was loud in its accusations against the Ramóns, St. Denis, and the French in general. He had arrived at San Juan Bautista on May 3 planning to continue without delay his journey to the San Antonio River so that he could plant crops immediately, and establish a mission. Seemingly, he had expected Commandant Diego Ramón to furnish him with the military escort. When Ramón did not, Olivares set out to petition Governor Alarcón for supplies and an escort.

Olivares wrote that he had not been able to continue his journey, for when he had requested an escort he was unable to secure it; he was told that Domingo Ramón "had gone to Coahuila to a bull fight, taking all the soldiers." Conditions were deplorable, he declared. "I have witnessed and experienced all that these holy religious in charge here suffer as a result of the negligence of Captain Ramón and the haughtiness of the Indians, who, encouraged by the Captain, have lost all respect for the padres. The whole country from Coahuila to the Tejas is in revolt." The soldiers killed mission cattle and abused the Indians, and the captain was too indifferent to punish them. As to the French, reported Father Olivares, Captain Diego Ramón and all his relatives were hand in glove with them, and the whole country north of Saltillo was full of "Ramonistas." In Coahuila there were three Frenchmen opening up a mine; at San Juan Bautista there were five, one of whom was to marry a Spaniard. Commandant Ramón, for appearances' sake, had placed an embargo on a few bundles of French goods but had allowed many more to come in unmolested. In conclusion, Father Olivares made the alarming prediction that if something was not done quickly the whole country would soon become a part of New France.

From a legal standpoint the priest had the easier side of the argument, and he felt that he was on the popular side with people of high position. But a number of factors weakened Father Olivares' statements. He went about with a chip on his shoulder. He had proved himself a poor observer.[3] As to the bullfight report, the garrison obviously did not spend the entire summer at "a" bull fight. Contemporary documents give no indication of revolt, and the missionaries, as a whole, are known to have respected and loved St. Denis.

Doubtless there was room for suspicion about activities at San Juan Bautista, but that all of Olivares' charges were well-founded is improbable. They nevertheless nearly ruined both St. Denis and the Ramóns.

Governor Alarcón was much impressed with Father Olivares' letters, which he took, characteristically, at face value. He proved to be a person who could amplify a whisper into a shout. In reporting to the viceroy he declared: "It is necessary that St. Denis be not allowed to return [from Mexico City] but that he be kept safely there." Both Diego Ramóns should be removed from their posts. Commandant Diego Ramón, his sons (Diego

[3] For instance, he knew enough about St. Denis and his activities to write pages and pages about him; yet in writing of his "probable" marriage he said: "Either Medar Jalot or St. Denis married at the presidio of Rio Grande a granddaughter of Diego Ramón, captain of the presidio . . . and although I do not doubt that one of the two married the granddaughter of Captain Ramón, I have not been able to determine with any certainty which of the two did." In fairness to Father Olivares it must be said that this was probably written before June, 1717. Nevertheless, he confused historians on the subject.

at San Juan Bautista, and Domingo in the Tejas province), the Protector Urrutia, of Nuevo Leon, and St. Denis were associated in a gigantic smuggling enterprise "in such a manner that all this country is full of contraband goods." The small amount of goods that had been seized was for effect only. The governor predicted that with the Ramóns removed the smuggling could be broken up more easily and the country could be developed into "a kingdom greater than that of new Spain." This final ambitious prophecy was penned with the delicate suggestion that this glory could come to pass only if his advice was followed and he was furnished adequate supplies and strength. To back up what he had said he attached letters from Father Olivares.

On July 12 St. Denis was back in the first quarters he had known in Mexico City—the national prison.

IX

For Freedom and Property

ON AUGUST 3 GOVERNOR ALARCÓN ARRIVED at San Juan Bautista to gather firsthand information. Captain Ramón called upon him without delay and presented him with a gift. And while these formalities were taking place, apparently, the "Frenchmen at the presidio" slipped out and took refuge in the church of the mission of San Bernardo.

The missionaries at San Juan Bautista were courteous enough to the ambitious governor. He was able to get them to admit that Captain Ramón was "lax in discipline and neglectful of duty," but this promising beginning came to nothing. He was unable to dislodge the Frenchmen from the mission, and he could get no information whatever about the Frenchmen or their goods. Exasperated, he summoned one Father Muñoz, who was president of the group of Queretaran missions at San Juan Bautista, and demanded that he speak for the missionaries and tell what they knew about the smuggled goods. Father Muñoz answered that he only knew "what everyone knows, namely, that the said French goods have entered." Again the governor had run into vague generalities with no more strength than rumor. When pressed further the priest said that he could give no additional information until he had consulted his superiors. This matter of "consulting his superiors" indicates that there was some sort of general agreement among the missionaries to protect St. Denis so that he, in turn, might be able to defend them against the Tejas Indians while they carried on their work. They held the work of the Kingdom of God above that of the kingdom of King Philip V. Whatever it was that the religious had in mind, the governor never saw through it. Disgusted, he turned to unofficial sources for his information.

Depositions of "disinterested persons" at the presidio brought him only vague, contradictory, confusing evidence at every hearing. He believed Father Olivares right when he declared the population to be "all Ramonistas."

The governor ordered Captain Domingo Ramón to deliver to him "the fifteen mule loads of bundles, numbering twenty-nine bundles and a box of merchandise" which had been seized from St. Denis. Alarcón was ready to see the evidence.

But he was frustrated again. The inventory revealed only thirteen bundles and a box.

Captain Ramón denied having knowledge of any other goods. He had delivered all that were in his possession. He knew of no memoranda or invoices; if anyone had them it was St. Denis. He had seen no reason for demanding them of the Frenchman, who would, if so requested, give them up in Mexico City as a matter of policy. There was nothing more that he could tell His Excellency.

It was a disheartening investigation for an executive who had started out so eagerly and so sure of success. He found little or nothing of real value to incriminate either St. Denis or his in-laws, but he heard enough to convince him that much more merchandise had been smuggled in than had come to light. It was his opinion that Diego Ramón and the mission priests were much more concerned with appearing to obey the letter of the law than with observing it in spirit. But he needed more than opinions to report to the viceroy after his vehement promises from Saltillo. His Excellency had gotten himself out on the proverbial limb.

The inventory revealed what goods were the trade favorites of that day and locality—laces and linens and twills; red and blue and green cloth; hose, red and blue and of the best quality. It was good substantial merchandise, but it also had color and delicacy to please the taste of the frontier people, both Spaniard and Indian.[1]

Governor Alarcón placed the goods in the keeping of Father Muñoz until the viceroy could order their disposal. Shortly after this disposition of the goods had been made the governor intercepted a letter from St. Denis

[1] The bundles were itemized as follows:
(1) 65 pieces of narrow Brittany linen of various lengths
(2) 37 pieces of the same
(3) 7 pairs of red woolen hose and twelve pairs of blue, of the best quality, and 179 bundles of Flemish thread
(4) 2 pieces of green twill and 28 half bolts of laces of all degrees of fineness, the 3 widest from Aberia [sic]
(5) 14 half bolts of laces of varying degrees of fineness and a piece of blue woolen cloth of the highest quality
(6) 6 pieces of blue twill, another piece of the same with a remnant of $16\frac{1}{2}$ varas, and a remnant of plush
(7) a whole piece of scarlet cloth, 2 pieces of green twill, 23 pairs of blue woolen stockings of the best quality, 28 bolts of laces of all degrees of fineness, and 2 pieces of Brussels camlet
(8) 21 pieces of wide Brittany linen
(9) 40 pieces of wide Brittany linen
(10) 4 pieces of Rouen linen, a piece of covering linen, and another of coarse brown linen
(11) 7 pieces of scarlet cloth and a remnant
(12) 7 pieces of light camlet, 12 pairs of blue woolen hose of the best quality, and some of red, and 3 pieces of heavy satin from France
(13) 7 pieces of scarlet cloth

written to Father Muñoz. It was a friendly letter in which St. Denis asked the priest to intercede in his behalf and look after his interest there. The letter gave the governor something to think about. He had just turned the goods over to Father Muñoz, who was evidently St. Denis' friend and supporter. The governor must have begun to feel that he was all alone. He felt that he had right on his side, but this was ineffective company. Soon he was even quarreling with Father Olivares, with whom he had been hand and glove.

Seemingly, the governor had run into a blind alley at San Juan Bautista, much to his political embarrassment. His flaming ambition temporarily smoldered, but he never lost sight of what he thought to be his duty or of the means for his advancement. He soon set out with renewed determination to capture the French traders at the missions. If he could not furnish satisfactory documentary evidence, he would send the culprits to the capital. That should be even better. The officials there would break them; they could be made examples of; and thus he would yet be the man responsible for breaking up smuggling in the northern provinces.

But no sooner had his intentions been made known than he received an upsetting letter from Captain Diego Ramón. The epistle was full of details as to the commandant's zeal and support of the governor's orders. He had done this and that. And the governor had but to call and he would be at his immediate service. At the end, somewhat incidentally, he informed the governor that the Frenchmen who had taken refuge in the church had fled. He informed the governor that he had immediately sent men in pursuit of the fugitives with orders to bring them back dead or alive. However, he did not hold out much hope for their capture; for, he added, "the fugitives' friendliness with the Indian tribes" would facilitate their escape.

This meant another report to the viceroy—not the kind Alarcón had hoped to send. However, he was not fooled, and he did not hide his opinion from his superior. He was sure, he reported, that the Frenchmen entered the country of the Indians "well provided for."

Alarcón was anxious to get on to the Tejas, but for one reason or another—investigations, lack of supplies, bad weather, confusing orders (or lack of them), or local quarrels—he was kept at the Rio Grande until April, 1718.

The Ramóns courted him and made the best possible show of obedience. They had early learned that the governor could not be tampered with.[2]

Delays in Coahuila grated on Father Olivares' nerves as well as on those of Governor Alarcón. Though the two had started out as allies, they were soon at each other's throats and tattling on each other to the viceroy.

Their disputes centered around the military escort with which the missionary expected the governor to supply him. The number of soldiers, their virtue, their ancestry—all were subjects of bitter arguments.

The governor also continued to clamor against St.

[2] As early as May, 1717, Don Domingo had written Alarcón from East Texas officially informing him of St. Denis' coming and saying that other Frenchmen were remaining there with their goods. No doubt the letter was a feeler to discover the governor's attitude toward the Frenchman's enterprise. He had given as favorable an account of St. Denis and his associates as he dared. Flattering the governor, he made it clear that no one failed to recognize the governor's position; he had given St. Denis strict orders not to leave the province until word could be received from His Excellency. Succeeding events had quickly made it clear that flattery would not turn the governor's head, nor had Ramón's evaluation of St. Denis impressed him. He formed his own opinion of St. Denis; and the trouble the man brought him, directly and indirectly, made his opinion something to reflect upon for a lifetime.

Denis and to warn the viceroy of the great danger of the French to the east. He had an ax to grind, and he had been in the service long enough to know that the best way to go about it was to warn against the French. He was following the missionaries' practice; if it had worked for them, it should serve him also. If he was to be a great and powerful governor he should have a large army to command, adequately supplied; if he could not establish the threat of invasion on the frontier, there would be no need for forces beyond the necessities for Indian protection.

Father Olivares' goal was reached on May 1, 1718, when the mission of San Antonio de Valero was established near present-day San Antonio. But he was soon complaining again. The Indians preferred to stay in the woods and hunt rather than to build houses and listen to long prayers. Alarcón supported the priest by sending out the word that if the natives did not come to the mission that he would put all of them to the sword. He was eager to get on to East Texas, and most of all he wished to be done with this troublesome priest. However, even Father Olivares did not agree with this proposed method of conversion, and he promptly obliged the viceroy with his opinion.

At long last, Alarcón reached the East Texas missions. But he was soon out of favor with the religious there. He had not brought them the long-awaited supplies and protection. He resorted to power he did not have in fact, and he rattled his sword when a soft tongue was needed. His boastful tactics served only to antagonize the Indians and arouse the fear of the French, so the missionaries reported to their superiors and to the government.

Criticism of Governor Alarcón finally came to a head in Mexico, and the governor was refused his soldiers and supplies. If he thought his threats to resign would bring the requested forces he was sadly mistaken. When his resignation was tentatively offered early in 1719, it was promptly accepted.

As to Father Olivares' jealous wailings and disappointments, only his death a few years later was to put an end to them.

This dissension on the frontier among the accusers and investigators of St. Denis had weakened the effect of their reports and confused their superiors. Most Spanish officials of this period who were sent out to the eastern frontier sank before they learned to swim in the unfathomable political current, and their ideals and good works perished with them.

While Governor Alarcón had been conducting his investigation on the Rio Grande, the viceroy had called in Don Juan de Olivan, an *oidor* of the *Real Audiencia* and the best investigator available, had given him special powers, had doubled his salary, and had told him to go to work on the St. Denis case.

No investigator of that country had ever had more inducements or encouragement, and Olivan set to work immediately. First, Olivan found three persons in prison who had been arrested upon suspicion of being connected with St. Denis' activities; a "connection" with him was sufficient cause for arrest. Olivan took the depositions of the prisoners, decided that no case could be made against any of them, and released them. One of the prisoners, a servant of St. Denis, stated in a memorial to the viceroy that he was penniless. He was unable to secure the 200 pesos which St. Denis owed him, because his employer was still in prison. He lamented on the dire needs of his family. His employer had declared that under the circumstances he had no means at hand to satisfy the demand. Seemingly, on the strength of this memorial, the prisoner secured an order for payment to be made to him from the confiscated goods.

Again, as in June, 1715, St. Denis was called upon to make a declaration.[3] St. Denis was still the suave diplomat whose memory had grown even worse. The whole truth might here have been considerably damaging for France and disastrous to St. Denis.

The prisoner was questioned in detail about his background. He answered that he was a native of Quebec; he was thirty-eight years of age;[4] he had been a soldier by profession; he had held the position of captain of Fort St. John on the Mississippi,[5] in the exercise of which he served the Most Christian King in peace and war against the Indians. He was, he inferred, an influential man among the Indians, whether in peace or in war.

As to his more recent past the declarant said that he was married to "Manuela Sanchez," a Spanish subject of Rio Grande del Norte. His residence was at the presidio of San Juan Bautista, where he was a citizen. He did not know the cause of his confinement.

He stated that he had made two *entradas* from Mobile, the first, four years ago; the present one had started two

---

[3] Considering the declaration as a historical document has led to much error and confusion. It was as a diplomatic instrument that it was most significant.

[4] According to the best documentary evidence, St. Denis signed the declaration on September 18, 1717, the day after his forty-first birthday. Some of the misstatements of the declaration have obvious purposes; some of them may have been carelessness; some seem to have no explanation.

[5] Referred to here as Rio de la Pilizada.

years ago.[6] As to the purpose of the second *entrada,* he explained that he was married at the presidio of San Juan Bautista and was living with the Spaniards and serving the Spanish king, even risking his life in the service. He had therefore forsaken his native land on account of the greater attachment which he and his wife held for the Spanish nation. He then reviewed his service to Spain, in the course of which he had led the hazardous expedition of 1716 and helped to establish missions.

He was asked why he had made the trip to Mobile after the expedition. This question might have tripped a less nimble wit, but St. Denis came up with the perfect answer: he had gone to get his few personal possessions so that he need never return to Mobile or the French, but could live with the Spaniards; he had married among them, and he wished to serve God and king in everything. He had had no other purpose.

He admitted that considerable time had been spent among the Tejas, providing corn for the established missions and helping to construct two new ones, at his own expense. He had worked strenuously until March.

Asked about other Frenchmen trading in Texas he answered that he set out alone from Mobile, but was overtaken by eleven Frenchmen at Fort St. John on the Mississippi; he did not remember their names. None of these men accompanied him into Texas. The merchandise which he brought from Mobile consisted of thirteen bundles and a case of thread, all from old France. St. Denis then made the *entrada* appear to be an innocent family affair; he stated that two first cousins assisted in

---

[6] It was only one year before that he had left. A contradiction later in the declaration gave the correct date.

the transportation as far as the Rio Grande. He supposed that they had probably departed by now because of his detention in Mexico. He estimated the merchandise was worth 5,500 pesos at Mobile.

On the matter of finance St. Denis told a touching story. To secure the money for this undertaking he had sold a cultivated farm and five Indian slaves which he had at Fort St. John; and had collected three years' salary, amounting to 1,200 pesos. He made it clear that this pay was for the time he served as commandant at Fort St. John and not for time spent among the Spaniards. For his property and service he was paid the bundles of merchandise now seized at the Rio Grande. The accumulations of his life's work had been taken from him by the country he served, he maintained.

The declarant was vague in his description of the goods contained in the bundles because he did not "remember such things well"; he had never "been a merchant." But he was not above an appeal to sentiment. In the bundles were two pieces of brocade for his wife. Señor Olivan did not appear to be a coldhearted man; he should understand how the loss of the gift would affect a thoughtful husband, particularly one who had just been presented with a beautiful baby daughter.

Asked why he was bringing the merchandise into Mexico, St. Denis stated that he wanted to establish his business for buying cattle and making other investments. In this way he planned to support his wife and "children," [7] who were at San Juan Bautista.

On the matter of geography the declarant was not

---

[7] This reference to "children" is inexplicable. It appears that more than one child was born at San Juan Bautista. Probably Emanuelle was expecting another baby, and St. Denis was informed of it; or perhaps the prisoner was trying to appear more of a family man than he really was.

specific. Seemingly, he wished to have the Spaniards think that he did not know much about the provinces which they claimed.

Information about Indians ran to great length.[8] He mentioned a few tribes friendly to the Spaniards and the Tejas who nevertheless "did not fail to be deceitful to the Spanish." He suggested that if the San Antonio River area should be occupied by five hundred veterans and the area of the Bay of Espiritu Santo with a hundred, the dominion of "the King our Lord will rest secure and many souls [will be] converted to the faith." How subtle! St. Denis knew this would give the militarists something to think about. Where would six hundred veterans come from?

Even as a prisoner St. Denis was able to throw fear into the Spaniards to the advantage of his native France. Just casually, to help the Spanish plot their strategy for any projected military expansion, he brought up the point that the natives west of the Tejas, where the Spanish might possibly conduct unmolested local recruiting, used bows and arrows. That the Natchitoches and some of the Tejas tribes, recognized by the Spaniards as being under control of the French, used firearms and, according to reports of the Spaniards on the frontier, possessed more firearms than they, were facts that all the Spanish officials knew and could not forget. If the Spanish overestimated this native military force and became unduly alarmed, St. Denis did not consider it his responsibility to calm their fears.

Sufficient information was supplied concerning the

---

[8] He was able to say which tribes wandered and which maintained fixed abodes, which were warlike and which peaceful. He could say who the natural enemies of most of the tribes were and could give a good estimate of the number of warriors each nation could muster.

Indians and their firearms to lend emphasis to Father Diez' letter of June 7, 1717, urging that St. Denis be allowed to return to the frontier to "prevent an Indian uprising." [9] Father Diez listed and emphasized the services which St. Denis had rendered the Spaniards in Texas. He urged that St. Denis be allowed to return to East Texas at once, because only his presence could prevent an Indian uprising, and because he "is the only protection which the poor missionaries have in that land." In view of these facts, the priest urged further that St. Denis' goods be released. St. Denis welcomed any lead that might get him out of his filthy prison.

From St. Denis' account of the tribes the inference was clear that the missionaries needed miracles wrought in this heathen land and that the best way to bring these miracles to pass would be by military control. It might be supposed that St. Denis was trying on this occasion, as on his first trip to Mexico, to picture himself as a man indispensable to the Spanish service.

The Spanish asked leading questions about journeys, fortifications, trade, maps, designed to bring out the truth and the man's true motives.[10] The prisoner ap-

[9] The declarant furnished sufficient data about the government and social customs of the Tejas Indians to leave no question about his being on intimate terms with them. Each nation, he related, was governed by its cacique, or captain, both when it was settled and when it was not. There was a chief who governed it in peace and war, but he had subaltern officers, some for the government of the nation in war and others, in peace. In regard to property the nations were communal, because that which anyone obtained by fishing or hunting was for the nation. As to wives, "these [women] are not communal, since they are married in their style to the Indian men; but the spinsters are." The husband had charge of the wife and children, but if she bore no children it was customary for him to abandon her temporarily, blaming her meanwhile. These Indians possessed horses and rode them but did not eat them, maintaining them to utilize among themselves. They did not cultivate the fields, which were fertile.

[10] There seemed no limit to Spain's interest in St. Denis. His inquisitors were interested in information about him personally; what he knew or might be sup-

peared to be well informed, but his replies were general and vague, as a whole, and had the ring of propaganda. In general he hinted that Spain had more to fear from England than from France, though there was never a suggestion that France might be pushed around by Spain, here or abroad.

Official Mexico had a great deal of respect for St. Denis' knowledge and opinions. Whether it was satisfied with his declaration is another matter.

Queer as St. Denis' actions and statements may appear there is no definite proof that he desired to live in New Spain or was ever intentionally untrue to his native France. He was practical, yes; never traitorous. There was nothing in his declaration that was detrimental to France or calculated to give Spain an advantage over her rival. Doubtless, most of the information he furnished about his native country, Spain knew already. He knew that Spain wanted information, and he played the game for what it was worth.

St. Denis' plight had progressed beyond that of the average defendant on trial. He was already in prison; his property—his life's earnings, according to his own report—had been confiscated; and probably the mildest punishment facing him was deportation to Europe or condemnation for years to a filthy Mexican or Spanish prison away from his family. St. Denis was in serious trouble

---

posed to know of the provinces of Spain, France, and England, as well as of the old countries; his journeys into explored and unexplored lands, the time involved, and the like; his conversations with persons of importance, and their plans and ambitions as he understood them; fortifications and military strength in various places; the richest and most promising lands; the locations and estimated production of mines; the favorite items of trade; the number and intentions of immigrants to New France; the work of the missionaries; the kinds of ships that came to New France; the handling of gifts to the Indians; the advantages and disadvantages of bays, ports, beaches, and mouths of rivers; and the availability of maps.

and, in spite of his self-confidence, must have realized it. Two months in an airless, eighteenth-century Mexican prison was enough to drive a man to the end of his wits. St. Denis possessed that rare talent so envied among diplomats of being able to make a falsehood sound more like the truth than the truth itself. He used that gift now and lived to serve colonial France in better days, when a man of his peculiar talents was needed.

It appears that Olivan would have been ready to release St. Denis after the declaration had been completed, except that he was determined to make the investigation as thorough as possible. Whatever the incentive—double salary, pressure from the viceroy, or his own sense of justice—Olivan's inquiry continued another two months while St. Denis waited in the government prison.

On November 4 Olivan submitted his voluminous report to the viceroy. It was entirely favorable to St. Denis.[11] Among other things, Olivan dismissed both the charges of Governor Alarcón and those of Father Olivares as "exaggerated reports." Instead of representing the defendant as an encroacher and menace, Olivan pictured him as a benefactor to Spain. He had abandoned his native country to become a Spanish subject, having married a Spanish woman; he had resigned his position as captain of the presidio of New France, Fort St. John, sold his property, and bought merchandise with which

[11] Olivan traced the history of French intervention in Texas beginning with La Salle, and what the Spanish had done to prevent it. What Governor Alarcón had reported "agreed with what the prisoner himself had stated—only thirteen bundles and a box had been found that belonged to St. Denis. No other evidence had been produced to prove that other merchandise had been brought in." No one else could be found to testify that the "whole country was full of contraband trade." A more conservative and levelheaded investigation on the Rio Grande might have been the undoing of St. Denis.

St. Denis was in serious trouble. . . .

to buy and cultivate lands in New Spain in order to serve the king in every way, and particularly in the conquest of the Indians, with whose languages and customs he was very familiar; he executed his commission as guide to the expedition to the Tejas in the most legal and efficient manner, and after reaching there he had aided the missionaries greatly.

St. Denis could have spoken for himself no better. In fact, one suspects that the charming prisoner may have obliged his Spanish interrogator by helping with some of the phrases.

In view of the evidence gathered, Don Juan de Olivan strongly recommended that St. Denis' goods be returned to him and that he be given the freedom of the city and its environs, provided some responsible person was willing to give bond for him. Despite his confidence in St. Denis, the investigator apparently knew how far to go in his recommendation.

In the meantime St. Denis addressed a petition to the viceroy, reviewing again his services to the Spanish in Texas and disclaiming any attempt to engage in trade. He explained that there was no profit in bringing merchandise across so extensive and hazardous a country, since the cost of transportation was prohibitive—a thin argument, but a talking point at least. The merchandise in question was not really commercial; it was his personal possessions with which he planned to provide the means of settling in the Spanish country. He asked to be released therefore and to have his goods returned. He hoped, in fact, that he might be given some commission "corresponding to the zeal displayed by him in the royal service." His first imprisonment had ended with such an arrangement. The idea should be worth a second try.

But neither his petition nor Olivan's report was enough. The viceroy either was not impressed with St. Denis' logic or was afraid to accept it because of what had happened to his predecessor. He would feel much more secure if all these French suspected peddlers were out of his way. The fiscal also failed to share investigator Olivan's point of view, although he finally agreed to accept Olivan's recommendation that the prisoner be released and his goods returned but advised that he be sent back to France.

The *real acuerdo*, in time, concurred in the first part of the fiscal's recommendation, but decided that St. Denis' deportation should be suspended until a more opportune solution could be arrived at.

A resident of Mexico City, one Don Juan Bautista Guizoldelos, immediately agreed to give bond, but the fiscal apparently had changed his mind again.

St. Denis wrote another memorial to the viceroy. He asked that some official other than the fiscal be authorized to attend to his case, as the hardships he was experiencing in prison would not admit to further delay. It was a pointed note for a prisoner to write to the chief executive of a vast province, but it succeeded. On November 22 bond was given and St. Denis at last stepped out into a limited freedom. He was still confined to the limits of the city.

Having gained partial liberty, St. Denis was more impatient than ever to get back to his family and property. He began to point out to officials and people of influence that the missionaries on the eastern frontier probably needed him. He had promised them he would return, and he wished to "fulfill his desires in extending the Holy Faith." He requested permission to recover and sell his goods at once. He was willing to pay just duties on these into the *real hacienda.*

St. Denis, if given an inch, took a mile—literally, in this instance. For, strangely enough, the viceroy gave permission for him to recover and sell his merchandise "in the most convenient places," except that he was charged not to return to Texas.

At this point St. Denis fades again into the fog of legend. There were good reasons for secrecy on the part of the Frenchman, as well as of those connected with him. The logical assumption is that he went to the Rio Grande to rejoin his family and sell his goods; some accounts mention sale of his goods, and some say that the money for the goods was paid to an agent, presumably a Spaniard.[12]

St. Denis did not take losses easily. It appears that he returned to Mexico City in an attempt to gain some remuneration for the goods,[13] for which he never received payment. This would seem a bold and presumptuous stroke, but it would not have been inconsistent with the character of the man.

When diplomacy failed to get action, one account runs, he threatened to use his influence among the Indian tribes to provoke an uprising on the eastern frontier.

But the Spaniards had the advantage of him. He was

---

[12] These accounts may refer to the known "thirteen bundles and a box"; but there were probably more goods, including those of his countrymen who for safety had made premature departures from the Rio Grande, and naturally had to dispose of their goods hastily. It would not be surprising to know that much of this merchandise was "lost" one way or another.

[13] One account states that he spent several months in the city hoping for some lucrative commission from the government.

in their city, not on the frontier among his faithful Indian warriors. According to legend the Spaniards threw him back into their dirty prison, where he remained until his wife's relatives interceded. The legend has some weaknesses. In the first place, the Ramón clan would scarcely have been bold enough to show a face in Mexico City, considering the political fire they were under at the time. Probably St. Denis heard of the plot before the Spaniards got their hands on him and, through the aid of friends, made his escape. September 5, 1718, is the accepted date of his final departure from Mexico City.

St. Denis had managed to get a horse fleet enough so that he could travel ahead of the news of his escape. But he must have taken a slower gait once he was out of reach of the Mexican police; for nearly six months passed before he reached Natchitoches—slow traveling, indeed, for a fugitive. Doubtless, he tarried a short while at San Juan Bautista; and once across, among the Indians and missionaries of East Texas, he could again do about as he pleased. For he was from a practical standpoint the most powerful man on the frontier, and everybody knew it.

Probably Emanuelle and Luisa went to Louisiana with him. However, he may have returned for them or sent for them a short time later.

There was no end to the accusations set off by St. Denis' two expeditions beyond the Rio Grande; as for an accounting of the goods involved, St. Denis was never to receive one. He may have been made a scapegoat; he may have lost the goods as he claimed; he may have been swindled out of them; or he may have become so involved that no true report could have been given about them for fear of ruining people in high positions.

But now, on February 24, 1719, at the end of a fantastic pilgrimage that had consumed nearly two and a half years, St. Denis was safely back in the town he had founded. Here he could talk business in French to Frenchmen, watch the familiar Red River glide peacefully past the storehouses he had built, and present a few gifts to, and talk tribal politics with, the gracious Natchitoches Indians, by whom he was loved so faithfully. Possibly all he had to show for the perilous years spent in Mexico during his two expeditions was a beautiful wife and tales of adventure, but even a vigorous, ambitious man may need no more to sustain him. These were the two driving forces in his long, restless life—Emanuelle, his wife and faithful hearth companion and mother of his children, and Adventure, a mistress he was to pursue as long as the blood ran hot in his veins.

X

Prosperity à la John Law

ST. DENIS LEARNED FROM CONVERSATIONS with his countrymen that many changes had taken place in Louisiana during his absence. Both depression and prosperity had reached new levels.

While the Spanish were successfully re-establishing their missions in Texas and occupying, in a manner, the vast province, stark failure was stalking the Louisiana colony at every turn: Crozat's ships of merchandise sent to Mexico and Central America had been turned back six years before. The overland trade had failed, from an official standpoint. The colonists were complaining and deserting because they were forced to buy goods only from Crozat's stores at his price. There were no other stores. No vessels or goods except those of Crozat were allowed to enter the province, and the colonists were forbidden to own seagoing vessels. Furs of the Canadian trappers were bought at prices fixed by Crozat's commissioners—which they considered insultingly low—and they were obliged to take their pay in merchandise at Crozat's own valuation.

But even with his monopoly Crozat could make no profit. Though the colonists thought their lot severe, their proprietor had troubles of his own. The crown had agreed to provide the garrison as usual, but neither pay nor uniforms for the soldiers arrived. Ragged, almost destitute, and unable to buy except from Crozat's stores, they began to desert to the English.

Crozat recalled Cadillac and replaced him with another governor, thinking that might help. But the new governor, one L'Epinay, turned out to be no improvement. To economize, he stopped the practice of sending presents to the Indians. This proved to be bad business as well as dangerous politics. The Indians turned to the English for presents, and, consequently, for trade.

In August, 1717, Antoine Crozat surrendered his charter. He was a tired, broken, disappointed man. He had dreamed fabulous dreams and had seen them shattered. Strange, unpredictable turns of politics and psychology had contributed to his undoing. For instance, the Spanish king, Philip V, grandson of Louis XIV, had been placed on the throne at the risk of his grandfather's French kingdom; yet no colonial trade could be arranged with Spain. Crozat may have witnessed the dramatic scene when the aged Louis proudly kissed his grandson and sent him off to his Spanish throne and the Spanish ambassador exultantly exclaimed that "the Pyrenees no longer exist." The Pyrenees barrier might melt away, but never the Rio Grande or Arroyo Hondo. No merchant would have expected such an unappreciative, monopolistic attitude as this. Thus Crozat found several million dollars' worth of merchandise on his hands and no buyers. One disappointment followed another. Expeditions in search of mines had proved to be costly failures; Indian trade had been limited and made unprofitable by English competition; his officials had become too engrossed in promoting their own private fortunes; and agriculture had been neglected.

It may have been his love for his daughter, as well as his economic and political adversities, that brought an untimely end to Antoine Crozat. She was the apple of his eye, and had been the inspiration of his Louisiana venture. As he watched his empire fade, he sadly watched the health of his beloved daughter also fade. Ambition left him. Perhaps it was just as well that he had no empire now; it had been a beautiful dream, but costly.

It was a desperate period for the Louisiana colony. The home treasury was empty, the government heavily in debt, the country prostrated by long wars, only recently concluded; the Spanish were steadily pushing eastward; the English were threatening from the Atlantic seaboard. The colony was facing a life-and-death crisis. What the outcome of the French colony would have been, but for the timely appearance of a financial genius, John Law, would be hard to say. A strange fate brought this savior to Paris.

John Law had been born in Scotland in 1671. As a very young man he went to London to seek his fortune, mainly by gambling. But he soon became too involved with members of the fair sex and their jealous husbands, and at last killed an enraged husband in self-defense. He was sentenced to hang for the crime, but two days before he was to mount the gallows he drugged his guards, escaped to France, and started all over again.[1]

He strutted down the streets of poverty-stricken Paris sporting a finely tailored suit and flashing a charm-

[1] The early days of John Law are shrouded in mystery. There are several versions of the incidents leading to his escape to France.

ing smile. He was handsome, courtly, and possessed of a polished tongue. His mathematical mind and knowledge of the laws of probability soon enabled him to recoup a good stake from gambling-table novices. This accomplished, he moved on to devising financial schemes and fiscal systems for European governments. He was two centuries ahead of his time, so the monarchs failed to take advantage of his genius. However, the treasury of France was in such a hopeless state that the prince regent, Philippe, the Duke of Orleans, was ready to listen to anyone with a plan to augment it.

The idea behind Law's "miracle" was new and quite simple. But it worked, and it might have made France the financial leader of the world if the regent had listened to Law and had not overdone it. Law suggested to the regent that he print money instead of minting it. The system immediately worked wonders. Prices rose, and soon the greatest boom of all time was on; millionaires were made by the thousands.

The national financial crisis having been turned into a period of unprecedented prosperity, Law gave his attention to "big business." He told the regent that he could produce prosperity in that struggling Louisiana colony just as he had in France. The regent was delighted to give him the opportunity to try it.

And so it was that John Law organized the Company of the West in September, 1717, and immediately proved himself one of the greatest promoters and advertisers of all time. People were actually crushed to death in the mad rush to buy stock in his new company.

Law expanded his enterprises and obtained control of the India Company, or East Indies Company, which held exclusive trading privileges with Asia and Africa. The

Company of the West was merged with the India Company in May, 1719, and Louisiana continued as a commercial colony controlled by the India Company.

The greatest need for Louisiana was settlers, so Law overlooked nothing that might attract them. On the walls of the cafés of Paris his placards pictured exotic Indian maidens; these placards bore the delightful caption that such beautiful creatures loved nothing better than to fall at the feet of the white man and become slaves. Young men left home in droves. Old men were promised youth. "In the country of the Natchitoches . . . we shall find [herbs] for the most dangerous wounds, yes . . . infallible ones for the fruits of love."

When Crozat had assumed proprietorship of Louisiana its population numbered a scant four hundred. Within a short time Law's publicity had caused nearly seven thousand people to sail for Louisiana, a fabulous region pictured as the new El Dorado, a land of riches, beauty, and health. When the enthusiastic colonists reached the unhealthy, unproductive swamps of Louisiana they were sickened with disappointment. But their fortunes had been spent in the enterprise. Some of them had sold old family estates for passage fare. For most of them there was no way back. Their struggles were grim and tragic, indeed. But the fantastic venture saved Louisiana for France.

St. Denis must have been encouraged by what he saw and heard at Natchitoches. Thanks to John Law, there seemed to be sufficient money to support the colony; settlers were pouring in; the Spanish along the border were neighborly; there were thousands of peaceful Indians under control; plans for an extensive commerce were under way; and most delightful of all, his old friend and co-explorer Bienville was the new governor of the colony. Although life in the colony seemed rugged to the new arrivals, to St. Denis, significantly, it seemed that the dangerous, hard times were behind.

On the Red River St. Denis may have met Bernard de la Harpe, who had arrived at Natchitoches in January of 1719 and "after a month" there proceeded up the river to forestall the Spaniards on that stream. St. Denis and La Harpe would have had much in common to talk about.

La Harpe represented the rejuvenated man of France. Now that Frenchmen once more had money in their pockets, their ambitions also began to bulge. And now that they had a taste of prosperity they did not propose to be hemmed in, or hampered in any way, by Spain. A man like John Law would surely expand the boundaries of his possessions as simply as he had raised the value of his stock. La Harpe had been sent over to the New World to "institute an investigation and ascertain just how far westward France could rightly claim." He had arrived in Louisiana the last day of April, 1718.

The revived missionary activities in East Texas and the bold talk of the Texas governor, Martin de Alarcón, had drawn La Harpe to the Louisiana-Texas border.

When the Texas governor had visited the most eastern mission in November, 1718, he immediately sent two soldiers to spy on Natchitoches and report to him on conditions at the fort. When they reported that the garrison consisted of twenty soldiers, most of them young boys, the governor again started rattling his sword and boasting. In his eagerness to be a general he announced that he would drive the French out of Natchitoches and away from the Red River. But the more practical-minded missionaries warned the talkative governor that he would without doubt stir up a hornet's nest—that if he persisted he would encounter a more forceful army than a company of twenty beardless boys. Evidently His Excellency had not been adequately informed on the local Indian situation. The governor heeded the warning, sheathed his sword, and turned to his more familiar work of writing reports and letters.

It is likely that the experienced St. Denis took these threats more lightly than the newcomer, La Harpe. For St. Denis believed and had convinced Governor Cadillac, among others, that the Spanish would remain in East Texas just so long as the French wished them there as it would be "easy to destroy or appropriate" the East Texas establishments.

But if St. Denis thought permanent prosperity and peace had come to the frontier he was misled. Events were then in the making that would test the colonists on both sides of the frontier.

XI

War of 1719

NEWS REACHED LOUISIANA ON APRIL 19, 1719, that war between France and Spain had broken out in January. On receipt of this information, the French officials felt that they were justified in undertaking expansion.

Governor Bienville immediately called a council of war, in which it was agreed to attack Pensacola at once. A quick decision and quick action brought quick success to the French, who descended upon the Spanish before they knew war had been declared, and by this advantage easily took the fort.

If St. Denis took part in the campaign no record of it is extant. He could hardly have reached Mobile in time to leave on the hastily planned campaign. One wonders if the Spanish wife may have influenced her warring husband not to fight her people, or if she pleaded with him not to risk his life so soon again.

The easy capture of Pensacola was not the victory it appeared to be. A large amount of supplies had been expected from the capture of the fort, but the expectation was doomed to disappointment. The French were obliged to feed themselves as well as their prisoners far from their base of supplies. This was impossible. So the prisoners were loaded on two ships and sent to Havana under a flag of truce. Here the French received their second surprise. In defiance of the flag of truce the ships were seized by the governor-general of Cuba and their crews made prisoners.

Apparently the governor-general considered anything fair in war, and he was not long in demonstrating this. He reloaded the French vessels with a strong force and sent them back with orders to retake Pensacola.

When the Spaniards drew near on their return, confusion and mutiny broke out among the French defenders, reduced in numbers because the main body of the French had withdrawn to Mobile. Chateauguay, the French commander and the brother of Bienville, tried to rally his men but failed. And again the Spanish flag went up over Pensacola.

Mutiny, confusion, and failure at Pensacola were grim forecasts for the whole French colony. Three hundred and fifty men, including Chateauguay, had either been taken or had gone over to the enemy voluntarily during the recapture of Pensacola; an attempted march from Mobile to reinforce Pensacola had shown the men unfit for vigorous action in the intense summer heat; and most alarming of all, it was known that several ships of war at Vera Cruz might be brought up against the French. The threat of support from Havana was another frightening speculation. With desertion rife in the ranks, equipment poor, supplies low, ships captured, soldiers physically unfit, morale low, a garrison possibly outnumbered severalfold, control of Louisiana was hanging precariously in the military balance.

Bienville must have rejoiced that St. Denis was back in Louisiana in time. He sent him word, apparently from

Biloxi, to mobilize the Indians while Mobile was being hastily prepared for defense.

This was no time for Louisiana's greatest warrior to stay at home importuned by his wife or influenced by respect for the nationality of his in-laws. The magic summons was sounded through the forests. The drums began to rumble, and runners beat the paths from village to village calling the braves to battle. From the banks of the Mississippi, from the bayous along the Gulf, from the northern woods, sleek Indian warriors, singly and in groups, came parting the brush making for St. Denis' camp. To have fought with the Great White Chief would be the boast of braves around campfires for many moons.

The time for preparation was short. On the night of August 13, less than four months after the news of war had reached Louisiana, a vanguard of three brigantines hove in sight off Dauphin Island. The Spanish commander, Antonio de la Mandella, without doubt knew his advantages. The French had put up only a shameful token fight in defense of Pensacola. Possibly he expected as easy a victory here; certainly the French were three hundred and fifty soldiers and two ships weaker now, by virtue of Spanish depredations.

Mandella demanded immediate surrender. He threatened to give no quarter if it was refused; he would mete out vengeance for the prisoners taken at Pensacola. He brashly announced his intention to take the whole French colony for the Spanish crown, and he had no time for diplomacy. Possibly, in a revengeful rage, he was trying to imitate the speed the French had shown in their first campaign against Pensacola. But all his huffing and puffing would not blow this French house down. He would need gunpowder, he was given to understand. And the battle began.

The first maneuver brought a blow to the French. Two small boats loaded with sorely needed provisions were captured, and the Spanish fleet pressed on into the harbor. Shortly reinforcements sailed in to join Mandella, and the harbor was blockaded.

The French ship *Philippe* had been drawn into the best possible position near land to defend the fort. It gave such a good account of itself that the Spaniards were delayed for some time in their frontal attack by sea.

Failing in this assault, they then landed with the object of flanking the fort.

By this time St. Denis had arrived with his army of Indians. His force was not yet large, but more red warriors were trickling in hourly. St. Denis had had little time to organize his forces, but the Spanish obliged him by giving him the choice both of field and of weapons. St. Denis, with his troops secured behind the natural barricade of the forest, prepared for the kind of fighting he excelled in and for which the Spanish were unprepared; he held his fire in order to let the invaders get far enough on land to ensure accurate shooting. And it was accurate; it resulted in pure slaughter.

Among the prisoners taken were eighteen Frenchmen who had deserted at Pensacola. And so overjoyed by the capture were the loyal defenders that they took time to celebrate by hanging one of the traitors on the spot, before his gaping comrades. The other seventeen were given more dignified consideration. They were taken to Mobile, tried, found guilty, and shot.

The Spanish refused to recognize this defeat as final.

Again they set out to sack the city by land. Forces were sent both to the east and west end of Dauphin Island. The number of Indian warriors had increased by now, and the French and the Indians knew the advantage of every tree and stream on the island. Only a remnant of the Spaniards got back to their ships.

The siege continued for several days with an exchange of random shots and ineffectual broadsides. Finally the once-overconfident, cocksure Mandella gave orders for the sails to be hoisted, and the fleet disappeared into the Gulf. Temporarily, the colony was safe.[1]

Hardly had the sails of the Spanish ships passed out of sight over the horizon when a fleet of two company transports and three battleships, under the command of a French count, one Champmeslin, appeared below the harbor. The battle-worn garrison relaxed.

The officers, however, immediately held a council of war on the count's ship. The consensus was that the French colony could never be free of danger as long as the Spanish held nearby Pensacola. They agreed that Pensacola should be retaken.

All haste was made in order that the attack might be carried out before reinforcements from Vera Cruz could reach the Spanish garrison. However, a delay of a fortnight was necessary to unload the ships, get the *Philippe* in trim and out to sea again, and await the arrival of more Indians.

As soon as preparations were completed, the regulars boarded the ships to join the command of Champmeslin; and Bienville, in command of a company composed

---

[1] Sources are inconsistent as to supreme command during this attack. Though Bienville, as governor, outranked St. Denis, it appears that St. Denis was placed in command of the defense upon his arrival.

WAR OF 1719   157

mainly of volunteers, set out in sloops for Perdido Bay, where St. Denis was waiting with five hundred Indians.

The eastward overland march to Pensacola began immediately. It is to be assumed that by virtue of Bienville's office he was first in command of the land forces. However, some evidence indicates that the governor left the tactics, and perhaps actual leadership of the land campaign, to St. Denis.[2] In the activities that followed it appears that St. Denis functioned as an equal with Bienville and Champmeslin.

On the evening of September 16 the French fleet was anchored outside the entrance to Pensacola Bay; the ground forces were stationed on the land side to avoid escape of the Spanish in that direction. The next morning Champmeslin's fleet plowed into the harbor, and the battle was on. The Spaniards proved to be much stronger than the French had found them the first time. For two and a half hours the small fort guarding the eastern end of the bay fought back with all it possessed. But in the end the Spaniards struck their colors.

The larger fort on the western shore, under the personal command of the governor, one Matamoro, was left to the land forces. When the governor saw the painted warriors of St. Denis' army decked in their feathered headgear and heard their terrifying war whoops

---

[2] Bienville seems by this time to have recognized St. Denis as his superior as an Indian leader. Bienville more than once nearly wrecked the colony by his poor judgment in Indian matters. The fact that Bienville had comparatively little to write or say about St. Denis' military achievements indicates that there may have been some jealousy on the part of the governor, and suggests that Bienville enjoyed the reflected glory from St. Denis' military and diplomatic success. St. Denis, though forceful and practical, was not a vain or overambitious officer. He took pride in doing his assigned job well. Had he followed the practice of many of his contemporaries who wrote long letters, diaries, and defenses some of the history of Louisiana and Texas might be much clearer.

he "surrendered at discretion"—the second time he had surrendered without a fight.

The formalities of the surrender were in order. The commander of the Spanish squadron who had faced Champmeslin went on board the count's ship and tendered his sword, but the count courteously returned it to him in recognition of the gallant defense he had made. Governor Matamoro was not so courteously treated. When he offered his sword the French commander ordered a common soldier to take it as a rebuke and a sign of contempt for his lack of courage in defending his post.

The surrender completed, St. Denis turned to another role in which he was unexcelled in those parts, that of host and toastmaster at a party to celebrate the victory. St. Denis would have been the first to think of this, to provide not only entertainment but the opportunity for the Indians to exhibit their war dances before Champmeslin and the other officers. The ease and effect with which St. Denis commanded the Indians and conversed with them in their own language entertained, as well as impressed, the count and the officers present.

Though the French had again been disappointed at the stock of provisions found at Pensacola there is no reason to believe that they lacked ample refreshments to cheer their party. The "plundering of the large fort was given to the Indians, who acquitted themselves as men who knew their trade; but there was no scalping." Doubtless the humiliated governor's best wine was poured; not, however, in his presence. He was probably behind bars, locked up with his privates and clerks. It is possible that the Spanish officers of the fleet may have had some part in the social aftermath of the battle, for gallantry and devotion to duty were the standards by which men of the profession of arms respected each other. The manner in which a commander fought and the bravery he showed was more important, from the standpoint of the individual enemy, than the principle or country he battled for.

There were other aftermaths of the campaign. Among the Spanish prisoners were found thirty-five French deserters. They were tried on the spot by a council of war; twelve were hanged from the mast of one of the recaptured French ships and the rest sent to the galleys. Men as well as forts changed hands in this war.

The Indians were paid their just due from the booty of the campaign—somewhat, it seems, in the way a show dog is fed a choice morsel for a trick.

History was repeating itself in a dizzy cycle. For the second time in a few months the French had captured Pensacola, and for the second time they had found too few provisions and too many prisoners. Again, in desperation, they were forced to send the prisoners to Havana; and again they realized that they were too weak to hold the fort after capturing it.

But the French had learned a few things. When the prisoners were shipped to Havana this time, the top Spanish officers were held as hostages against the return of the ships' crews and the crews captured on the previous trip under a flag of truce.

When it was realized that Champmeslin would return to France, leaving the colony without a fleet, and that forces from neighboring Spanish colonies would probably try to take the fort again, the French decided not to risk their troops again in an attempt to hold the fort. Instead they decided to destroy it and harass the Spaniards.

Most of the principal presidio was demolished before the main body of French returned to Mobile. Only one officer and a handful of men were left. They were instructed in the event the Spanish returned to cannonade the enemy, spike the guns, burn the buildings, and fall back on Mobile.

The maneuvers of this war on the eastern frontier resembled those of a football game, with opponents contesting the same territory only to have the final score nullified by a technical ruling of the umpires: the treaty signed in Europe at the end of the war gave Pensacola back to the Spanish.

The western frontier did not escape the war. Once hostilities began, the militarists could think of nothing but the glories and excitement of battle, loyalty to the crown, or fear of the enemy. The Spaniards on the western border—once valuable customers for the India Company—were now dangerous enemies. The French took advantage of the slow-moving Spanish and used the element of surprise on both frontiers. In mid-June, the commandant of Natchitoches, Philippe Blondel, received orders from Bienville to take the field against the Spaniards in Texas.

The campaign reminds one of small boys playing war with wooden swords and kitchenware helmets. But this childish game, played according to ancient rules by grown men of arms, made history in its own comic way.

Commander Blondel, when he received his orders, immediately had the bugle sounded to summon his troops —seven in number—and began the march to San Miguel de los Adaes, the easternmost Spanish mission, fifteen miles west of Natchitoches. Blondel had the element of surprise in his favor, as had been the case at Pensacola. The Spanish were always slow to move.

The approach of this conquering army was probably noted by nothing more apprehensive than a few lean dogs. The presidio was sacked in a matter of minutes.

Most of the excitement of the "attack" was caused by a "flurry and scurry" of the local flock of chickens, but even the last chicken was captured. The human captives consisted of a lay brother and one ragged soldier. The priest in charge of the mission was absent on a pious errand at the time, and thus saved himself from capture.

Blondel, satisfied with the success of the campaign, sacked all the sacred vessels, ornaments, and fixtures of the mission and began a leisurely, triumphant retreat toward Natchitoches. The fowls seem to have been the most resistive captives; they brought the only hazard of the expedition. The flapping of their wings and their squawking so frightened the horses that the commandant was thrown. And in the consequent confusion the lay brother escaped.

But this embarrassment was not allowed to dampen the glory of victory. If the booty seemed small on the return to Natchitoches, the psychological effect of the expedition was tremendous.

The escaped lay brother had remained a prisoner long enough to become well saturated with propaganda. He had learned from the French of the declaration of war, the capture of Pensacola, and "the intention of the French to drive the Spaniards from Texas." He had been told that one hundred soldiers were on the way from Mobile, and that the only hope for the Spaniards was to retreat as fast as possible across the Rio Grande. In his flight his alarm was spread among the inhabitants of the missions, especially the women. Miniature as the battle of Los Adaes had been, it frightened the Spaniards out of East Texas. Though the missionaries as a whole were reluctant to retreat, Captain Domingo Ramón could not ignore his panicky citizens and garrison.

The fluttering fowls of Los Adaes had served the French as well as an army. One of the most effective propaganda campaigns of that time was the indirect result of the chickens' alarm.

The retreat gave the vexed and disappointed missionaries the opportunity and stimulation to write "I told you so" at some length to the viceroy—such letters, perhaps, as only men of the cloth could prudently have written. The missionaries reminded His Excellency that they had previously warned him of the danger of the French, that their requests for troops and supplies had been overlooked. The Spanish had made no progress because these warnings and recommendations had been ignored. They hinted that a province "may have been lost" because of shortsightedness in high places.

The war news from the frontier grew increasingly terrifying as it spread back toward the interior. The escaped lay brother continued his unintentional cooperation with the French by hastening the retreat of the Spanish from Texas.

Some historians have credited St. Denis with driving the Spaniards from their eastern frontier, but such credit is unjustified.[3] He was busy fighting on the Florida border. And, as subsequent events would prove, it was for-

---

[3] Possibly the exaggerated danger was one of the reasons contemporary writers gave St. Denis credit for pushing the Spanish out of East Texas. Or perhaps one of Blondel's soldiers boasted that they might hear from St. Denis and his army of Indians next.

tunate for both St. Denis and the company that he was not on this frontier.

The aftermath of the war on the Louisiana-Texas frontier had a humorous twist. When the fighting was over, the company officials suddenly realized that they had no customers on the western frontier. French contraband trade was threatened with destruction. Business was at a standstill. It appears doubly ironic that Bernard de la Harpe should be in charge of the India Company's affairs in western Louisiana at the time—he who presumably had been sent to the frontier earlier to accomplish what Blondel later was ordered to do. The company officials now told La Harpe that something had to be done to reactivate trade.

La Harpe considered that inasmuch as Blondel had committed the "blunder" it was his responsibility to rectify matters. It was the old military game of shifting the buck as far down the line as possible. La Harpe, under pressure from above, addressed an order to Blondel, calling attention to the fact that Los Adaes was an important trade center which had been established with great expenditure of effort both by French and Spanish, and advised him to make immediate apology to the Spanish. Blondel was a soldier, and it is a soldier's duty to obey an order, whether it is to make war or to apologize for a war he has fought. He could not ask why this great expenditure of French and Spanish effort had not been thought of before.

Blondel's diplomacy was somewhat warped, as much diplomacy is. He dispatched letters to the missionaries expressing the fear that he had entertained for them on account of the Indians, who when they knew of the breach between the French and Spanish would have destroyed the mission. He had gone there to protect their reverences from the savages. Brother Manuel had not trusted his promises and had fled, abandoning the effects of which he had taken possession "to prevent their profanation by idolaters." Blondel neglected to mention the soldier he had captured.

This war, in the light of history, appears to have been rather futile. Nothing was gained except experience, which, as usual, was soon forgotten. In a short time the frontier was *status quo ante bellum:* the Spanish returned to Pensacola and to East Texas; John Law's Mississippi Bubble burst; and there was again a grim struggle for existence to the accompaniment of smuggling across the frontier, bickering over boundaries, and rattling of swords.

While St. Denis was away fighting her people, Emanuelle had time to become adjusted, to some extent, to his people and to the strange, damp, lowland of Mobile. It is possible that Emanuelle and the children had moved into a house there owned by St. Denis, for the map of 1711 shows that he owned lots in both the old and the new Mobile. However, if he owned a house, he probably did not have time enough to establish his dependents there before he was off to the Spanish war, but left them with one of the prominent families of the village. Emanuelle had not learned French thoroughly, and she was a stranger in a foreign land—a land that was very different from the mountain-rimmed desert home she had known. She needed someone to introduce her to the country and the people she had adopted.

She did not consider Fort St. Louis, which jutted out beyond the first street fronting the river, an imposing fortress. Constructed of cedar stakes thirteen feet high, it did not appear stable and sturdy like the solid Spanish forts of rock and adobe she had known. Its length from one point of bastion to another was ninety *toises*. Inside was the governor's house and the guardhouse. The officers, soldiers, and residents lived outside.

Emanuelle had never seen houses like those of Mobile. They were either of wood or of wooden frames filled in with plaster made from native shell lime. They seemed flimsy and unstable to one who had known the solid beauty and simplicity of Mexican adobe. A peculiarity of the architecture was the roofs, which sloped to the front and to the rear, with a sheltering eave projection. This was the gallery, which meant to the French what the patio meant to the Spaniard. Some of the roofs were of straw or leaves, though the more pretentious buildings were roofed with tile. Brick or clay-mud chimneys flanked the gabled ends. The houses stood in parallel lines facing the river. It did not seem possible that a town could be built without a plaza filled with shrubs and trees and flowers, where all the town could congregate. Architecture and surveying, she realized, reflected a system of life.

Back of the town towered a wall of mammoth trees bordered by matted undergrowth and brush and some cane, like the trees Emanuelle had seen for the first time on her trip across Texas. Here the great cypress and oak and hickory rose skyward out of the damp, dark soil—giants compared with the familiar dwarf trees of northern Mexico. It was a limitless forest, threaded with Indian trails and bayous, marked with marshes and lakes, stretching out mysteriously into the unknown distances.

In front, the Mobile River trickled by on its way to the bay that fronted Dauphin Island. It was difficult to tell where land and water met. The coast seemed subdued by water; the air was filled with it; it rose from the sea, thinly, sluggishly, but eternally. This was the new land of moisture—fog, mist, rain, mildew, perspiration—and endless talk of it. Emanuelle had left forever her land of shimmering distances, shining sands, and the dancing colors of brilliant sunlight splashed upon rocks and western clouds.

But if Mobile appeared drab and dank it was not without interests and excitements which even the most recent arrival might understand and enjoy. There was the inevitable politics, the Bienville and anti-Bienville factions providing a continual contest. The St. Denises were drawn to the governor. Bienville was of an old Canadian family; he was a cousin; and his brother Iberville had married St. Denis' niece. There were boundary disputes and discussions about illegal trade, except when there was war. To Emanuelle this talk had a familiar ring. There had been much discourse about scarcity of foods and provisions. But now, thanks to John Law, everyone looked prosperous. Governor Cadillac, before his retirement, had dressed his soldiers in decent garb—red coats with many silver buttons, silk-lined capes, silk hose for summer and wool for winter, strong shoes, trousers of white or gray wool. They looked smart and impressive, even if their forced enlistment made them worse rascals than they had been to begin with.

Slaves were pouring into Mobile with the stimulated immigration. There were Negro slaves and a great many Indian slaves, captured from the distant tribes. The free natives did not look down on the French or fear them because of their Indian slaves so long as the slaves were from the right tribes. They kept slaves themselves.

Just enough attention was paid to the presence of mulattoes to create mild gossip. It was considered in that locale that a man in the wilderness would make the most convenient liaison he could. Usually these matters were not referred to in public, but occasionally a father of prominence would recognize his child by a darker mother, who was, perhaps, a slave. The law forbade marriages between whites and blacks. And the Church at that time did not sanction marriages with Indians, although later these arrangements appeared in Church records as *mariages naturels*.

The unmarried colonists were encouraged by the governor to live among the Indians. Emanuelle had heard no end of talk about this unconventional French policy. Her people advocated the very opposite practice. Such a difference in viewpoint was enough to shock one who did not understand such things. This was a privilege of which most Frenchmen, all of whom were *coureurs d'aventures* if not *coureurs de bois*, eagerly availed themselves. The result was rare romantic frolics, if Penicault's accounts are to be taken as true; they well may be, for he spent much time with the Indians. This practice was called "summering" with the Indians.

To the clergy and the conservative wives of the town who asked about Governor Bienville's policy of encouraging the unmarried men in this practice, the governor explained that it was designed to save corn. Provisions were so low always! But every young bachelor had a pretty good idea as to what "saving corn" meant. This practice may have been encouraged partly as the lesser of two evils of the day. No longer were the colonists receiving shipments of virtuous girls chaperoned by nuns to provide wives for them, but rather prostitutes from the houses of correction of Paris.

As to the occupations represented in Mobile, that of the military was most prominent. A few merchants and traders were there, at least one tool sharpener, a locksmith, the keeper of the royal stores, a cabinetmaker, a midwife, and several carpenters. There was a lamentable lack of mechanics. There were some farmers, who principally raised indigo, rice, tobacco, and figs, but most of the food had to be brought in from France or purchased from the Indians.

The missionaries went about their duties in much the same way as those Emanuelle had seen at San Juan Bautista. The priests brought the natives in to baptize them and teach them the ways of virtue. The soldiers brought them in to smear them with war paint. The priests went out into the surrounding forest to save their souls, the soldiers hunted unfriendly Indians for their scalps. Every man to his own trade.

During the war the population of Mobile witnessed some gruesome sights. Emanuelle followed reports of the bloody work as the Frenchmen, her husband in the lead, subdued the Spanish and took their fort. The town turned out to see the French deserters shot. And at one time the Indians ran rampant, dragged seventeen Spanish prisoners of war into the streets of the town, murdered them before a gaping public, and threw their mangled bodies into the bay. But the cruelty of war was not reserved for the natural enemy. One deserter was placed screaming in a coffin, the lid nailed down upon his contorted face, and his body sawed asunder, a practice said to have been borrowed from the Swiss.

In time news came of the retreat of the Spanish from East Texas, to which St. Denis had led them, and where Uncle Domingo was commander. The campaign against Pensacola had been less personal. But in the West Emanuelle's own family was involved, their fortunes and positions at stake. Inasmuch as her relatives had received commands in East Texas after the re-establishment, she had hoped her family might be a link between the old and the new country. Now this hope was gone, swept away by the fickle fate that ruled the frontier. A note from Europe meant that neighbors must turn against each other, bear arms against former friends, and lose their homes and all their belongings in the process.

It is possible that the colonists no longer regarded such warfare a personal matter. They understood the jealousies, ambitions, and qualms of kings. A new world was in the making, and colonies were choice morsels in a cage of wild animals. There would be growling and fighting, and the morsel would in the end inevitably go to the stronger.

XII

Aftermath of War

THE WAR GAVE RISE, ON BOTH SIDES OF THE Louisiana-Texas border, to ambitious dreams of land. These ambitions clashed in a grotesque nightmare. On the Louisiana side, the French government dreamed of spreading colonial empires, and the India Company drew up statistics of anticipated customers and dividends. On the other side, Spanish officials were engrossed with visions of treasure lands that would restore Spain to her former prominence as the rich nation of the world, and the missionaries prayed for more land in which to convert savage souls for the Roman Catholic Church.

During these uncertain years St. Denis seemed destined to serve in either the reckless role of conqueror or the more stable one of balance wheel. On March 23, 1720, he re-entered the king's service and was commissioned a lieutenant. Later in the same year he was promoted to the command of the "Upper Cane [Red] River," a crucial command for which the right man was imperative. Recommendations for the post had specified that "it is necessary to have there a capable officer, who understands Spanish." St. Denis' commission was sent out from Paris dated July 1, 1720. It read in part:

It was judged necessary to appoint a capable, and experienced person as "Commandant of the Upper Cane River," under authority of the General Commandant in the Louisiana Province. We have chosen you for this place because of your worth, your capacity, and experience in the making of war; for these reasons, we by virtue of the power granted us by the King, do name, commission and appoint you. . . . For and in the absence of the Commandant General, Lieutenant Generals, and General Inspector of the troops and militias: you will command the inhabitants and strangers, those who are there and those who may establish themselves there, the soldiers who will be sent there and will be garrisoned in the posts and forts that you may judge necessary to establish and construct. You will give all the orders that you deem necessary and fitting for the glory of the name of His Majesty, the welfare of the Company and the maintenance and advantage of its trade in the said Province of Louisiana, without causing difficulty; for such are the intentions of the Company. . . .

The war had been regarded by the French government as a means of realizing its pent-up ambition to expand westward at the expense of the Spanish. In France the abstract of a plan was drawn for an extensive expedition against the Spanish of Texas, leading to the capture of the territory east and north of the Rio Grande. St. Denis was the man designated to lead the campaign.

But a mercurial, ironic fate seemed to rule—or to prohibit the rule of—the frontier. The royal order for the campaign never reached St. Denis. Instead, the Spaniards read the plan for the conquest of their province before any Frenchman in Louisiana knew of it. The ship carrying the order to America, so the story goes, was captured on the high seas by the Spanish.

If this important order had reached Louisiana, its execution would have made a dramatic story. There was much behind it. Paris had good reason to think that St. Denis was the one Frenchman who would most enjoy driving the last Spaniard out of Texas. His romantic courtship and marriage in Mexico were not the events of St. Denis' career most publicized in the French capital, but rather the hardships and imprisonments he had borne at the hands of the Spanish while attempting to open up trade for the company. St. Denis had lost much of his own goods, quantities of the company's goods, and months of his valuable time. And he was a man to let his superiors know that these losses were not taken lightly. France believed this, and was willing to support him in retaliation.

There is no indication, however, that St. Denis bore any grudge against the Spanish as a group. He was too practical and too busy a man to carry a chip on his shoulder. He had realized beforehand the risks he would run among the Spaniards, had taken them, had accepted his losses, and had enjoyed the fun and romance of it. He had brought the Spaniards back as customers; it is likely that he would have preferred to see them remain where he had placed them. But soldier that he was, there is little doubt that he would have led the fight against his in-laws and their superiors if the word from the king had reached him.

According to Spanish sources St. Denis was supporting the operations against the Spanish later during this period. Possibly he had received a delayed or modified order for attack from the French capital. In the winter of 1720-1721 he and several other Frenchmen were in the region to the west of the Tejas country working with the Indians there. By February they had assembled "several thousand" Indians between the two branches of the Brazos River, above the road to Texas. Several Indian nations were represented in the group, which was supplied with horses and guns and "drilled and given the rudiments of military training."

These reports on the threat of St. Denis may have been exaggerated by the missionaries and inhabitants to secure reinforcements from their government to protect themselves, particularly against the Indians.

That he was working among the tribes of the interior is shown by a letter from Bienville telling of an expedition of revenge against the Spaniards led by St. Denis. Just what type of a campaign, the extent of it, and even the actual existence of it cannot be made clear in the welter of propaganda, fear-inspired rumors, plans for personal and national defenses, claims and counterclaims, false and exaggerated reports. If St. Denis did have a campaign under way "with the sole aid of the Indians," it was a bold and risky project, but one he would have gloried in. Speculations have been varied. Did St. Denis actually plan to capture Texas, as the earlier French plan would have ordered him to do? Was he undertaking a great commercial scheme for the India Company? Was he taking advantage of international conditions to fatten his own purse? Was he merely establishing a background for future power with the Indians? Was he laying the groundwork for a gigantic smuggling enterprise in collaboration with his in-laws? The reason for his presence among the Indians that winter poses another riddle in the life of a mysterious man.

The peace treaty between France and Spain, signed on May 16, 1721, did not appease their respective passions for territory. In 1721 La Harpe was sent from Louisiana by sea to take possession of Matagorda Bay.

In addition to his military force he was armed with legal arguments. If the Spanish already occupied the bay, they were to be informed that they had no right to it as La Salle had taken possession of it in the name of the king of France. From the standpoint of international law La Harpe had a good arguing point. The nations of Europe, in parceling out the continent of North America, had come to regard two international laws as binding. One provided that when a European nation took possession at the mouth of a river emptying into the sea, that nation was entitled to all the territory drained by that river and its branches. The other provided that the boundary between such a discovery and another made at some distance from it by a different nation should be a line halfway between the two. Upon these laws France claimed the Mississippi watershed by virtue of La Salle's voyage and act of possession in 1682, and west as far as the Rio Grande, saying that that was halfway between the Lavaca River and the furthermost establishment of the Spanish in Mexico.

When La Harpe reached Matagorda Bay, the Indians proved so hostile that he was unable to effect an establishment. It might have been easier for him if the Spanish had occupied the site. His legal arguments did him no good. The Indians had already been impressed by the French with something more real than laws and claims written on pieces of paper.

The year before, an expedition led by a certain Beranger had left their shores, taking with it some of the natives' most attractive squaws and leaving a strange disease. Persuasion, gifts, show of force could not dissociate the La Harpe group from the cursed paleface seducers. Thus ended the last formal attempt of France to take possession of the Texas coast. Good arguments and international laws did little in determining the final ownership of the Southwest. Little episodes and little errors shaped the destiny of the shifting frontier.

The Spanish also had ambitions as well as bitterness. Their retreat in 1719 had been humiliating in the extreme. A proud and embarrassed people are sure to be spurred into action after such an experience. After longer delays than they had wished, they were finally ready in early 1721 to march back and retake their lost province and perhaps the French province to boot. Except for two circumstances, the treaty of peace on May 16 and St. Denis' convocation of frontier Indians, the conflict of 1719 might have been re-enacted in reverse two years later.

The expedition was the most formidable effort ever made to establish Spanish domination over Texas; and the force for the occupation was headed by an experienced and determined veteran, José de Azlor, the Marquis of San Miguel de Aguayo.

Just as Aguayo was about to start on the expedition he learned that peace had been negotiated between France and Spain, and he was instructed not to use force unless he found the country occupied by the enemy and resistance was offered. He was extremely disappointed with the prospect of a defensive campaign. His original idea had been not merely to drive the French from Texas but to pursue them across the Mississippi River. With his orders so tempered, he referred to the expedition now as a "sacrifice as evidence of my blind obedience" to the orders of His Majesty.

At the Rio Grande the marquis received news that St. Denis was holding a convocation with many Indians on the Brazos River and that he intended to attack the presidio of San Juan Bautista. Aguayo became more reconciled to the idea of obeying the letter of his orders.

Despite the various interpretations of St. Denis' activities in Texas, logic indicates that he was there simply to see that Aguayo did not get away with anything the French did not want him to. Just what St. Denis' instructions were in regard to the Spaniards at this moment and what he could have done if challenged cannot be said. To say the least, it was good politics to let the new Spanish commander see how many Indians he could muster, and to remind the frontier of his power with the natives.

This was another case in which the policy of the home government was at variance with the interests of the company, which wanted to bring the Spaniards back to the frontier area as customers. The royal government would have been pleased if St. Denis had been sufficiently strong and determined to keep the Spaniards south of the Rio Grande. It is quite probable that St. Denis again, as in 1716, let the Spaniards advance just as far as suited his convenience. He had just been granted a 5 per cent commission on the profits of merchandise which he sold to foreigners. It was therefore to his interest to have foreign customers near his property at Natchitoches. On the other hand, it was equally important to see that these foreigners did not push too far across the frontier and upset his base of activities.

AFTERMATH OF WAR 177

As Aguayo proceeded eastward he decided that the account of St. Denis' activities had been exaggerated; but missionaries and Spanish settlers all along the way warned him not to underestimate St. Denis. The man's influence was like magic among the Indians, they cautioned. He moved in ways forever mysterious to the Spaniards. As Aguayo marched onward he did not see any Indians along the route. It was not comforting to be told that they doubtless were assembled with St. Denis.

On July 8, near the Trinity River, he finally met a group of natives. Their equipment seemed quite significant to the Spanish commander. They carried rifles and ammunition of French manufacture. Aguayo began to ask more questions about this man St. Denis. The Indians gave him some interesting answers. But His Lordship would soon see for himself, they promised; the Great White Father was only a short distance to the east.

At the Neches River Aguayo had his first direct contact with St. Denis. The Frenchman had tarried at the abandoned mission of La Purísima Concepción, and from here he had dispatched a messenger to the west bank of the Neches, where Aguayo was encamped, to solicit an interview with the marquis. St. Denis' message stated that he wished to acquaint the marquis with the instructions he had recently received from the governor of Louisiana. The belligerent Spanish commander had seen and heard enough to make a diplomat of him. He sent a guarantee of safe-conduct to St. Denis.

When St. Denis arrived and presented himself to the Spanish leader he was not as well groomed as was his custom for such occasions. He had had a long, hard ride, it had been raining, and he had had to swim his horse across the river. But his poise and firm dignity and his fluent Spanish impressed the marquis. After paying his respects, St. Denis asked Aguayo to excuse him and permit him to retire for the night to rest from the fatigue of his journey.

St. Denis' bravery was not foolhardiness, and though he was not of the disposition to carry grudges, he never forgot the ominous fact that most men were. The Spanish had imprisoned him in Mexico, ordered deportation for him and his wife, and confiscated his property—actions not easily forgotten. He was the man most dreaded and feared by the Spaniards, and he knew that, among other things, he was suspected by many of them of having led the attack on Los Adaes. The marquis had been cordial enough, but St. Denis had met other cordial strangers in Spanish territory who had brought him no good. He cautiously sought out his old friend Father Espinosa, and the other missionaries in the camp. Here he was among friends.

The following morning, August 1, the Spanish commander called his officers together for a council of war. St. Denis was summoned and asked to state frankly the purpose of his visit. He replied that he had been informed of the peace signed between the two nations; he wished to know if the marquis intended to observe peace. If he did, St. Denis would do likewise. Aguayo replied that in accordance with his instructions he would observe the peace faithfully, provided St. Denis and his men immediately evacuated the entire province of Texas without hindering the reoccupation by the Spanish of all the territory they had previously held, up to and including Los Adaes.

The Spanish records portray Aguayo again as a military hero, saying that his superior numbers forced St.

Denis to make protest and retire. These documents relate that St. Denis tarried for three days among the Indians seven leagues beyond Concepción, where he counted his forces, reflecting that his schemes had been frustrated by the decisive action of the marquis. Before returning to Mobile to report to the governor of Louisiana St. Denis without doubt made protest against farther advance of the Spanish. How much of it was sincere and how much was intended merely to sound impressive for the record is something to guess at. In any case, Aguayo proceeded to Los Adaes to re-establish the most eastern mission.

As soon as the Spanish expedition reached Los Adaes, a messenger brought the news of its arrival to Natchitoches. Renaud, the commandant, immediately dispatched a protest to Aguayo, informing him that St. Denis had departed for Mobile upon his return from his interview with Aguayo. Renaud had received no instructions to permit the Spaniards to settle, he continued, and he therefore requested Aguayo to abstain from acting until St. Denis should return. St. Denis' absence from the frontier at this climactic time was a characteristically expedient political maneuver.

Aguayo was firm in his reply, stating that he was determined to carry out the orders of the viceroy. However, his tone was diplomatic rather than militant, pending the opportunity to promote some spying activities. He sent his reply by no less personages than Don Fernando Pérez de Almazán, who was the lieutenant governor, and Don Gabriel Costales, a captain. These men were instructed to keep their eyes open while acting as messengers.

The two officers reported to the marquis on their return that the Natchitoches fortification consisted merely of a square stockade without any redoubts, the garrison consisted of fifty soldiers and five civilian settlers, and the French depended mainly for their defense on the river itself, which formed a moat around the island, and the labyrinth of bayous in the immediate vicinity. Information about the Indians was the intelligence to cause most concern and speculation. On another island, they reported, were a number of Indians—unfortunately they did not know how many—armed with rifles and skilled in the use of them.

The messengers had advised Renaud of the marquis' orders to reoccupy the entire province of Texas and had emphasized his determination to carry them out. The French commandant had replied that he had no orders either to oppose or to consent to the occupation of Los Adaes, and that consequently he would take no action. He asked permission to present his respects to His Lordship.

Eight days later Renaud rode over from Natchitoches. For months opposing frontier commanders had attempted to outdo each other militarily and diplomatically. Now they tried to outdo each other socially. Renaud thought that after his long journey His Lordship would enjoy some fresh food for his table; so he had considerately brought a dozen chickens and some melons and vegetables. Spanish hospitality seldom suffered by comparison, and the marquis did not stint himself in returning the courtesy. During the course of the banquet the Frenchman complimented the marquis' wine and brandy. This was the lead for the host to make his peace offering. He gave Renaud some spirituous refreshments to take back with him to the French post. The two at least enjoyed each other's food and liquor, and that was a good start toward understanding, and a potential war for possession of a province resolved itself into a party.

The marquis sent his routine report to the viceroy, emphasizing that he had made it clear to the French commander that there would be no more trade in merchandise or supplies.

As he wrote, the troops at Los Adaes were out of corn because, so Aguayo said, of delay caused by floods. While looking for corn he had found two French settlers to the west of Natchitoches who agreed to let him have fifty or sixty *cargas* of grain on the specific condition that the marquis send for it after dark in order that the French commander might not find out about their bargain. The settlers had just been warned about the new regulation concerning trade with the Spaniards.

The war was over; the peace had been signed; claims and counterclaims had been voiced. Courageous and bold ambitions had been announced, protests made and recorded, and reports sent in about it all. Now the frontiersmen were ready to settle down to more mundane business.

XIII

Tale of Two Cities

SHORTLY AFTER ST. DENIS RETURNED WITH his family to his headquarters at Natchitoches, he was honored with one of the highest distinctions that could be conferred upon a Frenchman—the knighthood and military decoration of St. Louis. The French government must have been highly pleased with St. Denis' work on the frontier.

The India Company also recognized him as the man of the hour. Early in 1721 the company had noticed his success in boosting trade on the frontier and had proceeded to encourage him in his commercial activities. St. Denis had not been chosen commandant of the upper Cane River solely because he could speak Spanish and was an experienced soldier. The company wanted a trader-businessman to handle and encourage the Spanish trade to the west; it was willing, moreover, to offer inducement for the right man, possibly to hold men to the interests of the company instead of their own. An order to St. Denis and a colleague, one Weillard d'Auvilliers, illustrates this policy:

> The Company knowing that the Sieur de St. Denis, Commandant on the Cane River, and the Sieur Weillard d'Auvilliers, senior commissioner of the same post, wish to use

their abilities and their experience in opening and establishing trade abroad, on the other side of the ocean. Wishing to reward their cares for the success of the enterprise, the Company has granted them a commission of 5% on the profits of the sale of the goods, which they will take from the said Post to foreigners; this bonus they will divide in half during the time that it pleases the Company to retain them in its employ. The Company asks and orders the Commissioner and Directors of the Colony of Louisiana to pass on and allow expenses against the Accounts of the General Store of the said Post, upon receipt of the aforesaid Srs. de St. Denis and Weillard d'Auvilliers and the records in due form of sales made by them to foreigners. Allow the 5% accorded them as explained above. For such are the intentions of the Company; done at Paris in the offices of the India Company, on March 31, 1721.

St. Denis had been maneuvered into the most strategic position in Louisiana at that time. His title gives no true indication of his status or functions. Contemporary and more recent commentators have remarked that St. Denis, by virtue of his ability, character, influence, and experience, should have been governor of the colony. But St. Denis served France better as commandant because he was able to devote himself to holding the frontier against the Spanish, keeping peace with the Indians and developing trade among them, and conducting foreign business for the company where it was most promising and tedious. Los Adaes, fifteen miles away, was now the capital of a province, the strongest fortification in Texas, and the spearhead of Spain's threat to Louisiana.

In 1722 St. Denis was made Commandant of Natchitoches. His previous title, Commandant of the Upper Cane River, sounded more impressive, but this new title indicated the strategic importance of France's westernmost barrier against Spanish aggression; the appointment of St. Denis showed that his peculiar abilities were fully appreciated.

Though Natchitoches was still a crude, isolated establishment of log cabins, storehouses, a stockade, and Indian wigwams, the place had a long, colorful history behind it, beginning with a legend about an old Indian chieftain who lived on the banks of the Sabine River. Calling his two sons to him, he had commanded them to found new tribes. They were to walk in opposite directions—one to the east and one to the west—from sunup of one day until sundown of another; wherever each was at that time he was to establish himself. In time the two destinations became Natchitoches, Louisiana, and Nacogdoches, Texas. Geography lends credence to the legend, for the towns are located almost equidistant east and west of the Sabine River, and each is a well-balanced two days' journey therefrom. Their names also are in peculiar contradistinction to one another. Natchitoches, in the tribal language, meant "papaw eaters"; Nacogdoches meant "persimmon eaters."

Almost from the beginning of history in the new world "Natchitoches" became a well-known word. The papaw eaters were among the first Indians to be discovered by explorers. During the dawn of the white man's history in the Southwest they entertained many famous travelers, and because of their friendly attitude they were always popular with the Europeans. After the death of De Soto, his followers, under the leadership of Luis de Moscoso, came to Natchitoches while seeking a route to Mexico in 1542. According to one account La Salle visited them in 1687. In February, 1690, De Tonti, on his search for La Salle's colony, halted among the Natchitoches. This was one of the most timely visits ever made to these people, for they were at that time at war to the death with the Tensas. De Tonti made peace between the two tribes, a diplomatic act which perhaps saved the Natchitoches for their later beneficial role to his countrymen. St. Denis favored this tribe from the time of his first contact with them. While commanding Fort St. John on the Mississippi River he had removed this nation, or most of them, to live around him there. When he had returned to the Red River they, in turn, had come again to be with their Great White Father.

A census of Natchitoches, dated the year St. Denis took command, listed thirteen men, five women, five children, thirteen Negro slaves, eight Indian slaves, and forty-two horses. In the country around the fort were fourteen men, ten women, ten children, twenty Negro slaves, eight Indian slaves, twelve horned beasts, and seventy-four horses.

On the western side of the river, to the south of the fort, St. Denis built his home on high ground overlooking the two important islands where the fort and storehouses stood, and where farther on the Natchitoches Indians camped. St. Denis lived between two worlds of contrasting beauty.

To the east, across the river, lay the spreading lowlands and swamps of the Red River valley, reaching to the horizon; they were matted with cane and reed and willow and webbed with unending bayous and lakes, which, though inconvenient for a French traveler, formed a natural system of fortifications. And towering over them all, the mammoth cypresses rose majestically from shadowed, knee-studded waters. Moist silt brought in by the river and deposited there through the long centuries had made this a fabulously fertile land of lush growths. It was still a mysterious valley of intriguing secrets.

To the west, toward Texas, were the forests that grew from high, dry, poor soil, in supreme contrast with the one across the river, a region without the monotonous, floorlike flatness and the dense growths that shut out the sky in the jungle-rich valley of Natchitoches. To the west there were more kinds of growth than any man had ever counted, and hills, valleys, and streams in endless variety. On the dry sandy hills the tall pines towered over their realm as did the root-soaked cypresses across the river. St. Denis seemed to have preferred the rolling hill country, where a man could ride a horse among the trees without bogging or tangling, where flowers, berries, and grapes glowed with the sun, and streams ran with a merry babble instead of creeping silently, like snakes. For it was where the hill country jutted into the valley like a blunt, ragged spear that St. Denis established his town; and it was on the first real hill that he built his home.

In 1772, for the first time, the frontier was showing signs of stability. Although Los Adaes and the other presidios to the west were stronger, more customers were therefore at hand for the French. Aguayo had enforced the viceroy's law concerning contraband trade and the penalties therefor, while he himself became more bewildered and underfed because of it. Before the end of the year he handed the command to his lieutenant, Almazán, turned his back on the frontier, and marched into the interior. Frontier trade thereupon burst out into the open. Doubtless the marquis had needed French corn and French clothes enough to convince him of the impracticability of certain royal orders. St. Denis and the French had long been ready for such a situation.

St. Denis' commission of 5 per cent of profits on goods sold to foreigners must have set him off to a very profitable start in the new boom. It seems to have been a custom of the day—a custom encouraged by the French—that rulers were also the chief traders. St. Denis' store of merchandise, real estate, prestige, and personal goods increased abundantly.

Shortly after St. Denis took command at Natchitoches one Sieur Diron made an inspection of Natchitoches and the Red River country and reported that the commandant exercised great power among the Indians on both sides of the frontier. In spite of the existing peace and the fact that St. Denis appeared to have the situation under control, Diron recommended the continued strengthening of the post in view of the Spaniards at Los Adaes. He must not have expected any immediate action, for he recorded that the general at Los Adaes had promised St. Denis to supply him with cows. He was happy to report that a new arrangement had been made in the method of paying the soldiers at Los Adaes. They had recently been allowed half their salaries in cash, "which will mean," Diron commented, "money coming into Natchitoches, where the Spaniards go and buy what they cannot find at home."

El Camino Real, the road between Natchitoches and the Texas capital became a well-beaten highway. Grain and French finery were the goods most frequently exchanged for livestock and Spanish silver.

Although he was now a settled family man, with responsibilities which increased as his family grew, St.

Denis continued to develop new interests. He turned to stock-raising, farming, and vine-growing. He reported that the wild grapes found in the woods between Natchitoches and Los Adaes could make wine as good as that of France, and that the grapes would bear a year after the vines were planted. As early as 1722 he found time to experiment with the local vines and have a vineyard of his own. St. Denis did not overlook the other natural resources of the country. He made personal investigations and was always alert for suggestions for new trade potentialities—pelts and game, wild fruit and nuts, flax plants, mulberry trees, and honeybees.

The source of St. Denis' power continued to be his control over the Indians. As a permanent neighbor he was now better able to cultivate their trade and friendship. In this work, though he was ever-confident, St. Denis never became careless. His was a cool, silent dignity that was magnetic to the Indians. This may have been an inherent characteristic of a man born in the mute Canadian woods, a characteristic which gave him a natural bond with the Indians, who considered a frugal use of words a fundamental virtue; he may have grasped it from the natives; or he may have simply improved a natural inclination by his association with the Indians —a people who found many vivid and effective ways to express themselves other than by conversation. He had learned that an Indian was more impressed by stately bearing and a bright cloak than by diplomatic phrases. A contact between men who spoke different tongues would naturally lead to sign languages, or a blend of words and signs. Even after the Indian had learned the white man's language, or the white man his, however, the Indian continued to use words sparingly and resorted to dramatic gestures which, though not so exact as words, were effective.

In dress as in speech, St. Denis knew the value of a vivid impression. And so he wore gaudy surtouts of brilliant scarlet and blue and green, and glossy black, cut from the finest velvet and taffeta and damask, fringed with silver braid and garnished with gold and silver buttons; beneath, he wore scarlet- and gold-embroidered vests, yellow taffeta waistcoats, and red jackets. His breeches were usually scarlet. Thus decked, he walked about with the air of one who is master of all he surveys, and the Indians were attracted, and believed without question that he was, indeed. That the Spaniards never understood him did not bother him. He overshadowed them completely.

On the other side of the frontier the presidio and mission of Los Adaes quickly became the capital of the province of Texas and the strongest garrison north of the Rio Grande. It has been called the second most important site in the old Southwest, San Antonio being given first place. However, during its half century as a provincial capital, frontier listening post, barrier against foreign aggression, strong mission, and trading center it was probably considered of foremost importance by colonial Spain.[1]

When Aguayo returned with his strong force of Spaniards, he chose a site for Spain's easternmost establishment half a league east of the original mission, which had been abandoned in 1719. The new location was far-

[1] It was because of its sudden and tragic end that Los Adaes was forgotten. When Louisiana became a possession of Spain by treaty in 1762, Los Adaes was needed no more. A signature on a piece of paper in Europe made a ghost town of the provincial capital.

ther along the road to Natchitoches, a mile northeast of the present town of Robeline, Louisiana. It was given a new name—Nuestra Señora del Pilar de los Adaes.

Aguayo gave his personal attention to the building of the establishment. Though a number of factors—the treaty of peace between France and Spain, advice from the missionaries, and St. Denis' influence over the Indians—had made a diplomat out of the aggressive Spanish commander, he still wanted to build the strongest possible fortification to guard the gateway to Texas and to put the fear of Spain into this all-sufficient lord of the frontier watching him from Natchitoches.

But Aguayo had not lived on the frontier long enough to learn its mysterious and treacherous secrets as had the French commander across the border. Most of the governors sent out to occupy Los Adaes came to the frontier with some glorious dream of making the capital a Garden of Eden, of extending the territory of Spain eastward, or at least of getting St. Denis out of the way. One after the other they failed and retired without knowing exactly wherein they had failed. Aguayo, however, stayed long enough to taste some of the grim realities of the turbulent border country.

First the marquis found that he had no engineer to supervise the building of the fort. "In fact," he wrote, "there is no one who knows the first principles of that art." The expected native labor did not show up; the Indians kept sending promises that they were coming to live at the presidio, but that was all. The hope of building a strong fortification of brick or stone soon vanished; there were no building stones to be found, and though over ten thousand adobe bricks were made, they proved to be more artistic than practical.

The marquis had traveled a long way and led a great force on a glorious mission; he was determined to build a fort—even without engineers, labor, or stones. One fundamental material for building was plentiful—timber. So the marquis set his troops to hewing stakes and beams from the local forest. And the fort was built with sharpened stakes driven one fourth of their length into the ground. The hexagonal structure contained three bastions, each provided with two small cannons mounted in such a manner as to protect two curtains of fifty-five varas each. There were six ramparts. The fort was designed to suit a company of one hundred troops, and it was strategically located on a hill dominating the whole countryside. Aguayo had done the best he could.

Under the protecting guns of the presidio a temporary chapel was erected to serve until the Indians could be collected and a more suitable mission built. The missionaries and soldiers were so enthusiastic that they could not wait until the presidio was completed to celebrate its erection and dedicate it to Spain and the Church. During late September or early October, 1721, the Spaniards staged the biggest celebration that frontier means could provide. Possibly the gay and elaborate dedication ceremonies were designed to minimize the marquis' hopeless failures and to dull his worries. Anyway, the missionaries spared no pains to attract the Indians, even if they had no power, as yet, to hold them. There were dances and masquerades, and a drama was staged—doubtless to propagate the power and emphasize the goodness of Christ and Spain.

After the festivities, optimistic letters were dispatched to Mexico City telling about the accomplishments of the reoccupation: the French had been driven out of

Texas without firing a shot; the natives were rejoicing at the arrival of the Spaniards and would be deserting the French to flock to the missions in droves; the French had given up and were making no more protests—almost anything might happen.

The commander of the French also received reports on the Spanish outpost. His Indian friends brought him details, and frequently the Spaniards came themselves, when they lacked some small item essential to their building program. St. Denis was glad to supply them, though doubtless with tongue in cheek. The Spaniards at Los Adaes may have fooled their superiors to some extent with their cheering and confident letters, but the French commander was to be neither fooled nor frightened. The letters he wrote were orders for more goods for his customers.

Officially, Los Adaes prevented contraband trade and infiltration of the French into Texas. Actually, it prevented neither. But it was an important administrative center, and a seat of grave diplomatic meetings, Indian councils, and treaties. It was a fragile blossom on the withering tree that was colonial Spain.

The provincial capital was not without a grosser side. The most corrupt practice at Los Adaes was one so common that it was taken for granted. The colonial governors and presidial commandants were in a preferred position for graft, and most of them were not above taking advantage of their position. Did not a man of the class likely to become a commander sacrifice much when he abandoned the comforts and pleasures of the metropolis to represent Spain in a remote outpost? Surely he was justified in supplementing his meager salary. Soldiers were paid chiefly in food, clothing, and equipment, secured by the governor and lesser rulers and dispensed to local troops at great profits. The position of governor or commandant was as much that of merchant as leader. As an example, it was charged that one of the later governors pocketed over 80,000 pesos on sales to his troops at Los Adaes, not including his profits from trade with the Indians, the missions, and the French, and from his stock ranch, all conducted without private expense through the labor of his soldiers.

At the other end of the scale, life was simple. Around the presidio and mission, along the streams that broke the thinly soiled hills sprang up the abodes of the families through whom the empire would thrive or collapse. Neither the local earth nor the damp climate approved the Spaniard's favorite dwelling, adobe. And so he made his house as Aguayo had constructed the fort, by driving stakes into the ground. But his house of stakes, the ever-present red mud, the long, damp, rainy winters, the surrounding hills, and the towering walls of the forest hemmed him in and made him homesick for his old world—adobe, dry air, sand, and vistas of unlimited distances and bright colors. Since colonial policy would not permit him to go home, he brought a touch of old Spain to his adopted land. Bright flowers appeared in his windows, pepper plants by his door, and the Spanish dagger—his favorite flower—in his blossom-studded yard. Poor, exploited, neglected, he became a part of the poor landscape he inhabited. Troubles do not dig deeply into a man's soul if he can content himself with simple things. Worries for Spain or the Church he left for those who had possessions to guard, ambitions to satisfy.

A province and a people had taken root.

XIV

The Natchez War

IN 1730 A COMBINATION OF MISFORTUNES WAS descending upon the Louisiana colony. The year opened to a woeful din: disgruntled French troops murmuring of revolt, bankrupt India Company stockholders lamenting the now-inevitable collapse, and Indian war whoops resounding from border to border.

For more than a decade war clouds had been forming above the colony—mere flecks in a peaceful sky, caused by rash judgment or savage revenge. The winds of good will or retribution would drive them to the edge of the horizon, but they never disappeared. By 1729 these clouds had formed one direful shadow that threatened to blot out the entire colony.

The real trouble started with the Natchez, the most highly cultured, powerful, and peaceful nation of the province. The fact that these Indians endured atrocities for nearly fifteen years attests to their natural desire for peace. Certainly there were days when a levelheaded, broad-minded peacemaker might have settled the trouble without war.

Just when individuals of the two races began to kill each other and who was first to begin would be difficult to state; Bienville's treachery in 1716 set a high example for the Natchez to match; after this date their trust in the French was never restored.

Although Bienville was one of the prime movers, he was not alone in his foul play against the Indians. Governor Cadillac had also been guilty, as a result of jealousy between him and Bienville, who wanted to be governor. It is accepted political strategy for a politician to remove a strong rival or placate him if possible. According to Bienville, Cadillac had tried the latter; he had proposed a marriage between Bienville and his daughter. Bienville flatly turned down the proposal and continued to strengthen his clique against the governor. Not only that, he wrote the home government, in answer to subsequent criticism, giving his side of the story and brazenly informing the king that all his opposition was caused by "Cadillac's animosity to me in my having refused to marry his daughter."

This move having failed, Cadillac, early in the year 1716, determined on "the alternative." He devised a plan to destroy Bienville—or so Bienville and his supporters interpreted the plan. The governor summoned Bienville to him and informed him that some Frenchmen had been murdered by the Natchez. He directed Bienville to take fifteen soldiers and nineteen able-bodied men to punish the Natchez and build a fort in their territory.

Bienville asked the governor if the latter expected him to wage war against eight hundred warriors with only thirty-four men.

"Why not?" the governor retorted. He told Bienville that at Detroit he had controlled six thousand Indians with fewer troops. "Does the great, invincible Bienville tremble?"

Bienville was a man of great pride and, despite his

many faults, was no coward. He accepted the governor's challenge and set out to the Natchez nation to make the best of his assignment. He built a stockade below the Natchez nation and sent word to the tribesmen that he had come to establish a trading post.

After a time a delegation of the Natchez, including three principal chiefs, called at the fort for a powwow. The Indians were invited inside the stockade after depositing their weapons outside. Here they offered the pipe of peace, which Bienville brushed aside. He told them that he knew of the murder of the five Frenchmen by their tribesmen. He had come to demand the delivery of the men who had murdered the Frenchmen. The defenseless visitors were thunderstruck. Before they could recover from their shock they found themselves shackled in a prison built especially for them. They began to sing their death songs.

After a night spent in communion with the Great Spirit the chiefs asked Bienville for the privilege of sending one of their number to the village to apprehend the murderers. Bienville consented, but with the warning that at the slightest sign of treachery or attack the hostages would pay with their lives. Chief Little Sun [1] was chosen for the heartbreaking mission.

On the fifth day Little Sun returned and threw three heads at Bienville's feet.

"These are not the right heads," Bienville shouted at Little Sun. And finally the Indians confessed that a guilty chief, White Earth, had fled, and his brother's head had been brought instead. Bienville disbelieved the story and said that the heads were those of slaves, the heads of the

---

[1] The chiefs of the Natchez claimed to be descended directly from the sun, and therefore were known as Suns.

innocent who had died for the guilty. Then it was revealed that four of the five guilty ones were among Bienville's prisoners, two chiefs and two tribesmen. If any of the prisoners were to be spared the guilty ones must pay with their lives. Furthermore, they must swear to put to death the Chief of the White Earth as soon as he could be apprehended. All the slaves and property taken from the French, or the equivalent in pelts, must be delivered to Bienville. The chiefs must require of their people that twenty-five hundred logs, each thirteen feet in length and ten inches in diameter, be delivered to the governor at a spot to be designated on the Mississippi; out of the logs a fort was to be built. Also the bark of three thousand trees must be delivered for covering the houses of the Frenchmen. The imprisoned Indians were in no position to bargain. They agreed.

The four guilty Indians were led outside the stockade, and bound hand and foot to stakes. One of the chiefs shouted defiance to the last, in words that, as recorded, anticipate a Revolutionary hero: "My regret is that my death will prevent me killing more Frenchmen." To his relatives looking on he shouted: "Slay all these French dogs who come prowling and stealing over the beautiful land of our free country! . . . We will be avenged!" What a prophecy for a patient, peaceful people to fulfill. But the French soldiers had no ears for the death cry of an Indian prophet. They were listening for Bienville's command to fire. The order came. The defiant wailing silenced. The two great chiefs and the two tribesmen slumped forward. According to a few historians, the first Natchez War had ended.[2]

[2] Accounts of this treacherous expedition vary as to the number of chiefs killed and the way in which they were trapped. However, accounts of the methods and results are consistent.

But, rather, a war had only begun. Though hatreds smoldered and deep wounds appeared healed, the Natchez chiefs had seen things that day that would never be forgotten. For the first time a Natchez had seen a ruling Sun put to death. Treachery was something they could match. And they could be submissive while awaiting their day.

The terms of the treaty were carried out to the letter by the Indians, who helped the French to build Fort Rosalie. Bienville returned to Mobile, to have Cadillac pronounce his conduct as an outrage "against the rights of humanity, and execrable." One wonders just what Cadillac expected.

The Natchez were a proud and sensitive race. They were not ordinary savages. They could not forget grievances as easily as could other Indians. And they were subtle and patient enough to mislead the French. There is a tradition, with some evidence to support it, that they were related to the Aztecs of Mexico. They were a distinguished tribe, advanced to a cultural stage beyond any of their neighbors. Not dissipated by warfare, they had directed their efforts to internal economics, the development of a religious system, and a governmental organization. They were a tall, strong, robust and well-proportioned people, handsome of face, and of a proud bearing. Their women were noted for neatness in dress and extreme cleanliness.

The most unusual feature about this nation was its odd caste system. There were two classes, the nobility and the common people. The lower class spoke a language somewhat different from that of the nobility, and were called stinkards by the French. The caste status of a child was always that of the mother. The offspring of a noble father and a stinkard mother was a stinkard. If the papoose was born of a stinkard father and a noble mother it was a noble. Such a child, if male, remained noble during his lifetime, but could not transmit his status of nobility to his descendants; if female, she was not only noble herself but her children were of the nobility.

The Indians had explanations and, usually, good reasons for all their doings, and this caste arrangement in which nobility was transmitted through the mother and not the father was no exception. The women of the tribe were given to promiscuity and looseness. A noble married to a stinkard woman could never be sure of the paternity of his wife's offspring. The real father might be, and often was, some stinkard lover. No chances must be taken. Should this child be allowed to inherit the status of his putative father one of the common stock might be raised to the rank of a Sun. This would never do. The gods would be displeased.

But one could always be sure that the offspring of a noble mother was of noble blood, at least on the mother's side—and that was enough. The noble women seemed to have had the best of it throughout. A princess of the blood never married one of her own rank, but always took a spouse from the lower class. Such a princess had only one husband, but according to tribal society it was quite the fashion for her to dismiss him at will and take on another. It was quite proper also for the Sun princess to have a number of lovers. The husband must keep quiet. It was his duty to see to it that she was properly flattered and admired. The husband of such an exalted one had to conduct himself with profound respect when in her presence. He never partook of meals with her. If he was found guilty of infidelity his head was immediately chopped off. The only compensation for his henpecked life was his exemption from all work. When the female Sun died it was the duty of the husband, as a final tribute, to escort her to the next world. His journey began with strangulation.

A ruling Sun chose a wife outside his caste for very obvious and practical reasons. If he married a female Sun and she died first, he would promptly have to drop the business of government to fulfill his obligation as an escort. It was too great a risk to run.

For a number of years it appeared that these busy people, who had so much to think about besides war, might forget Bienville's treachery and consider the score balanced. But in the fall of 1722 an incident occurred to revive bad memories. Following an argument over a debt, an old warrior was shot in the back. The relatives of the victim appealed to the commandant of the post for justice. The murderer was let off with a light reprimand and the relatives told to make the best of it. Certain individuals, perhaps led by relatives of the victim, retaliated by a few ambushings and destruction of French property. Bienville demanded the head of Old Hair, the chief Sun of the White Apple village, with that of a Negro renegade. This was a tragic demand. A ruling Sun was above the law, subject to no punishment. But Bienville got his two heads.

The Village of the White Apple was the hardest hit by French demands, for a very human reason. It was laid in the most beautiful and desirable of all the picturesque country of the Natchez Nation. A domineering bully was in command of Fort Rosalie. He desired more than a commission. He wanted to be a land proprietor. He summoned the chief of the Village of the White Apple before him and informed him that his ancestral village must be abandoned, immediately. The chief was dismayed. But he knew the force behind the demand; and the memory of the unprecedented end of his predecessor was fresh upon his mind. He played the best diplomatic game he knew. He pleaded that the corn had just sprung up and that the hens were setting; to abandon everything at this time meant famine for a whole year. The plea was of no avail, until the Sun suggested that the commandant be paid to grant a respite until the crops could be gathered. It was granted, after the bargain was struck at a very high rate. Many fowls, pots of bear's oil, baskets of corn, and peltries were the graft. The chief went away. Seemingly, all was well. But soon there were secret councils, and the news of the outrage spread to other tribes. To add to the danger of the blundering Indian policy of the Louisiana French was that of the presence of English visitors from the Carolinas who were exerting some influence among the Louisiana tribes. The English quite naturally were generous with their advice and expressions of sympathy and astonishment at the mistreatment the Natchez were receiving from the French. The dwellings of their fathers, the homes to be inherited by their children, could not and would not be abandoned. The French must be destroyed. The campaigns began.

In November, 1729, the entire white male population of Fort Rosalie, with the exception of a tailor and a carpenter whom the Indians needed for their own use, was massacred, and the women, children, and slaves made prisoners. Over two hundred white men were slain.

For the next two years the history of Louisiana is a series of tales of bloody horror. It seemed at one time that every strong tribe of the lower Mississippi Valley would be employed against the French. But because of lack of organization or a strong supreme commander or because of intertribal treachery the Indians were never able to strike with all their forces at the same time. Without these weaknesses they might have wiped out the entire colony during the early days of the war.

After a long series of battles, cruel and treacherous on both sides, the French seemingly had the Indians trapped on Black River. But the clever Natchez escaped. For a while they wandered northward among the Washitas collecting their scattered warriors. Then they reorganized and reinforced. They were ready for the decisive blow. They started toward the land of the Natchitoches.

The Natchez were well versed in the legendary powers of the Great White Chief at Natchitoches. The French would never be driven from the hunting grounds of the red man so long as this greatest of white chiefs commanded his warriors. Just what their sentiments, reasons, plans were as they advanced for this fateful attack cannot be said. Here was stark irony, drama, tragedy, a subject more fitted for fiction than military history. Next to the Natchitoches the Natchez had been St. Denis' favorite tribe. When St. Denis had visited them during his first days in the Louisiana wilderness thirty-one years before, their sentiment toward the tall, charming, pale-faced visitor had been love, no less. No more pleasant contact had ever been made in the wilderness than that between St. Denis and the intelligent Natchez. But after he left, there had come other Frenchmen, among them those who had confiscated their property, shot their braves, and demanded the heads of their chiefs. Doubtless, all Frenchmen had come to look alike to the embittered Natchez.

St. Denis received early information of the approach of the Natchez. If the attack had come during normal times there might have been little in it to have alarmed the experienced Indian fighter. But conditions were everything but normal. The boom days of John Law were past. The India Company had struggled along after the bubble burst, but had never recovered. In fact, the staggering expenses of the Natchez War was the final blow that collapsed the Company. It had been only a matter of weeks since St. Denis had heard that the company had been dissolved. The expenses of the war which the company officials referred to in their petition for surrender of the charter had not been spent on the Natchitoches post. The town was pitifully low on everything needed to wage war, including morale. Arms were at a low level; supplies were short; the troops were ragged and poorly fed, and possibly hated the company officials more than the Natchez Indians.

Never before had St. Denis faced a situation so alarming. Many times before he had fought the Indians with superior odds against him, in the swamps, along the rivers, the coast, and on the plains of Texas; but never had there been so much at stake, a retreat so uncertain. The army descending upon him now was no hit-and-run raiding party, but an army organized and experienced by years of battle in a long, single-purpose war, infuriated by years of humiliation and injustices—a maddened legion with the basic alternative before it of destroying or being destroyed. Everything St. Denis possessed was at stake facing destruction before this ravaging army: his wife, family, home, and accumulated property; his livestock, crops, stores; his reputation and prestige in the eyes of the French, the Spanish across the border, and the surrounding friendly Indians. A man in such a singular military-diplomatic position might lose his most cherished possessions—his wife and children, his fine home, his merchandise and property—and still be an official of importance for his colony and country; but to lose his prestige by military defeat would ruin his position forever. For it was chiefly by virtue of military prestige gained by victories in the past that he would stand or fall at this climactic time. This was St. Denis' hour of greatest military need. If the Indians rallied behind him in this crisis it would be mainly because they thought no one could lose when led by the Great White Father. It was this power over the surrounding Indians and the military strength that resulted from it that had kept the Spanish in place. Power was the guiding light and driving force in these wilds, an element that both the simplest and most complex minds understood beyond the strength of words. A frontier leader could not be without it; prestige and "face" might be more important to a man and the country he served than anything else. What St. Denis depended most upon now was what he stood in greatest danger of losing and what he could least afford to lose—military power. But even a complete and unprecedented influence would be limited in this instance by local native manpower, because of the pressure of time.

St. Denis dispatched a messenger to New Orleans in all haste with news that his post was the next objective of the Natchez. This was a poor quarter in which to seek help. The colonial troops were already reduced and

. . . he walked about with the air of one who is master of all he surveys. . . .

exhausted. Supplies were low. However, help started, a company of sixty men which collected a hundred Tonikan Indians on the march. But the troops never reached Natchitoches. At the mouth of the Red River the forces received news that the battle was over.

In the meantime, the Natchitoches commandant sent out runners to the Caddodaquois and Asinai, tribes which he considered in position to give him best and quickest aid. It took some time for them to make medicine and get on the march, but within a shorter period than usual they started coming into the fort in little groups. The White Chief was in a hurry. So they did not take time to go through all the rituals and organize. Some of the braves came singly, and every one was a cherished recruit.

When St. Denis took stock of his local armory he found that it held weapons enough to arm only forty-two men. He not only condemned the company for this terrifying shortage but blamed the war on its blundering and mismanagement. Later, when reporting on the matter, he did not hesitate to denounce the narrow, careless, stupid policy that permitted this company-breaking, colony-destroying conflict. He gave no indication that the company had not received a just reward in the fact that this war put them out of business.

St. Denis needed trained, well-armed soldiers, and he needed them in a hurry. Again his prestige and singular diplomacy paid off in a strange way. Just a few weeks before, a new governor of Texas, Captain Juan Antonio Bustillo, had arrived at Los Adaes to take up his duties on the frontier. St. Denis had traveled to Los Adaes to pay his compliments. He found the captain a pleasant and practical man, not too hard to influence. Spanish wine and Spanish conversation flowed freely, and when they parted the men felt that they understood each other. Evidently Governor Bustillo had been inspired. He had even obtained official permission for the Spaniards to trade with the French at Natchitoches—just in certain articles, of course, but the foot was in the door. Now St. Denis assumed that Bustillo was his friend both officially and personally. A horseman was sent dashing over El Camino Real fogging the air with dust behind him, carrying an appeal for help. And, apparently without taking time to think of the advantages his country might gain by his refusing to aid Spain's traditional rival and enemy, the Spanish governor dispatched sixteen Spanish soldiers and a contingent of Indian allies to fight under the command of the Natchitoches commandant. The Spanish might have thought of old military scores to settle; they might well have reasoned that if the Natchez destroyed the French this would be their long-awaited opportunity to push across to the Mississippi, join Texas and Florida together, and make the Gulf Coast a solid province of Spain. What would have been the action of the viceroy had there been time to consult him cannot be said. The important thing at the moment was that St. Denis and Bustillo were friends, and it was, indeed, a unique and timely friendship.

On October 5, 1731, the Natchez struck. Only a few Indian allies had arrived. And the Spaniards and their contingent of Indians had shown up without arms. This was a staggering disappointment. How a mistake of this sort could have happened at such a critical time is a subject of much speculation. The Spanish may have rushed off in too big a hurry to bring their arms. But this does not sound like professional soldiers, and Governor Bustillo was a professional military man. It is equally possible that the error resulted from St. Denis' having overplayed his hand on some previous occasion in impressing the Spaniards with his talk of strength of arms. Also, the Spanish were forever short of weapons, and they may not have had them to spare, or considered them too inferior for their rivals to see.

The Natchitoches bore the weight of the first attack. These Indians probably possessed firearms, provided in more prosperous days. They used them courageously as best they could, but they were hopelessly outnumbered. Every hour of delay they provided was precious. But the onslaught was overwhelming, and they were forced to fall back to the fort, pursued by the Natchez.

When the Natchez approached the fort they sought to gain entrance under pretense of friendship, planning then to slaughter the garrison, according to one account. The account does not state under what guise they requested entrance. Did they appeal to the old friendship that had once existed between them and the white commandant? Did they approach him as if seeking a mediator or peacemaker to end the long war? Did they explain the clash with the local Natchitoches Indians as a misunderstanding? The answer died in the drama that ensued.

St. Denis was too experienced an Indian fighter to be misled by a ruse. He refused admittance.

For nine days, while he waited for reinforcements, St. Denis stopped the Natchez from advancing by "resorting to skirmishes day and night." And what a place for skirmishing. Around the edges of the town wound a labyrinth of tangling streams and irregular ridges fringed with bogs and filled with tall grass, matted cane, little thickets of bushes and vines, and stumps and logs. There was usually a tree or knoll for the Frenchmen to use for cover, but there was likewise a place of concealment for the enemy. It was a nerve-racking job of scouting and stalking, like beast against beast. St. Denis was trying to hold the enemy at a distance to save as much of his town as possible, and above all things to keep him at a sufficient distance from the fort to prevent its being destroyed by fire.

The Natchez pushed in ever closer. They gained footholds which they used to build fortifications of entrenchment and embankments and even a small fort. The French were powerless to stop them. It was evident that this was not a senseless, resourceless, or unorganized band of savages. The enemy, in good order and without delay, provided themselves with an adequate water supply; they brought up provisions under the very noses of the French. Then they laid siege to the fort.

St. Denis was waiting for reinforcements from New Orleans which would not come, and also for more Indian allies. The Indian allies, however, did come; St. Denis' frontier diplomacy and justice paid off when payment was most needed. One way or another they crept into the fort, or were slipped through the lines by scouts sent out to meet and direct them.

The stubborn resistance, almost passive at times, was less than the Natchez expected of the Great White Chief. Why did he not come out in the open and give hand-to-hand battle like a great warrior? The Great Chief was biding his time, making the best of his ammunition, arms, and men, and waiting for the reinforcements that must surely come. The tension began to tell on the Natchez. They determined to bring this battle to a point. To do so, on October 13, they brought out a French woman captive, erected a stake in plain sight of the French fort, and tied her fast, while the incredulous defenders looked on. If the French thought this was a bluff they were soon to find out how mistaken they were. Amid her screams of horror and anguish, they saw the Indians set fire to the woman and burn her alive.

This was too much for red-blooded men to see and remain on the defensive. St. Denis changed his tactics. At the head of his mixed army of Frenchmen, Indians, and Spaniards he rushed from the fort and charged into the nearest Natchez. At the onrush the Natchez scurried back and tumbled into their trenches. St. Denis' men plunged on. The Natchez steadied themselves and fought back with savage fury. The battle they had been waiting for was on. The Natchez began to fall, but when one brave went down there was another to rush in and take his place. After a time, lines began to waver and break, but the violence only increased. Over logs and ditches, from tree to tree the furious hand-to-hand battle raged.

Then, after six days and nights, the Natchez asked for a truce. They admitted that they had lost seven great warriors. St. Denis dictated his condition. They must surrender their weapons. The Natchez gave evidence that the terms were acceptable, filled the holes they had dug, and knocked down their fort. And then, at a moment when they thought the French had relaxed, they fiercely resumed the battle. And for three or four days more it raged.

Finally the Natchez seemed to weaken. The French sensed victory. Into the swamps, the marshy woods of tall cypresses and stubby cypress knees and brush, onto the sand bars of the Red River, across the patches of corn and the pasture meadows they pushed the Natchez. Several Indians, mortally wounded, jumped into the river "rather than leave us their scalps." The drive gained momentum, and the battle turned into a rout.

The Natchez attempted to retreat down the Red River. But by now they were scattered, disorganized, low in supplies and ammunition, almost leaderless. The Natchitoches, who perhaps had suffered most, were the most furious in the chase.

St. Denis stayed at Natchitoches to patch up the fort and the town, bury the dead, manage for critically needed food and supplies, arrange for the sick and wounded, survey the damage—especially to himself, the heaviest loser without doubt—demobilize the Indian allies, and try to provide gifts for them. And to write a letter.

The letter was dated November 2, 1731, and was addressed to the *ordonnateur*. St. Denis was not in one of his best moods and for obvious good reasons. "As quickly as possible," he wrote, "I am dispatching one of my officers to inform you that the Natchez who came here have run away. At the same time I wish to inform you of the trouble we went through: The Indian Nations that came to help us numbered two hundred fifty, not counting the Natchitoches. Since the 5th of October (when the Natchez attacked us) I have had with me men and women of the Natchitoches tribe. I have been obliged to kill oxen and cows to feed these people. To crown all this a hundred Caddodaquois have just arrived —a little late. I have been terribly hard up to find merchandise and weapons for all the nations."

St. Denis railed against the company. "I do not know why all posts have been undersupplied," he continued. "I blame the Company for it. The Company ought to be made to pay for the Natchez war, for it is responsible for it. Had my post been well manned by troops, maybe the expense would not have been so great and the rout of the Natchez would have been complete."

St. Denis reported that he would not stop pursuing the enemy. He said that the Natchitoches expected to defeat them "all around here." He attached a list of what had been supplied and by whom, expressing the hope that the addressed might be able to meet the expense "so that on future occasions we may call on these people again." The only booty was a few slaves. On this subject the commandant wrote: "The Natchez had with them six negroes, three of whom surrendered to us, saying that they had no other master but the Company; so I hope you will find it agreeable if I keep them for myself. I have given the other three to some inhabitants until I can send them back home. One of them claims to belong to Champinel; another to a man called Cidou, who, I learnt, was killed in the Natchez massacre; if he has no heirs and has paid the Company, I shall keep his negro since he is a prisoner of war. I have sent a few slaves, of whom the savages made me a present, to the Spaniards in order to keep them away from the French settlement."

The commandant lamented about the destruction of his corn, which he said would be a loss of a thousand gold coins. He asked for no compensation for this, but he said he would like to be reimbursed for the cattle which he had been forced to kill in the service of king and company. He asked reimbursement for "the guns." One wonders whether the forty-two guns which he reported were merely all that belonged to the company or the king, and whether there were additional ones used which belonged to him personally. Considering the magnitude of the battle and the nature of the commandant the latter is quite probable. St. Denis concluded his letter by requesting three or four pirogues for the king's service "to come and bring news as well as to transport supplies for the store." He made it clear that transportation and the handling of intelligence had affected his campaign. He was not too subtle in emphasizing that he considered the risks and losses of this life-and-death struggle uncalled for.

St. Denis' letter was dispatched before the final outcome of the battle was known. If he had waited he could have given a brighter report. For his troops did better in pursuing and defeating the Natchez than he thought would be possible in such a short time. So hot was the chase that the Natchez were never able to give much organized battle afterwards. They fell back, following the course of the river southward to a lake about three miles west of the present town of Cloutierville. Here they made a stand and fought back desperately among the willows and reeds and cypresses, with their backs to the lake. Their supplies and ammunition were going fast. The French and their allies closed in. Foot by foot the Natchez fell back, first into the swamps, then the shallow edges of the lake, and finally into the depth of the lake itself where the deep water cheated their enemy of their scalps. It was wholesale slaughter, annihilation. The lake became known by the French as Sang pour Sang.

St. Denis' generalship and sacrifices did not go unheralded. Commendations came without delay from his superiors. The entire colony was grateful. Historians recorded his part in the struggle as "the only really brilliant success in all the wars with the Natchez won by French arms."

The Natchez had not effected any extensive damage to the town of Natchitoches. Some superior strategy or method of primitive defense must have accounted for this miracle. And all accounts agree that the number of casualties were surprisingly light among the whites. As an Indian fighter St. Denis had had one of his "brilliant" days.

The Natchitoches commandant was grateful for the support that had helped him to save so much. He did the best his limited means would permit in expressing his thanks. Trinkets and supplies, a feast and scalps were rewards to his red warriors. To his friend, Governor Juan Bustillo, went a present of some captive Indian women. Spanish blood had been spilled in defense of a rival French fort. A strange co-operation was being rewarded by an equally odd gesture of appreciation. Perhaps it was the best St. Denis could do. The Spanish governor, incidentally, declined the offering with thanks.

This was a battle the frontier Indians never forgot. So long as the Adaes and other neighboring tribes remained on the frontier, their part as warriors of the Great White Father in his greatest battle became a part of tribal tradition and frontier oratory.

A few Natchez escaped destruction and were absorbed by the Chickasaws. But the Natchez as a nation passed into history. Their name lived on, however, not only in legend but in the name of a beautiful town inhabited by their white enemy, a quaint little town nestling upon picturesque bluffs overlooking the Mississippi. A unique civilization had been destroyed. A blundering, bloody, tragic era was ended.

XV

Boundaries

IN 1735 ST. DENIS DECIDED IT WAS TIME TO establish a boundary between Louisiana and Texas. He came to the decision at that particular time because of a storm of protest raised at Los Adaes when the Spaniards heard that he planned to move the Natchitoches fort a gun-shot's distance further to the west of Red River because of the uncomfortable situation made by high water. A rise in the river caused the water to surround the fortification, isolating it. On the surface this would not appear to have been a move of great import, because many French settlers lived west of the river and there had existed a sort of "understanding" that the Arroyo Hondo, a stream about midway between Los Adaes and Natchitoches, constituted the line limiting Spanish and French influence. To the north and south the boundary was about as fluid as St. Denis wanted it to be. This arrangement had seemed practical, but it had been only a tacit agreement. At the first sign of a move the French were charged by the Spaniards with "expansion," "encroachment," "invasion." The alarm became so widespread that it was a heated topic in the capital cities of Madrid and Paris.

The controversy revived old claims and boasts and

inspired some new threats. It was an old fire with new fuel and a fresh draft.

During the early periods of exploration and colonization, each country had made vain and expensive excursions to expand its territory at the expense of its rival. Now the time had come when both sides could see the importance and practicability of becoming developers rather than conquerors. Each recognized the increasing strength of the other and realized that invasion and colonial wars were grave and serious matters, especially when thousands of Indians who now carried European weapons might be involved.

But where should the boundary be placed, and what should be the basis for its establishment? For years there had been claims and counterclaims, almost without exception extremely biased. Some Spaniards claimed territory as far east as the Mississippi River, and many French claims demanded the Rio Grande for Louisiana's western border. During the long controversies diplomats fretted; archivists, research agents, students and officials spent many perplexing hours over old maps and claims, faded letters and documents in Mexico City, Madrid, Natchitoches, New Orleans, and Paris. The problem had been passed back and forth through diplomatic channels for years, becoming more confusing all the time.[1]

It would appear that the man least worried about the boundary was the one most involved. Like a ruler sure of his reign, St. Denis had let the storm blow over his head through the years without getting ruffled by it. He, among all people, would know when the proper time and circumstance arrived to bring the matter to a point.

---

[1] This boundary was never permanently settled. The United States tried to establish it after the Louisiana Purchase of 1803, and the problem came very near precipitating our war with Mexico in 1806 instead of forty years later.

And so the "time" turned out to be the year 1735, and the cause of it, St. Denis' decision to move his fort.

The lieutenant governor, Ensign Joseph Gonzales, was in command at Los Adaes at this time, Governor Manuel de Sandoval, Bustillo's successor, having retired to San Antonio on other business. As soon as the lieutenant governor got wind of what was going on at Natchitoches he wrote the governor about it. And the next day, November 13, Father Vallejo, a Franciscan, also wrote the governor contributing his rather interesting interpretation of the French move. He informed Sandoval that the foul work of the French was inspired by the treacherous designs of his archenemy, Father Pierre Vitry, the Jesuit priest at Natchitoches. He explained to the governor that the black-robed padre had just returned from New Orleans with orders for the removal of the fort to the west, hinting in unmistakable terms that the orders were the "results of the Jesuit's machinations."

Among the many strict orders which the provincial governor carried in his portfolio was one stating that he was to resist any effort of the French to pass beyond their boundaries. Without sufficient thought or preparation on the subject, Sandoval assumed an impossible position. He immediately took the view that the French were encroaching beyond their borders. He talked too fast and too loud. The thunder of his voice was all out of proportion to the number of his troops. Worst of all, he had not been in Los Adaes long enough to know the schemer he resisted.

It seems logical to assume that if the positions had been reversed, had the Spanish, that is, decided to move Los Adaes a few yards eastward for some simple convenience and had St. Denis found himself too weak militarily to resist, he would have overlooked the matter—at least, until his position could have been sufficiently improved —and would possibly have supported the argument of his adversaries in his reports to his superiors. The issue seems a mere technicality now; but Sandoval lost both his position and fortune by his ignorance and lack of both common sense and a sense of humor. When Sandoval attempted to defend his position on the grounds of history and geography, St. Denis immediately made a fool of him, so completely that even the Spaniards could see it.

Governor Sandoval and Gonzales spent considerable time writing protests and reports. For instance, on December 19, 1735, Ensign Gonzales wrote to the Natchitoches commandant, saying:

> I am notifying you that I have received orders from my superiors: In order to perform my duties I informed them that you intended to build a fort on our land, on the other side of the river. To fulfill these orders, I implore you, Sir, to remain on the land which has always been known as the Crown property of the very Christian King of France. I am obliged, Sir, for the first time, in the name of His Most Christian Majesty (May God protect Him), Philip V, my master, the King of Spain and America, [to demand] that you stop this work already begun. Do not overlook this demand. Disastrous results would follow such an expected novelty as the building of your fort.

St. Denis never had time for lengthy letter writing. He was a master at the enviable art of brevity and possessed a rare insight into its powers and virtues. His reply to Gonzales was so blunt, so complete, so pointed as to be almost unanswerable:

I, Louis de St. Denis, Knight of [etc.], am notifying you, Lord Gonzales [etc.] . . . that I have received your ultimatum.

I read in your opposition that, under the obligation to obey orders of your superiors, you notify me for the first time to remain within my frontier boundaries and not to continue the transfer to my fort, which I have already begun. You have done your duty.

For the first, second, and third time I answer that I am obeying orders from my superiors and will continue to do so. However, I am sending word to his Honor the Governor General of the Province of Louisiana stating your position and that of your Lord Governor and your opposition.

Work continued on the fort without interruption.

By 1735 Los Adaes had reached a new low. Soldiers and civilians were in rags, and starving. For the past few years there had even been talk of abandoning Los Adaes. In fact, nature and circumstances had about determined the fate of the post without benefit of royal order. The poor soil, laziness of the colonists, their inability to make farmers of the Indians, and the great distance from the base of supply placed the Spanish on starvation rations. Pinched stomachs had made the border Spaniards blind to petty trade laws, and so they depended, in the main, upon the French for their corn, beans, and other food supplies. During the hard years this practice became so open that Spanish rulers condoned it and saved, to some extent, their official faces by proclaiming that trade would be limited strictly to food supplies.

During the winter of 1734 it had been reported that the wives and children at the presidio were so poorly clothed they could not attend religious services without offending common decency. The men were forced to go about their duties wrapped in dirty blankets or in buffalo hides. Ensign Gonzales lamented that the soldiers often went weeks at a time without meat. As a result of the reduced corn crops and the spoilage of much of this grain at the French post because of the damp season, Los Adaes was without this staple. In a desperate effort to gain lard the men had hunted in vain for bear. A supply of butter and cheese which the lieutenant governor was saving for the governor, to be used on his visit, which was expected daily, was seized in desperation. This brought no social embarrassment on the presidio for it seems that the governor read the glum reports and stayed at San Antonio where butter and cheese were more plentiful. The lieutenant governor closed one of his reports with a plea for a pair of pants for himself. In the spring of 1735, just as St. Denis was getting ready to move his fort, Gonzales sent a significant dispatch to Sandoval at San Antonio relating the condition of Los Adaes. It appears that his superiors had been prodding him on the matter of bringing the fort up to an adequate state of defense. He stated that the stockade was full of holes and in sad need of repair. Another report a little later stated that Los Adaes resembled a cattle pen more than anything else. He tried to make the situation show some promise by saying that the timber for repairs had been cut, but explained that the few men who were not sick were repairing their own living quarters. This had become necessary because in late January a severe storm had swept across the country and leveled to the ground part of the weakened post.

Sandoval replied by directing Gonzales to repair the fort at once. However, the governor continued to issue orders from his more comfortable quarters at San Antonio.

According to St. Denis, the French at Natchitoches also had suffered from the severe winter, and were not in a position to furnish the vitally needed aid to the Spaniards. St. Denis set up an "Office of Price Administration" in Natchitoches in 1735. A minimum price on corn of two pesos per *fanega* (approximately two bushels) was fixed by the Natchitoches commandant. This was a higher rate than the Spaniards were accustomed to paying. Gonzales complained about this price regulation and the consequent hardship caused at his garrison. After expressing to the governor an opinion of St. Denis' selfishness, he proceeded to the more practical and pressing task of promoting some illegal trade on his own behalf. A few weeks later he boasted that he had secured fifty-nine *fanegas* of corn and six barrels of red beans from the French.

The Spanish commander well might have made the most of his accomplishments in smuggling. For he had a very short run of luck. A few dark nights later his emissaries were caught red-handed on the Natchitoches highway by St. Denis himself. The enraged St. Denis put the fear of God and the law into both the Spaniards and French. That was the end of the black market on the frontier, until St. Denis was ready to permit it again. If it takes a thief to catch a thief, one might say with equal accuracy that it takes a smuggler to catch a smuggler. No one on the frontier could have known more angles on this delicate art than the French commandant. Neither Spaniard nor Frenchman could fool the old master in this business. The Spanish might not be able to stop smuggling, but *par dieu*, when he said there would be none, people had better forget about it. And they did, as long as St. Denis remained in his determined frame of mind.

It hardly seems a coincidence that St. Denis chose a time to move his fort when his opponents were ragged and starved, their fort was rotting down, and they were harassed by sickness, storm, and flood. St. Denis knew that ambition, patriotism, and the zeal to fight are not very strong in worried men who have empty stomachs.

If St. Denis was a crafty general who knew just how much fight was left in the enemy, he was nonetheless a shrewd politician and a farsighted businessman. He was too cunning to allow the proverbial tail to get into a crack to be nipped off by Spanish politics or an effective embargo against French goods. A political or diplomatic breach might strain relations, but he did not wish the gap to become irreparable. St. Denis was determined to move his fort, but he was also resolved not to lose his customers in the process, or at least, not permanently. As a suave diplomat and tactician he knew how to present his side of a question if the annoying practice of arguing became a necessity. So he took it upon himself to score a few points when individuals across the border spoke of his actions as selfish. He explained that his people had lived through the same severe winter about which the Spaniards were complaining so loudly. He reasoned that he had to take care of his own first, and this included the Indians. If the friendly Indians needed corn, naturally their need came before that of the Spaniards, for they were his "reserve" troops. If this unconventional philanthropy caused the Spaniards to regard him as a base character for considering the hunger of a "savage" in preference to a white man, it also gave them something else to think about along the line of military strength, which was always the final "line" in St. Denis' scheme of things.

St. Denis had an impressively long memory. However, knowing how easily some men forget, he understood the necessity, as well as the methods, of taking advantage of inconvenient moments to teach his adversaries lessons not to be quickly forgotten. For instance, at this time the Spanish semiofficially permitted trade with the French only in items they had to have, not in goods the French most wanted to sell nor those which would bring the most profit. Almost any businessman might have used a little pressure against such a one-sided system.

The exact motives behind St. Denis' actions during the controversial years of 1735–1736 may not be entirely clear. But it can be said, without risk of contradiction, that his timing was perfect.

Embarrassed and outwitted, Ensign Gonzales continued to send protests to St. Denis. He relayed irate letters from his superior, Governor Sandoval; he made outright personal threats about military force and about cutting off the commerce which, officially, had already been cut off. He was between the devil and the deep blue sea—the governor and the Spanish administration on the one side prodding him against the French, and St. Denis, against whom he could do nothing, on the other side. He wrote Sandoval that the French move should have been opposed by force from the beginning. But who was going to drive St. Denis out? Not the governor; he liked it at San Antonio very well, indeed. Not the lieutenant governor; he was too short on everything, including pants, to launch a campaign. For fear that the governor might agree with him and yet order that force be used, he informed His Excellency that the strength of the French garrison had been doubled by enlisting the settlers of Natchitoches. This may have been a true report, but it may also have been made just so the record would show an excuse for his not having already resisted the French with force. It would appear that these two seemingly inconsistent letters were penned in the hope of saving both the lieutenant governor's face and his troops. Gonzales kept on writing letters to Governor Sandoval and to St. Denis and worked himself into a rage; the more helpless his position, the more furious he became. And Governor Sandoval continued to compose well-phrased official communications and to enjoy the comparative ease of San Antonio, at a comfortable distance from the annoying controversy. St. Denis began moving settlers to the island from which the fort was being transferred.

But one Sunday in April of 1736 Gonzales' cup of bitterness ran over. When he and his family—or rather a part of it—came out of church he discovered that his daughter Victoria was missing. Gonzales sensed a plot at once. He disliked Frenchmen in general, and in particular Jean D'herbanne, a soldier stationed at Natchitoches, who had been boldly courting his seventeen-year-old daughter.

He learned that Victoria had been seen leaving the church through a side door which led to the blacksmith shop; a few minutes later she had been seen with a French soldier; but now she had disappeared. A frantic search about the town convinced the father that an elopement was under way. This unwelcome foreign suitor had stolen his daughter right from under his nose while he was at worship.

The garrison broke into a confusion resembling a stampede. Guards were called; soldiers were summoned from their barracks. Horses were quickly saddled. The commandant lost no time in organizing a company to pursue and capture the lovers before it was too late. Soldiers dashed out over the road toward Natchitoches with great hopes of capturing the commandant's daughter and a reward or promotion at the same time. Troops were posted along the road, and guards were placed at all approaches to Natchitoches.

But they found not a trace of the eloping couple. While the excitement was at such a peak at Los Adaes, and curses were shouted against the French, the lovers were quietly but hastily rowing down a small, winding stream toward Spanish Lake to the north.

D'herbanne and three companions had secreted a canoe in the brush on the stream nearest the church and, at the close of the services, had slipped through the woods to it with Victoria. Now the men were pulling hard at the oars, afraid even to breathe under the strain and haste. It was not a stream suited for canoeing. It was so shallow in places that the French companions had to wade into the water often and push the boat over sandbars and gravel beds. Cane and limbs hung low over the creek, and care had to be taken lest telltale hats be left behind or wedding clothes ripped by brambles.

Finally they reached Spanish Lake, a large lake hemmed in by tall cypresses and oaks that crowded the water's edge. They set their course far enough from the banks to make recognition difficult, and without detection they arrived at the outlet of the lake, a larger stream that flowed gently into the Red River.

When they gained the Red River their hearts did not pound so heavily. The sun was sinking. The red current would speed them on, and they could hug the tall banks to hide them from sight in the direction of the Spanish country. Night would soon cover them.

They came to the towering bluff known as Grand Ecore. Under its moon-cast shadow Jean and Victoria drew closer to each other, and whispered that they had just a few more miles, around one more great bend, and they would be safe in Natchitoches, where the priest awaited them. And yet while they spoke of hope and luckier days their ears were trained for the pound of a horse's hoof, the splash of an oar, or a Spanish command to halt.

In a little church of logs and mud and bark at the very edge of the rust-colored river that had brought them, Victoria and Jean said their marriage vows before the Jesuit priest Father Vitry in the flickering candlelight at midnight. They had dared, raced, and won. And they had given the frontier an elopement to talk about for generations to come.

The entire Spanish capital had been fooled, and the lieutenant governor heartbroken and embarrassed no end. Already there had been hints that he had not shown a sufficiently strong hand in dealing with the French, that he did not have the frontier situation under control. Now a lack of discipline and control had flared up in his very household. Father Vallejo wrote letters to the superior Spanish officials, along with Gonzales, defending the lieutenant governor's position, and ranting against the French. Vallejo accused the Jesuit of having disregarded all church regulations in marrying the runaway couple at midnight. Ensign Gonzales wrote a pathetic letter to the governor, referring to the matter as an "outrage," affirming that he had most emphatically refused the union, and further explained that he had disowned this daughter, who had brought shame upon his greying hair. He related how D'herbanne had tried to persuade Father Vallejo to intercede with him for his daughter's hand and how the priest had refused to have anything to do with the affair; how the Frenchman then came in person with two companions to ask him for the girl's hand in marriage. Gonzales had emphatically refused to consent to the union because of the difference in their ages and because of his position.

At least there had been some delightful gossip to relieve the tense, frontier monotony, something to talk about besides the dangerous new French fort and the shortage of corn and clothes.

St. Denis, of all men on the frontier, would have understood Jean D'herbanne's escapade. It reminded him of his own risky international marriage. He probably had a toast and a sly French wink for his bold soldier who had braved a whole fort of Spaniards and stolen a lieutenant governor's daughter in broad daylight at a place where the whole town was congregated. Here was a man after St. Denis' own heart, one who had the courage to go after what he wanted.

While the rival Spanish commandant was writing letters of apology and defense to his superiors, St. Denis had his laugh, and then set out to do some writing of his own—of a more studious and permanent nature. He took time off from his fort building and his trading business to compose some rather lengthy arguments on the defense of France's claim to the Red River country—perhaps the strongest and most logical local treatises on the subject up to that time.

In this correspondence, the Natchitoches commandant insisted that the French had been the first discoverers of Texas; that the French settlements west of the Red River had been there at the time of the coming of Aguayo and his followers—the first permanent settlers—and that neither Aguayo nor his successors raised any objection then; and that earlier, in 1716, Ramón had been furnished supplies from Natchitoches. He stated that the Spanish owed their occupation of Los Adaes and the founding of their missions to St. Denis himself; that the French represented the Natchitoches Indians, who possessed land on both sides of Red River, without objection from the Adaes, a lesser tribe whose claims the Spanish had inherited; and there was no reason why the Spaniards should appropriate all the undivided seven leagues between the two garrisons. He emphasized that the French had always had their fort west of the river, not east, as the Spanish wished to claim; that the water which surrounded the west side of the fort at times was only a tributary or backwater which was dry parts of the year.

He answered some official protests from Sandoval, informing the Spanish governor that he was acting under superior orders and could not remain passive if attacked with arms. He would defend himself with them, and the consequence of the result would rest upon the governor. He insinuated that he had heard enough on the subject, that His Excellency might do one of two things—fight or drop the subject.

If the Spanish governor ever had any idea of fighting he should have set about it instead of sitting at his desk writing long letters of protest. The governor still preferred to write rather than to fight—militarily, doubtless, the safest and practical thing to do, but a procedure which ruined him politically and financially in the end. During the summer of 1736 Sandoval drew up a proclamation prohibiting all trade between Los Adaes and Natchitoches, which St. Denis had already accomplished. This was incongruent, humorous face-saving, for the Spaniards needed French supplies worse than the French needed theirs. But Gonzales had written him that the corn and bean crops were much more promising this year. The governor felt that he had to get some show of action into the records, and this was about all he could think of at the moment.

Sandoval, despite his apparent lack of energy and diligence, was a pathetic victim caught between the French on one hand and the home government on the other. As a politician, he had political enemies, and it is the business of politicians to take advantage of any blunder or misfortune of a rival. In the latter part of the year Governor Sandoval was replaced.

It was most unfortunate for Sandoval as well as for the province that he was superseded by an impetuous egoist by the name of Carlos Benites Franquis de Lugo, who took the position that he had been appointed god of Texas. Franquis' background was obscure. But he descended upon Texas like a whirlwind, insulting, ignoring, and bluffing officials and missionaries on his hasty journey to get to Sandoval, a choice target requiring his immediate attention. Had not Spain sent out a man of his superior caliber to straighten out a mess made by this weakling? If the world had not heard much of him before, it was high time. He arrested Sandoval on sight. He was eager to let his virtues shine by contrast with those of his unfortunate predecessor.

The chief charge against Sandoval was his failure to prevent the French from building a fort on "Spanish soil." For approximately a decade legal actions were instigated against the ex-governor. Witnesses were examined on both sides of the frontier, old claims were reviewed, and evidence was collected until the proceedings of the case totaled thirty volumes of manuscript. If Sandoval had overlooked some clauses of Spanish technicality or had shown undue lenience toward the French, Franquis was determined that he should answer for every bit of it.

Sandoval was finally acquitted, but the mills of Spanish justice ground exceedingly slow, and Sandoval was a bankrupt, broken man before the trial was ended.

Franquis made a lot of fuss everywhere he went. He loudly denounced Sandoval for not having driven the French across the Red River, but somehow he missed the opportunity to take advantage of his position to do it himself. As a matter of fact, he spent so much time boasting and threatening that he was a little late getting to the business of straightening out the frontier, for which he recommended himself so highly, and was anticipated by St. Denis. The clash between Franquis and St. Denis arose over a trading incident and was but remotely connected with the boundary problem, but St. Denis stood firm and promptly outwitted his opponent. St. Denis demonstrated that His Excellency's mouth worked much faster than his brain.

In April, 1737, Jean Legros, of Natchitoches, was sent by St. Denis to trade among the Caddodaquois Indians. He possessed a passport which had been obtained in February from Fermin de Ybiricu, lieutenant at the Spanish capital, permitting him to pass through Spanish territory. While on his journey he was arrested twelve leagues from Nacogdoches by Sergeant Antonio Losoya, and five soldiers from Los Adaes acting under orders from Lieutenant Ybiricu. At the time of arrest he had the trader's equipment common in that day. He rode a horse and led two pack horses carrying his wares. He was accompanied by an Ais squaw. He was escorted to Los Adaes, put in the stocks, and ordered given a ramrodding, but someone interfered. His goods, however, were confiscated and part of them were burned by Ybiricu in the presence of witnesses.

Apparently Legros was not held long at Los Adaes, for by April 17 he had made his way back to Natchitoches and told St. Denis what had happened. On this date the Natchitoches commandant addressed a letter to Ybiricu. He wasted no time calling in secretaries or translators. The letter was written in his own hurried hand, in Latin —one of his typically piercing, questioning epistles that put the cleverest recipient to a strained task: "Perhaps we are at war," St. Denis wrote, "or perhaps you mean to prevent us from going to Kadodachos [sic]. What is meant that five soldiers should be sent by a sergeant to arrest one of my Frenchmen who was going to Kadodachos by the direct road? Did you not know that he was sent by me? For [even] if you are ignorant, you should know that he was. You confiscated all his goods; on what grounds? You put him in stocks; perhaps he is a Spaniard! You wished to ramrod him; where is your justice? You were wise that you did not do so, that's all I've got to say!" He demanded that all appropriated goods be restored at once, or, he continued, "I will close all commerce with you from today, and will pursue you in the name of the king even to the viceroy, or even to the king himself, if that should be necessary."

No satisfactory answer had reached St. Denis when blustering Governor Franquis made his appearance at Los Adaes. When the new governor began telling about the things he would do to the aggressive, encroaching French, St. Denis' letter was respectfully handed him.

The details of the workings in which St. Denis browbeat the Spanish governor into compliance, spoiled his taste entirely for the frontier, and brought about the unexpected and unhappy turn of events against Lieutenant Ybiricu are not complete. A few interesting details, however, have survived: During their first clash it would appear that St. Denis so talked the governor down that he was left with only the most trite of all political answers—he would make an investigation. St. Denis spared no pains in seeing that the investigation was made—promptly and without subterfuge. St. Denis had demanded satisfaction, and before the investigation was very far along the befuddled governor was hard pressed for any placating answers. Evidently Ybiricu's activities had not been above suspicion, or so the French inferred. Ybiricu may have been made, to some extent, a scapegoat. His sins, though perhaps extensive, were in the main personal ones—the sort that create no public stir as long as they are handled discreetly, out of reach of rivals, but are very unsavory when made public.

In the course of the testimony it was brought out that

Legros had used his passport as a license for trading with tribes in Texas. Under the existing regulations this would have been sufficient grounds for arrest. But St. Denis brushed the point aside as a mere technicality and muddied the water by suggesting that the trader was arrested after he and Ybiricu had quarreled over the Ais squaw. Ybiricu was then charged with keeping French women at Los Adaes. St. Denis might have been content to overlook such an arrangement as this and to leave the amorous lieutenant to his pleasures, if he had just not meddled with trade. But St. Denis knew colonial officials, policies, and prejudices too well to overlook the political aspect of Ybiricu's reputed intimate relations with French of either sex. "Undue intimacy with the French!" The mere hint was sufficient to shake confidence in an official. Proof, even circumstantial, was fatal to his career.

There was evidently talk about Ybiricu on both sides of the border. So Franquis decided to resolve the gossip by locking this frontier Casanova in jail, safely away from his squaws and Frenchwomen and out of sight of jealous or tattling Frenchmen.

The incident was prolonged by the reaction of the Indians, who were angered at the arrest because their trade had been cut off. Fourteen Indian chiefs formed a delegation to call upon St. Denis to complain about interference with their commerce. Perhaps some astute Frenchman pointed out to the Indians their inconvenience at being denied trade with the French by the Spaniards and subtly suggested that the Great White Chief at Natchitoches might be able to do something about it. A convenient route for the chiefs on their way to Natchitoches would have been along the old highway through Los Adaes. Actually their route is not known, but the French commandant may well have arranged for them to march through the very streets of the Spanish capital on their way to make complaints to him against the Spaniards. The wishes of fourteen disappointed chiefs were no casual matter on this frontier. Even an inexperienced Spaniard knew that. Such a demonstration might have more power of persuasion than volumes of diplomatic correspondence.

All in all, the affair must have given the frontier a rather severe shaking up. Even the belligerent mission president, Father Vallejo, who had once written critical letters about the French and freely volunteered his opinion as to what should be done about certain events and certain people, now wrote with a changed tone. With other missionaries in Texas, he was beginning to criticize Franquis. However, Vallejo made a report to his superiors in which he commended the governor for "so prudently placating St. Denis." The "placating" seems to have been entirely in a negative form, but everyone seemed happy that St. Denis had been silenced; no one could tell what this omniscient Frenchman might stir up against them. The political-minded priest also wrote a personal letter to the governor thanking him for satisfying the French commander so promptly. Father Vallejo had had time on the frontier to live and learn.

When the delegation of chiefs reached Natchitoches, the international issues of the case had already been adjusted. The White Chief simply told the Indian leaders that he was now satisfied, but that was enough. Then, and only then, was the matter completely settled.

Franquis had passed through the country roaring like a lion, and Texas had trembled. Now that he had reached the end of his journey, this aggressive St. Denis stood up and hissed right back in his very whiskers. This had all happened before discussion of the boundary got under way. Then, when the hiss turned into a growl, the Spanish governor recalled that he had passed over some important matters on his eastward journey which demanded his immediate attention.

And so it was that Franquis turned his fiery energy instead toward the interior, suppressing the missionaries, making big talk about how he would annihilate certain unconquerable tribes, but in the main using the labor of the mission Indians and the troops for his personal enterprises.

Franquis was so obnoxious with everything he did that the next year the viceroy pulled him down from his self-made throne; and like Sandoval he, too, was sent south under arrest. He now knew the taste of his own medicine. Sandoval rejoiced at his rival's downfall. Possibly there is no hatred that smolders so long and dies so hard as that between rival politicians. But Franquis still had influence enough to keep Sandoval's pot of bitter brew boiling.

Before the end of 1736 the French had established themselves in their new fort. St. Denis had won every one of his contentions. The Arroyo Hondo was recognized as the boundary between the two provinces.[2] And while Spain kept her governors and ex-governors busy answering tedious questions about their own conduct and their relations with the French, St. Denis took advantage of the distraction of the rulers to rebuild a flourishing contraband trade.

[2] This was by only a temporary agreement. Actually the Franco-Spanish frontier disappeared before a permanent boundary was officially established.

XVI

Contest for Control of the Indians

THE FRONTIER PRESENTED MANY PARAdoxes. For instance, St. Denis, reportedly a religious man and a faithful Catholic, helped build and supply the Spanish missions, encouraged and supported the Spanish padres, and was in turn universally loved and respected by them at a time when most of the Spanish military and civil authorities on the frontier looked upon him as their worst enemy. Yet, while the Texas missionaries were singing his praises, he was far from being unanimously loved and respected by the religious of his own country. For many years he supported the missionary program in the "enemy" country, at a time when there was no resident priest in his own town. The search for an explanation of these ironic riddles reveals much of the colonial machinery of France and Spain, and the character of the agents who shaped their western empires.

The struggle for supremacy in this part of the New World resolved itself, in the main, into a contest for control of the Indian tribes. The competition was keen and took many queer turns. Chief devices used for native control on the Franco-Spanish frontier were Christianization, trade, distribution of gifts, diplomacy, and military force. The first was paramount on the Spanish side, the second on the French side, but all were used to some extent by both factions simultaneously.

To understand the men engaged in the task of controlling and using the Indians to build personal empires it is necessary to know something of the natives themselves.

When the European explorers discovered the Indians they found them in a land of plenteous beauty in harmony with their nature, living their simple lives, rearing their families, worshipping their gods. They were uncivilized, but not unhappy about it.

The Indians of this region worshipped many deities. In childish confidence they prayed to their gods about the things that concerned them, and in simple and consuming faith accepted their fate as the gods' decree. There was one all-seeing and omnipotent spirit, whom they called Manitou. If an Indian had been brave in war and faithful to his conception of duty, he trusted that after death he would be carried away on the wings of the wind to the happy hunting grounds, where, in a joyous world, he would resume the chase on his swiftest horse, with his dog and bow and arrows. If destruction came to him, if he lost in battle, or if the spear of heaven-fire turned his squaw to cinders, it was because the Great Spirit was angered.

The appearance of the palefaces from the unknown east was an amusing novelty. As the natives observed the polished armor of the soldiers, the long robes of the priests, the bright and elaborate costumes of the officers, they marveled; but when they heard the roar of great guns echoing through their hunting grounds, felt the queer effects of firewater and the pain of the white man's strange diseases, and were introduced to a more restricted life, their childish souls were disturbed. Their confusion was usually more than the missionaries could understand.

The missionaries had come to inform the Indians that their religion was wrong. When the fathers presented the Christian religion to the natives with its beauty of ceremony, symbols and images, bright candles, the rosary, and colorful paintings, the Indians marveled. And when they heard the solemn chants of the priests and were shown the tender kindness of a Great Being above, expressed by His mediators—these pious men in long robes —they were touched. Many were baptised. It was not until these preachers told them of sin, that the great merciful Father was also a wrathful God who sent the wicked and disobedient to an eternal destruction of hellfire and brimstone, that the congregations became disturbed and trembled with fear. Their Manitou would not torture his children so cruelly. Some understood only enough of what the priests said to be frightened at what would happen to them in the next world. Moved by fear, some had a vague idea that remaining near the fathers might save them. Others, however, betook their troubled souls to the forests and plains to forget the decrees of the wrathful God of the white man and soothe their spirits again in the chase.

Such an ancient system of life and philosophy as the original Americans possessed could not be changed overnight—not even as fast as great European powers could appropriate new lands.

Different methods of Christianization were applied on the two sides of the frontier; and the differences showed prominently in the military, civil, commercial, and territorial success of the rival powers.

If the Spanish Franciscans were any more zealous and sacrificing than the French Jesuit and Capuchin missionaries, it perhaps meant only, in the final analysis, that their failures were larger. The Spaniards were much more strict and formal than the French. Though the Franciscans' zeal never waned, their methods and procedures were not flexible enough to meet the necessities of the ruthless, practical wilderness.

As a first step toward Christianizing the Indians, the Franciscans considered it necessary to induce them to adopt settled habitations. They were to be taught to love God more than their hunting grounds. When kind treatment and persuasion did not yield a proper crop of converts the missionaries extended their excursions to surrounding tribes. The soldiers were valuable allies in this effort. Reliable Indians were also sent out among their wild brethren to bring them under the shepherds' care, so that they could be instructed in the mysteries of the Christian faith and of agriculture.

The process was usually tedious, with little understanding on either side. The Indian had no background for a comprehension of the God of civilized nations. For him to show obvious kindness to his mother, wife, or daughter was a sign of weakness; to love one's enemy was unheard of—to scalp him was the duty of every brave. These errors the Franciscans sought to correct by insisting upon the observation of regular, rigid rules of living, while the Indians were indoctrinated in a faith made impressive by colorful images of saints, pictures illustrative of the passion of the Saviour, fasting, hymn singing, and long prayer.

The daily routine of a mission Indian was a dull existence, completely at variance with his natural desires and instincts. At dawn the mission bells rang out, calling the Indians to religious service. The Lord of the white man would tolerate no laggards or drones. After service the adults were assembled in front of the church for about an hour's instruction in the catechism. This was usually given in Spanish, but for those who could not understand the language, the lesson was explained through an interpreter. Then the natives were allowed to eat breakfast. After eating, some of the men were led to the fields by one of the missionaries or a soldier who acted as overseer and instructor in the science of agriculture; others went to the workshops. The women worked at the looms, made pottery, or cooked; the children spent the morning in school. In the evening the entire populace was congregated for a period of catechizing. Afterwards the priests visited the native dwellings to minister to the sick, give instructions, have prayers, or sing hymns. Any Indian who missed any part of the daily routine without a good excuse was whipped in the presence of the other Indians.

The regulation of the Indians' domestic life also came under the supervision of the friars. Huts for the converted Indians were erected a short distance from the mission buildings. The unmarried of either sex were placed in separate cabins and locked in by the guardian fathers, who carried the keys. The violation of chastity was punished by public or private whipping. The young natives were divided among the older and more deserving Indians, who held them in servitude until they were of a suitable age to marry. When the fathers considered the time opportune for matrimony for a couple, the two young Indians were married in the church.

This confinement of the Indian in a Spanish fort, in which he was forced through a tiresome round of formal religious services and manual labor, was hardly likely to make him love either Christ or the Spaniard. Without his freedom the red man was a convict, without a purpose for living. To him this life was a type of good-intentioned slavery promoted in the name of Christ.

On the other side of the frontier, the French worked differently. Whereas the Spaniards relied chiefly upon the missionaries for control of the Indians, the French depended largely upon the trader. While the Spaniards were seeking fabulous cities with gold and pearls, the French traders, in their congenial way, were seeking Indian villages with hides and furs. Whereas the Spanish padres restrained the Indians by tedious ceremonies and uninteresting prayers, the French Jesuits went with their flocks on their hunting excursions, joined them in their feasts, and praised them for their skill in the chase. The Jesuits possessed a twofold advantage; they had the power of dispensing with detailed formalities, and they enjoyed the aid of the cheerful, talkative, open-hearted French traders.

The Spaniards held themselves in cold reserve; but the French traders adopted the ways of the red man, and far from their European home to which most of them had no intention of returning, they found a new home among them. Here was a land that beckoned to the imaginative spirit of the Frenchman. France in this colorful age held many youths who were idle, reckless, and intent on pleasure. The offices and trades of that day offered no promise of quick wealth, but stories of America thrilled them. They heard how, in the fur trade, they might make a fortune, return to France, and shine again in the vivid life of Paris. But once they came, few ever returned.

Another group of Frenchmen, not so closely associated with the missionary effort as the traders, also contributed toward establishing French influence in the Louisiana colony; this was the group called the *coureurs de bois*.

In the secret wilderness there was no correcting eye of parent, restrictive law of government, or priestly regulation. Here was the wild liberty of the endless forests. Such were the charms of the wilds that settlements were all but depopulated of young white men. Wherever the Indians went the *coureurs de bois* followed, living for the most part a savage life, to the disgust of the missionaries. These picturesque youths, despising conventional domestic life and commonplace labor, were at times of little use to the growing and needy colony, but upon their wanderings France was to base her claims to the interior of a great continent, even as Spain used those of her gold-seeking conquistadors.

Many of these freehearted Frenchmen married Indian girls and became home builders. Around their homes the influence of France was firmly planted. The *coureurs de bois* learned the ways of the wilderness as no others ever have, and they became a part of it.

St. Denis understood the strengths and weaknesses of both the French and Spanish systems of Indian management. During his first days in Louisiana he observed what he considered flaws in the French missionary system —church politics and rivalry among religious orders. His observations and resulting decisions may have been why he was later accused of not pushing religious activities in western Louisiana.

Before arriving in Louisiana St. Denis had become acquainted with Iberville's chaplain, Father Paul Du Ru, who had come out from France on the same ship with him. Father Du Ru was a highly educated, sensitive, observant man with a liking for the strangeness of the new unexplored world, and an ambition to spend his life among the simple, contented people he found in the Louisiana forests, converting and instructing them. He probably was a close friend of St. Denis, for they were together on the famous expedition up the Mississippi River in early 1700. St. Denis had opportunity to watch first hand the zealous padre start his work in the wilderness with enthusiasm and faith in the land he loved and had adopted; and then St. Denis saw his missions and authority taken from him and, in 1702, his deportation to France because of a clash over ecclesiastical authority.

During this period the Seminary of Quebec was a branch of the Foreign Missions Organization of Paris. From this seminary Capuchin missionaries were sent to work among the natives of the lower Mississippi. Iberville, however, had been decidedly partial to the Jesuits and had gone to special pains to bring along a member of that order on his second voyage. Thus was Father Du Ru brought over, and thus did he take up work for the Jesuits below the Red River and claim Jesuit jurisdiction in that region. Soon there was a dispute over regional authority. No satisfactory settlement of the counter-claims could be reached in Louisiana, so the matter was taken up by the superior authorities in Paris and Du Ru lost his place. The priest had been caught in an impossible position, in a religio-political cross fire. During the course of the controversy some uncomplimentary terms, such as "insubordinate," had been applied to him, which had not contributed either to his happiness or to his effectiveness where he most desired to be effective—among his flock in lower Louisiana. It seems that for all his sensitivity Du Ru was a practical man who became adapted easily to the wilderness life and, impressed and inspired by the glorious freedom he saw there, became a little careless about channels, realms of jurisdiction, superiors, discipline, and the like. Viewed from staid, conservative European circles perhaps he did appear insubordinate and stubborn as he went about the work of learning a new language and preaching, neglecting painful attention to ancient rules. St. Denis must have loved such a man, though he doubtless kept his opinion to himself.

Father Du Ru's case was typical. There were vital lessons and morals in it for an observer like St. Denis, who had a highly controversial international political boundary running alongside his district. For him to have taken part in a religious dispute might have added a new factor to his problems. Religious friction would without doubt have lowered the prestige of both the Church and France in the eyes of the natives. St. Denis' type of practical, abstract reasoning could not vision any good this would accomplish in the long run politically, economically, diplomatically, or even religiously. The Natchitoches commandant believed that organization and unity gave strength in all things; and peace and harmony among the Indians was a requisite for frontier unity. Rival factions fighting over territory in which to convert Indians and developing systems for imprisoning wild rovers of the forests in missions were best left to his enemies to weaken them.

St. Denis had reached an unbiased, broadminded outlook upon life and religion which was rare in his age. If even one man on the Spanish side of the frontier had possessed St. Denis' practical slant, his wisdom, or his influence over the Indians, Spain might have broken over the dam which St. Denis built and held during the formative years, and the flood might have washed across the French strip into Florida and made the Gulf of Mexico a Spanish sea.

Circumstances, more than the conscious efforts of St. Denis, may have determined missionary policy during this period. But if so, St. Denis was a man to make the best of circumstances. It was a period of heated church politics throughout New France. The bishop of Quebec, who claimed jurisdiction here, sought to bring everything in his vast diocese into strict regularity by precise rules and regulations, and he suffered no infringements on what he regarded as the rights of his see. His administration was turbulent, indeed. The local conflict between the Jesuits and the Capuchins lasted for a considerable time. The India Company made special contracts for missionaries. And for a time religious boundaries and jurisdiction appeared as controversial and conflicting as the international boundaries. Even if St. Denis could have obtained a French priest for Natchitoches during the early days, he probably would have preferred to use the Spanish missionaries from Los Adaes and keep his community clear of French church politics and disputes.

Whether by design or circumstances beyond the commandant's control, Natchitoches was without a resident priest until 1728, and for long periods of time after that no priest was stationed there. No church was erected before the latter part of 1729. It was sometime shortly before 1733 that a church was built. Even then the house of worship was a small, unimposing edifice with only one door and two windows.

When the Natchitoches fort was moved, a better and larger church was built. It was only of log and clay covered with shingles, but it was twenty-four feet wide and had six windows and a small sanctuary. And outside was a pride-raising bell weighing thirteen and a half pounds. A comfortable house thirty feet long and eighteen feet wide had been built for the priest.

By the time the fort was moved and the new church finished, the religious controversy had reached Natchitoches and come to something of a head. It appears that St. Denis and his associates had always favored Jesuits in preference to Capuchins. In 1738, ecclesiastical authority decreed that Natchitoches would be served by a Capuchin, not a Jesuit, whether the inhabitants liked the idea or not. Now that they had built a church to be proud of and had finally been blessed with a priest to live among them and administer unto them, one whom they loved and to whom they had shown their affection by building for him a comfortable home, they were much grieved and disappointed to hear that he was to be taken from them. The Jesuit was Father Pierre Vitry, whom the Spanish authorities had hated so vehemently. But how the French loved him! It was he who had waited long into the night on the edge of the river for Jean D'herbanne and Victoria Gonzales when they eloped from Los Adaes two years before and had married them at midnight by flickering candlelight before the tiny altar in the little log church. There was a thing to touch a Frenchman's heart. The people of Natchitoches did not submit without a contest. They drafted and signed a petition asking that Father Vitry be allowed to remain with them. Even after the father had left, a second petition was sent out, with a letter from the commandant, stating that the people were determined to keep the Jesuit missionary. The populace even offered a pension of 700 livres for Father Vitry. But authority had spoken, and their pleas were of no avail.

When the people found that a Capuchin was going to be forced upon them they suggested that the new missionary reside at the fort, and not at the home they had built for their beloved Jesuit, and that he confine his activities to duties as chaplain for the garrison.

Even before Father Vitry had come, when the friendly Franciscans came over from Los Adaes for services, there had been more freedom and less turmoil, the people thought. They preferred the services of foreign priests to those of bickering rival French missionaries.

Before a church had been built in Natchitoches the Spanish priests apparently officiated at a private chapel in St. Denis' home. One historian states that "There is no questioning St. Denis' piety and his devotion to the church. . . . And true it is also of his very religious Spanish wife. That he gave good example in every way possible among the French inhabitants of the post is known, attending to his religious duties and doing what he could for the establishment of the Church and the spread of Christianity among the Indians and Negroes, always assisted and seconded by Señora Manuela, his wife."

If St. Denis appeared lacking in religious zeal for his territory or in personal fidelity, he doubtless had the far-reaching motives of an exceptional administrator.

During St. Denis' administration at Natchitoches he saw nearly a dozen governors and rulers at Los Adaes recalled in disfavor or political ruin; he saw officers come and go at a rapid rate in his own province; he heard the roar of the storms that swept them away. He had learned to discern the important from the unimportant. He knew when to stand like a mighty oak and when to sway like a sapling before the storm. Through all the changes one policy stood supreme in his administration—control of the frontier Indians. The methods he employed in maintaining this control may appear to have been puzzling and contradictory; but St. Denis felt that the objective justified any reasonable means. Control of the Indians meant Louisiana for France, commerce for the administration, a livelihood for the traders, protection for the inhabitants.

XVII

In the Day of Prosperity

IN 1737 A RARE AND REMARKABLE EVENT OCcurred in France: the national budget was balanced. French factories began to hum, and goods poured out from them at an unheard-of rate. Natchitoches immediately felt the boom, which coincided with a period of peace on the frontier. Men now thought of making customers rather than casualties out of their foreign neighbors, and they took time to relax, dress up, and improve their homes.

It was a guady era of brilliant costumes—bright colors, elaborate laces, and flashing buttons. Not only the French but the Spanish and Indians as well loved these pretty things. There had never been enough of them on the frontier. Now they poured into the colony—satins, damasks, taffetas, printed cottons, laces, silk braids, velvet, and muslin. Fine china and etchings and even wigs found their way to the Natchitoches stores, where they were sold to the limit of the supply or of local purses.

The Indians, too, took part in the boom. Sparkling French glass, shiny beads, tools, the inevitable brilliant cloth, and a beauty preparation manufactured for their special taste—vermilion paint—were bought in reckless quantities and paid for with decorated pottery, grotesquely designed woven cloth, tobacco, corn and melons, furs, and innumerable other products of the forest that had a ready local or foreign market.

The Spanish were willing customers, but they were impoverished. Unfortunately for the French merchants, the Spaniards' purses never equaled their tastes. But they raised stock, and in good years they had grain to sell; most helpful of all, they hoarded some silver from the interior mines. As long as the alluring French articles were displayed at Natchitoches the envious Spaniards would find a way to buy some of them; even when Spanish laws forbade trade.

Despite the boom and renewed good feeling between the French and Spanish, the usual Spanish laws and technical regulations had to be contended with—edicts designed to prevent any foreigner from setting foot or eye upon Texas soil. There was no waning in the jealousies of Spanish officials. Regarding the province as a bewitching mistress who was as charming to rivals as to her keeper, Spain went into a resentful rage when any competitor cast an eye upon her. No convent rules were ever stricter to guard its charges than those of Spain to protect its northern province.

The prohibition of French trading on what Spain considered her territory was a never-ending nightmare for Spanish officials. French traders had poor eyes for boundaries. They were traveling salesmen of a bold and superior type which the Spaniards could never match. The French knew their Indian customers and did not look down on them as did the Spaniards; they liked them, and they liked to trade with them; they peddled the wares the natives wanted—not what some official in Madrid declared was best for them. They dominated trade wherever they went.

The promotion and regulation of trade, though an important and absorbing function of a French colonial commandant, was only one of many varied duties.

First and foremost, he was commander of the king's troops stationed to guard the western boundary and to keep the peace in general.

He was an Indian agent extraordinary, whose duties took many queer but practical turns. Of prime importance was the maintaining of friendship between the natives and the French, and among their own tribes. There could be no strong confederacy for him to use against the Spanish or English if the native tribes were weakened by warring among themselves. The promotion and maintenance of a solid, workable, and lasting peace called for more than official formalities, execution of royal policies, announcement of proper laws, or even the show of modern military might. It required among other things the maintaining of a healthy, just, and sensibly regulated trade. The Indian wanted to think that there was some profit in the white man, just as the white man expected to profit from the red man. The distribution of gifts was a practical necessity. It was the basis of diplomacy, a fundamental in wilderness etiquette— a type of thoughtfulness, consideration, and good neighborliness the aborigines could always understand and respond to. A little lagniappe never hurt any trade or caused ill feelings, except between competitors. The Spanish even suggested that presenting gifts was an unethical practice, but this was jealous clamoring. Though they distributed gifts to some extent, the Spanish never saw the real profit of gifts. Indians from deep in Spanish Texas continued to look to French traveling salesmen and to Natchitoches for gifts. And friendship and trade usually flowed toward the source of the best and most appropriate gifts.

St. Denis was ambassador-at-large among the tribes. He sat in their powwows, heard discussions of their troubles, intertribal and domestic, usually spoke his judgment in a few direct, brief words in Indian fashion, and saw the problems settled quickly and finally without argument. Justice was respected second only to power on the frontier. The Indians never, so far as record or tradition reveals, disputed St. Denis' maintenance of either.[1]

He was head of the civil government, a sort of Lord Mayor. On occasion he was both prosecutor and judge. According to the laws and customs of the day, all important transactions were effected by order of, or with permission of, the commandant. For instance, all notarial deeds had to receive his permission to become legal. He granted military personnel permits to marry and to buy land. He posted the king's laws and saw that they were enforced. He policed the town and surrounding country to make sure that order was maintained. He investigated murders and other crimes. He gave adequate protection to property sales and transfers, assuring legal and proper procedure. At times he annulled sales and assessed fines, which were paid to the Church. He granted leaves of absence, permission to travel, and passports. His personal attention was given to finding proper guardians for orphans and to supporting the Church. The witness-

---

[1] The Natchez War was not a conflict of St. Denis' making. And if the tribe had known St. Denis better they might not have made their fatal mistake.

ing of weddings and wills took no little time. The commandant assisted wherever emergencies arose—fire, flood, disease, military threat, or transportation difficulties—these, and many other details great and small were his personal concern. Everyone had the right to protest injustice and appeal directly to the commandant, and the documents of the period attest to the exercise of their rights.

The commandant was the chief businessman of the town. He kept, or supervised, the accounts of the official trade of the district. He not only kept books but watched the market and saw to it that traders were protected. He presided over auctions of goods and local produce. Besides his official duties, St. Denis carried on numerous private enterprises—merchandising, real estate, farming, stock raising.

But all was not work and controversy for the Natchitoches commandant. He, too, had moments for refreshments in the shade. He never lost his taste for Parisian finery, and no forest was ever dense or remote enough to make him a slovenly dresser, no occasion informal enough to shake his dignity. St. Denis did not take the wilderness as an excuse for a man to turn himself loose and forget his pride, or even the niceties of life.

Indications are that St. Denis lived extravagantly, and beyond his means. His house was the finest and most modern the place and times could afford, his furnishings the best that could be made locally or imported. Inventories show his silver, china, and wardrobe to have been magnificent. The commandant was well equipped to play his assigned role.

In France these were the luxury-loving days of extravagantly designed, colorful costumes. Men wore knee breeches with silver buckles and ribbons at the knees, bright silk hose and high-heeled shoes, corsets, wigs, and coats with fluffy cuffs; they carried lacy handkerchiefs, bejeweled snuff boxes and gem-studded walking sticks; they perfumed themselves; and they even wore earrings. Natchitoches was a part of this France. Documents of the period—inventories, bills, receipts, contracts—show that the frontier post kept abreast of the times.

Here, as in old France, men preferred breeches of soft velvet or smooth silk, dyed red, lavender, or blue. For their coats of sleek velvet or shining taffeta, brilliant tones of scarlet, blue, or gold were chosen. Other stylish shades were cinnamon, black, pink, silver, and grey—almost anything except yellow. Coats were often lined with fur as an added flourish. Vests were made of rich materials, plain, flowered, or embroidered, with fancy pockets and bright buttons; they might match coat or breeches or contrast with them. Stockings of silk, linen, or cotton were sometimes a sober white or black, but blues and reds came and went according to passing fancy. Lavish ribbons, silk scarves, laces, frills, feathers, and sparkling jewels put the final garnish upon the well-dressed Natchitoches male.

St. Denis was not a man to be outdone at anything, particularly in the matter of clothes. He was, accordingly, the best-dressed man on the frontier. An inventory of his belongings supports this claim, and offers a specific example of an eighteenth-century Frenchman's wardrobe:

> One damask surtout (coat) braided with silver lace at the bottom of the flares.
> One black taffeta surtout with silver braid on the bottom

One damask surtout with silver braid at the bottom
One black velvet surtout with silver braid at the bottom
One scarlet surtout with silver braid at the bottom
One scarlet surtout with silver braid at the bottom [*sic*]
One green damask surtout with gold braid at the bottom
One black taffeta surtout with silver braid at the bottom
One damask surtout with silver braid at the bottom
One blue taffeta surtout with silver braid at the bottom
Four surtouts in [illegible] of India
A coat (cloth) with gold buttons
A scarlet cloth vest with goatskin buttons
A gold embroidered vest
A man's dark dress with gold buttons
A yellow taffeta waistcoat
A red jacket with cotton blouse
Monsieur Don Louis' dress—russet brown color with silver waist and waist coat
Scarlet breeches
Five caps, different kinds of taffeta
A red velvet cape with gold braid all around
A wicker basket, in the shape of a chest, which contains several things such as capes, muslin and other trifles
A bolt of cotton material, nine years old
Two hats, one of which is new
Another hat

In this day of long trousers, it would seem odd for a man to make a point of attractive legs. But the styles of that day forced a man to give considerable attention to his figure, or, in tight-fitting knee breeches, he would be the target of an uncomfortable share of jokes. The feminine frame, of course, was carefully obscured by long dresses and many petticoats. In public or mixed conversation it was not even conceded that women had legs. It was the male who exhibited and accentuated his lines.

St. Denis came in for distinction on this score. In view of the mode of the day it is interesting to find that in

Indian writing St. Denis was "the Beautiful Leg"—sometimes more carelessly or uncomplimentarily translated "Big Leg." The written symbol for the Natchitoches commandant was the drawing of a shapely leg. This Indian nomenclature does not seem to have risen from any knowledge of French modes or attempt to be complimentary. According to the best accounts, St. Denis was a large man of powerful strength, well over six feet tall, with the figure of a well-proportioned athlete. His long expeditions in the wilderness and his continued physical activities must have developed powerful legs. French tastes being what they were at the time, a prominent man would scarcely have discouraged the complimentary tag.

The ladies of this period came in for finery and exquisite styles in their own way. Receipts and bills of the day indicate that St. Denis provided his Spanish wife with the best and prettiest that the market afforded. From the day he brought his first present to her at the Rio Grande she was ever in his mind when he was trading. Wherever his travels took him, he was on the alert for a present that would put a sparkle in the dark eyes of the beautiful girl he had smuggled out of Mexico. He was a cavalier at home as well as abroad. Her exotic loveliness, the Spanish accent that remained in her speech, the enthusiasm for her adopted country and new people, the touch of daring and romance in her spirit intrigued and sustained him. His references to her speak only of a love and happiness that is genuinely touching and rare —a blend of youthful romance and mature affection. To the last, she was his ideal.

XVIII

Last Days

SUDDENLY IN 1741, GRIEVOUS FAILURES BEgan to descend upon St. Denis. Old accounts he doubtless had thought settled or forgotten were presented. He was called upon to make payment for goods lost or taken by the Spanish on his risky, speculative expeditions into Mexico over a quarter of a century before. Some debts were comparatively new; perhaps he had expected that in the process of trade and exchange the books would balance in the natural course of events.

Seeking an understanding for the peremptory demand for prompt settlement at such a late date leads into a long and speculative story involving changing and fickle administrations, antique auditing systems, slow-moving governmental action, and perhaps the psychology of a busy man too concerned with important affairs to give proper attention to details. It is a hazy story that reveals no definite conclusions, but one thing is certain. Once the matter of debts was brought to a showdown, St. Denis took the burden of his debts with extreme seriousness. Financial troubles completely shadowed his last days.

Many times St. Denis had been in more serious trouble. But he had been a younger, more vigorous man. Now time was behind him; the fire of youth that had burned at such a fierce rate was flickering. It was as if he had reached a promising citadel only to peer over into a barren chasm that held neither excitement nor promise. There were moments when his poise appeared shaken; the few existing letters of his trying days reveal an acridness that was not in keeping with his old dignity. But, withal, there was a melancholy nobleness in his last struggle.

The decline was personal and psychological rather than public. To the last St. Denis held the unwavering respect of his home government, the Spanish, the Indians, his countrymen. The reverses were his and Emanuelle's alone. But to him that was where reverses counted most. His country could do without him now; he had seen the colony created and then lived through its hazardous infancy; the great crises had passed. He worried now most of all about Emanuelle, and the struggle reminded him vividly that their days together could not go on forever.

The old warrior began to fight back. In May of this year he traveled to New Orleans and pressed a lawsuit before the Superior Council to recover losses realized during his trading expeditions to Mexico while serving under Crozat. St. Denis had courage and confidence; he had always been a successful man when arguing cases. For nearly thirty years he had browbeaten, outwitted, or flattered Spaniards to win suits even while in prison, alone, and even when his life was at stake.

The case dragged on. Either the old power or the luck or both were gone. Fronting his own countrymen, countering the government he had spent his life serving, his arguments were but feeble wailings. He lost the case. He lost in other contentions about his accounts. Auditors "appointed by edict of the State Council for the business of the India Company" worked over his books in long impersonal calculations. By December 6, 1742, they had completed their audit. The statement showed that St. Denis owed the India Company—or, rather, the agency which had taken over its accounts—18,361 livres, 5 sol, 4 deniers. He gave his note for the amount "annulling all bills which might come up later for credit or debit of said account."

St. Denis possessed property of sufficient value to settle his debts; but to pay them off meant lean times in his last days with Emanuelle and, further, that she would not be well provided for financially upon his death. St. Denis could not bear the thought of either.

An inventory of the commandant's property of this period lists, among other things, "Four hundred and fifty jars of oil, twelve negroes, male and female, . . . twelve small negroes, male and female, three big savage [Indian] women, one savage man, five small Indians, male and female, a hundred cattle, big and small, . . . twenty mattresses, . . . fifty horses." The amount of land he owned cannot be determined. Old records testify that he possessed, at one time or another, considerable scattered holdings, but extensive as they were, they were not to be sufficient, after his death, to settle his debts without much sacrifice and discomfort to his widow.

St. Denis worried more about Emanuelle than about the children. The boys were young and could make their way; the girls would marry good husbands. His letters and actions show constant thought of Emanuelle during these last days. His dream, as far as the records reveal, was to spend his last days with Emanuelle back in the Mexico they had known in their joyous youth. If he could recapture some of the thrill of those days, he would have something to sustain and revitalize him now that his heart was beating more slowly from the strain of long, fatiguing years. In his ever-romantic soul he fancied that in Mexico his last days might be as gloriously exciting as had been his youth. And so the still-restless commandant sat down and took up his pen to make one last request of the government he had served so long.

In January of 1744 the king's officials in Paris were pondering over his letter. They considered it a most bewildering document: Louis Juchereau de St. Denis, whom they recognized as "one of His Majesty's most distinguished officials," requested the king to relieve him of his command, pleading as a cause the infirmities of his old age. And surprisingly, for one who had served France so long and faithfully, he asked that he be granted permission to move to New Spain with his wife and family and a few slaves, to spend his final days in that land.

Another letter of this period primarily concerns a gift to his nieces in Canada of a deed to a plot of land belonging to him in his Canadian home of Beauport. But it tells much more. It shows him a warrior to the last and reflects his mood, his disappointments, an ambition that was never realized, and his love for "the young lady whom I married." It was dated "Natchitoches, April 3, 1741," and was addressed in particular to Mme. Aubert de la Chesnaye:

> I have received your letter of the 12th of May, 1739, sent in care of M. Rouville. You would have had an earlier answer had it not been for the war with the Tchicachas which kept me from getting an opportunity to send it to Canada, because it was necessary that I go myself to New Orleans

to have the deeds drawn for the donation you had asked [of] me, according to law so that you would have no trouble about it, and since I could not get off before the month of June, the convoy of the Illinois having already left, I was obliged to postpone until now.

It is through the kindness of the dear Jesuit priests that I am sending you this letter. They have promised to see that you get it.

You will never know how glad I was to receive news from you and your dear husband. You will always be dear to me and I still feel keenly the separation from a family that I have always cherished and shall always cherish; but God disposes of everything as He pleases and it is our place to conform to His will. You know that there were twelve brothers and sisters in our family and I am today the only one left, sixty-seven years old. I had always hoped to see my dear country and my dear family, but the discovery of Mexico kept me from doing so. It was there I met the young lady whom I married. I have never regretted this step, because I have been very happy with her. We have seven children. God called two of them and we have five left, two sons and three daughters. Even though we have no fortune, God has not forsaken us, and we live a quiet and peaceful life. I have not had the consolation of seeing a single one of my relatives in this country. I am too old now to hope ever to see them again. After all, I do not advise any of them to come, for I can assure you that it is a very worthless country; happy he who can get out of it and infinitely happier is he who has never come to it, and no matter how old I should be I would wish with all my heart to be out of it. . . .

The letter continued with comments and predictions regarding international politics. There were references to prominent international figures—"the death of his holiness the pope, that of our Bishop of Quebec, that of the Emperor, and that of the great Turk." He signed himself "My very dear niece, your very humble and very obedient servant and very affectionate uncle." The communication showed the writer well informed and still keenly interested in important happenings of the world. It was a sharp contrast to his pointedly brittle and often scathing official letters. It revealed a tenderness and mellowness, in spite of the surprising sour and dejected tone at the end. His tone of fatalism is another difference, for if ever a man in his youth and middle age seemed self-confident enough to trust the molding of his fate to his own wits, that man was Louis Juchereau de St. Denis.

There is an account of obscure origin which relates that before the end St. Denis became lame. It is an ironic thought that the "beautiful leg" may have become the "crippled leg." Hardly any personal misfortune could have brought the proud, active commandant more embarrassment and disappointment than a physical infirmity which would hamper his movement and mar his appearance; it would have done much to sadden his last days.

On March 26, 1744, St. Denis made his will. The opening paragraph indicated physical handicaps: ". . . physically ill but mentally sound, . . . knowing that the hour of death is uncertain and not wishing to be found unprepared," it begins. The will revealed further information about his debts and his concern for Emanuelle. "He orders that all his debts be paid before anything else, by the executioner of his will. . . . Fifteen hundred *livres* will be given M. de la Freniere.[1] Seven hundred *livres* will be paid by M. Denoyan, to Mme.

---

[1] This amount seems to have been set aside for the publication of his memoirs, rather than for a debt, but if they were published, the writer has been unable to find account of them. No evidence has been found to verify the writing of any extensive memoirs.

d'Hyberville. Eighteen hundred *livres* that I, St. Denis, still owe the King for a loan given me in New Orleans. Nine thousand *livres* to the Company."

Emanuelle was given authority to execute the will. She was devised half of his property, the other half to go to the children.

The old warrior must have known that his days were numbered. His final engrossing dream of an interlude in Mexico with Emanuelle must have faded painfully as his physical decline progressed rapidly and as he waited wearily for an answer to his request for retirement and permission to go to Mexico. During early 1744 his petition was moving slowly through channels in the French capital. Official correspondence on the subject reveals that the government was disappointed that he should wish to leave the service. Who was there who could capably replace him? The communications were most complimentary to his record, but the aging commandant spent many anxious days waiting, while high officials pondered his request and stalled for time in the hope that he would change his mind. Government action was too slow and cumbersome to cope with personal desires and feelings.

His desire for rest and peace and a few quiet days in private life with Emanuelle, away from the trials and responsibilities of the turbulent frontier he had won for France and guarded for close to half a century was never realized. On June 11, 1744, just as the sun was setting in the distant west toward the land of his romance and final dream, he too passed away as quietly as the evening shadows. He had died as commandant.

The funeral was the most elaborate the frontier had ever seen. From whatever regions word of the death had reached, acquaintances and friends came to pay their last respects—the current Spanish governor, Boneo y Morales; the French-baiter, Father Vallejo; and other Spanish dignitaries from the capital at Los Adaes; Indian chiefs; braves who had fought under the White Father; the entire Natchitoches population.

St. Denis was buried in the Natchitoches church, the Westminster Abbey of the French frontier. A mixed congregation, experiencing emotions also mixed, hovered around the grave that day—governor and slave, priest and *coureur de bois,* white man, black man, red man. The charming Spaniards, with long faces, using their most polite and sentimental phrases, expressed their sorrow and condolence to the bereaved Emanuelle. It was a few days later that their true feelings were revealed when the governor reported the occurrence to the viceroy in language which meant in effect, "St. Denis is dead, thank God; now we can breathe easier!" [2] No one realized better than the Spanish the part St. Denis had played as an empire builder of France.

Other than the grief of the family, the deepest grief was that of the Indians. Theirs was a sorrow which only a savage could experience at the loss of one of his gods. Staidly, silently, with arms folded, they stood about the grave and the church, gazing into the distance. They did not know any fine phrases such as the Spaniards spoke. They accepted the decree of the Great Spirit in a reverence beyond words or tears. Manitou had borne their most wise and just one away—surely to a happier hunting ground where there were wider plains, greater mountains, and longer trails to follow.

[2] Herbert Eugene Bolton, *Texas in the Middle Eighteenth Century* (Berkeley, 1915), 41.

A mixed congregation . . . hovered around the grave. . . .

Bibliography

No attempt has been made to list all the travel books, general histories, journals, and the like which have been read for an understanding of the background. Guide books and modern feature articles have been omitted. This is a selected list of sources.

MANUSCRIPT SOURCES

Collections

Archivo General y Público, Mexico.
Cabildo Archives, New Orleans.
Library of Congress: Paris Archives National Colonies, French transcripts.
Library of Mrs. Cammie Garrett Henry, Melrose, Louisiana.
Nacogdoches Archives, Courthouse, Nacogdoches, Texas.
Natchitoches Parish Courthouse Records, Natchitoches, Louisiana.
St. Francis Church Records, Natchitoches, Louisiana.
University of Texas Library Archives, Austin.

Individual Manuscripts

Barham, Alice Verdian. "A History of Nacogdoches, Texas" (Master's thesis, George Peabody College, 1926).
Guardia, John Edward. "Successive Human Adjustments to Raft Conditions in Lower Red River Valley" (Master's thesis, University of Chicago, 1927).
Shelby, Charmion Clair. *International Rivalry in Northeastern New Spain, 1700–1725* (Doctoral dissertation, University of Texas, 1935).

PRINTED SOURCES

Bancroft, Hubert Howe. *History of the North Mexican States and Texas.* 2 vols. San Francisco, 1886.

Baudier, Roger. *The Catholic Church in Louisiana.* New Orleans, 1939.

Belisle, John G. *History of Sabine Parish, Louisiana.* Many, La., 1912.

Bolton, Herbert Eugene. *Athanase de Mézières and the Louisiana-Texas Frontier, 1768–1770.* 2 vols. Cleveland, 1914.

———. "The Native Tribes about the East Texas Missions," Texas State Historical Association, *Quarterly,* XI (No. 4; April, 1908), 249–76.

———. *Texas in the Middle Eighteenth Century.* (University of California Publications in History. Vol. III.) Berkeley, 1915.

Bossu, N. *Travels Through that Part of North America Formerly Called Louisiana,* tr. John Reinhold Foster. 2 vols. London, 1771.

Brown, John Henry. *History of Texas, from 1685 to 1892,* . . . St. Louis [*c.* 1892–93].

Buckley, Eleanor Claire. "The Aguayo Expedition into Texas and Louisiana, 1719–1722," Texas State Historical Association, *Quarterly,* XV (No. 1; July, 1911), 1–65.

Bugbee, Lester D. "The Real Saint-Denis," Texas State Historical Association, *Quarterly,* I (No. 4; April, 1898), 266–81.

Butler, Ruth Lipham (tr.), *see* Du Ru, Paul.

Castañeda, Carlos E. *Our Catholic Heritage in Texas.* 7 vols. Austin, 1936———. Vols. I–II.

———. (tr.), *see* Morfí, Fray Juan Agustín.

Chambers, Henry E. *A History of Louisiana.* 3 vols. Chicago and New York, 1925.

Clark, Robert Carlton. *The Beginnings of Texas.* (University of Texas Bulletin No. 98, Humanistic Series No. 6) Austin, 1907.

———. "Louis Juchereau de Saint-Denis and the Re-establishment of the Tejas Missions," *Southwestern Historical Quarterly,* VI (No. 1; July, 1902), 1–26.

Coopwood, Bethel, "Concerning Saint Denis," Texas State Historical Association, *Quarterly,* II (No. 1; July, 1898), 97–98.

Cox, Isaac Joslin. "The Louisiana-Texas Frontier," Texas State Historical Association, *Quarterly,* X (No. 1; July, 1906), 1–75; XVII (No. 1; July, 1913), 1–42.

———. "The Significance of the Louisiana-Texas Frontier," Mississippi Valley Historical Association, *Proceedings,* III (1910), 198–213.

Dunn, Milton. "History of Natchitoches, Louisiana," *Louisiana Historical Quarterly*, III (January, 1920), 26–56.
Dunn, William Edward. *Spanish and French Rivalry in the Gulf Region of the United States; the Beginnings of Texas and Pensacola*. (University of Texas Bulletin No. 1705.) Austin, 1917.
Du Ru, Paul. *Journal* (February 1 to May 8, 1700), tr. Ruth Lipham Butler. Chicago, 1934.
Espinosa, Isidro Félix de. "The Espiñosa-Aguirre Expedition of 1709," tr. Gabriel Tous. Texas Catholic Historical Society, *Preliminary Studies*, I.
———. "Ramon Expedition: Espinosa's Diary of 1716," tr. Gabriel Tous. Texas Catholic Historical Society, *Preliminary Studies*, I, No. 4, April, 1930.
Foik, Paul J. (tr.), see Ramón, Domingo.
Ford, Lawrence Carroll. *The Triangular Struggle for Spanish Pensacola, 1689–1739*. (Studies in Hispanic-American History, Vol. II.) Washington, D.C., 1939.
Forrestal, Peter P. (tr.) see Peña, Juan Antonio de la.
Fortier, Alcée. *A History of Louisiana*. 4 vols. New York, 1904.
Foster, John Reinhold (tr.), see Bossu, N.
French, Benjamin F. *Historical Collection of Louisiana* . . . 5 vols. New York, 1846–1853.
Garrison, George P. *Texas*. New York, 1903.
Gayarré, Charles A. *History of Louisiana*. 4 vols. New Orleans, 1903.
Hamilton, Peter J. *Colonial Mobile*. Boston and New York, 1897.
Hackett, Charles Wilson (tr.), see Pichardo, José Antonio.
Hardin, J. Fair. *Northwestern Louisiana*. 3 vols. Louisville and Shreveport, n.d.
Hassall, Arthur. *The Balance of Power, 1715–1789*. New York and London, 1900.
Heinrich, Pierre. *La Louisiane sous la Compagnie des Indies, 1717–1731*. Paris, 1867.
Hodge, Frederick Webb (ed.). *Handbook of American Indians North of Mexico*. (Smithsonian Institution, Bureau of American Ethnology. Bulletin No. 30. 2 vols.) Washington, 1907–1910.
King, Grace. *Jean Baptist Le Moyne: Sieur de Bienville*. New York, 1892.
———. *Sieur d'Iberville*. New York, 1893.

La Harpe, Bernard de. *Journal Historique de l'établissements des Français à la Louisiane.* New Orleans and Paris, 1831.
Le Page du Pratz. *Histoire de la Louisiane* . . . 3 vols. Paris, 1758.
Margry, Pierre. *Découvertes et Établissements des Français dans l'ouest et dans le Sud de l'Amérique Septentrionale* (1614–1754). 6 vols. Paris, 1879–1888.
Martin, François Xavier. *History of Louisiana from the Earliest Period.* New Orleans, 1882.
Morfí, Fray Juan Agustín. *History of Texas, 1673–1779,* tr. (with biographical introduction and annotations) Carlos E. Castañeda. Albuquerque, N. Mex., 1935.
Murphy, Edmond Robert. *Henry De Tonty.* Baltimore, 1941.
Ogg, Frederick Austin. *The Opening of the Mississippi; a Struggle for Supremacy in the American Interior.* New York and London, 1904.
Peña, Juan Antonio de la. "Diary of the Aguayo Expedition," tr. Peter P. Forrestal. Texas Catholic Historical Society, *Preliminary Studies,* II, No. 7, January, 1935.
Pennybacker, Anna J. Hardwiche. *A New History of Texas.* Palestine, Texas, 1895.
Pichardo, José Antonio. *Pichardo's Treatise on the Limits of Louisiana and Texas,* tr. Charles Wilson Hackett. 2 vols. Austin, 1931–1934.
Portré-Bobinski, Germaine. *French Civilization and Culture in Natchitoches.* (Peabody College Bulletin, No. 310.) Nashville, 1941.
———, and Clara Mildred Smith. *Natchitoches, the Up-to-Date Oldest Town in Louisiana.* New Orleans, 1936.
Ramón, Domingo. "Captain Don Domingo Ramón's Diary of His Expedition into Texas in 1716," tr. Paul J. Foik. Texas Catholic Historical Society, *Preliminary Studies,* II, No. 5, April, 1933.
Reed, Charles Bert. *Sieur de St. Denis and Jallot, his Valet de Chambre.* Chicago, 1934.
———. *The First Great Canadian—Iberville.* Chicago, 1910.
Robertson, James Alexander. *Louisiana Under the Rule of Spain, France and the United States.* Cleveland, 1911.
Roy, Pierre-Georges. *La Famille Juchereau Duchesnay.* Quebec, 1903.
———. "Louis Juchereau de St. Denis," *Revue Canadiene,* XIX, N.S. (1917), 49–60.

BIBLIOGRAPHY 271

Schmitt, Edmond J. P. "Who was Juchereau de Saint Denis," *Texas State Historical Association, Quarterly*, I (No. 3; January, 1898), 204–15.

Shea, John Gilmary. "The Beginnings of the Capuchin Mission in Louisiana," *United States Catholic Historical Magazine*, II (1886).

———. *The Catholic Church in Colonial Days . . . 1521–1763*. New York, 1886.

Shelby, Charmion Clair. "St. Denis' Declaration Concerning Texas in 1717," *Southwestern Historical Quarterly*, XXVI (No. 3; January, 1923), 165–83.

———. "St. Denis' Second Expedition to the Rio Grande, 1716–1719," *Southwestern Historical Quarterly*, XXVII (No. 3; January, 1924), 190–216.

———. "Projected French Attacks Upon the Northeastern Frontier of New Spain, 1719–1721," *Hispanic American Historical Review*, XIII.

Smith, Clara Mildred, and Germaine Portré-Bobinski. *Natchitoches, the Up-to-Date Oldest Town in Louisiana*. New Orleans, 1936.

Stoddard, Major Amos. *Sketches Historical and Descriptive of Louisiana*. N.p., 1812.

Surrey, Nancy Maria Miller. *The Commerce of Louisiana during the French Regime, 1699–1763*. New York, 1916.

Tanquay, Cyprien. *Dictionnaire Genealogique des Familles Canadiennes*. Montreal, 1871.

Tous, Gabriel (tr.), see Espinosa, Isidro Félix.

Vogel, C. L. *The Capuchins in French Louisiana, 1722–1766*. Washington, 1928.

Watrin, Philibert Francis. "Memoir of the Louisiana Missions," *American Catholic Historical Researches*, XVII (1900), 89–93.

Yoakum, H. *History of Texas. . . 2 vols*. New York, 1855.

Index

Adaes, Los; see Los Adaes
Adaes Indians, 228
Aguado, Father Juan López, 82
Aguayo, Marquis of San Miguel de; see Azlor, José
Alabama Indians, war of, against French, 28-31
Alarcón, Martin de, governor of Texas, 114, 120-23; investigates St. Denis at San Juan Bautista, 125-31, 138
Almazán, Don Fernando Pérez de, 179-80, 186
Anya, Don Gaspardo, governor of Coahuila, 61, 65
Apache Indians, 49, 115
Arroyo Hondo, 146, 215, 235
Asinai Indians, 38, 206; St. Denis trades with, 45, 46
Azlor, José de, Marquis of San Miguel de Aguayo, 228; expedition of, to Texas, 175-81, 186, 189-92

Barr, Captain, 4
Bayogoula Indians, 32; visited by French, 10; treaty with French, 13-14; at war with neighboring tribes, 22
Beauport, 59, 260
Bernardino, chief of Asinai Indians, 46, 48
Bienville, Jean Baptiste Le Moyne, Sieur de, 34, 173; expedition of, up Mississippi, 5-18; expedition of, to Caddodaquois nation, 18-21; returns to Biloxi, 22; takes command of Fort St. John, 27; becomes governor of colony, 27; directs war against Alabamas, 29-31; in war of 1719, pp. 152-60; on "summering with the Indians," 167-68; sent against the Natchez, 195-98, 200
Biloxi, 2, 23, 41
Black River, 202

Blondel, Philippe, commandant of Natchitoches, 160-64
Boneo y Morales, Justo, governor of Texas, 264
Boundaries, 18; Franco-Spanish controversy over (1735), 215-24, 227-30, 233-35
Brazos River, 106, 173, 176
Bustillo, Juan Antonio, governor of Texas, 206-207

Caddodaquois Indians, 15, 21, 206
Cadillac, Antoine de la Mothe, Sieur, 67, 78, 111, 112, 166; as governor of Louisiana, 37-42, 146; relations of, with the Natchez, 195, 198
Camino Real, El, 109, 187, 207
Canada, 58, 260
Cane River, 182, 183
Capuchin missionaries, 243, 245, 246, 247
Champmeslin, ———, 156-59
Chandeleur Islands, 25
Chateauguay, Antoine, expedition of, up Mississippi, 5; in Pensacola campaign, 153
Chickasaw Indians, 12, 26, 31, 214
Cloutierville, La., 213
Coahuila, 65, 66
Colorado River, 47, 115
Comanche Indians, 49
Concepción, La Purísima, 177
Costales, Don Gabriel, 179-80
Courcelles, ——— De, 59
Crozat, Antoine, 78; granted commercial monopoly in Louisiana, 34-37; fails in Louisiana, 145-49

Dauphin Island, 154, 156
Davion, Father, 33
Deer Island, 1
D'herbanne, Jean, 224-27
D'Hyberville, Mme., 263
Del Toro, Joseph, 102

Denoyan, M., 262
De Soto, Hernando, 184
Diez, Father Joseph, 118-19, 136
Diron, Sieur, makes inspection of Natchitoches and Red River country, 187
Duchesnay family; see Juchereau, St. Denis
Du Ru, Father Paul, 242-43, 244; diary of, 5-10, 14

East Indies Company; see India Company
England, as threat to France, 3; Indian policy of, 12, 28, 201
Espinosa, Father Felix Isidro, 94, 95, 100, 101, 104, 105, 106, 108, 178

Foreign Missions Organization of Paris, 243
Fort Rosalie, 198, 200, 201, 202
Fort St. John, 27, 28, 69, 132, 133, 134, 138, 185; abandonment of, 34
Fort St. Louis, 165; see also, Mobile
Foucault, Father, killed by Indians, 33
France, claims of, to Louisiana, 1-3; to Texas, 40
Franquis de Lugo, Carlos Benites, governor of Texas, 229-30, 232-35

García, Lorenzo, 101
Gonzales, Joseph, lieutenant governor of Los Adaes, 217, 218-19, 220-21, 229; daughter of, elopes with Frenchman, 224-27
Gonzales, Victoria, 224-27
Grand Ecore, 43, 226
Guerra, Anna, 103
Guizoldelos, Don Juan Bautista, 141

Havana, Cuba, 153, 159
Hernandez, Alférez Francisco, 114
Hidalgo, Francisco, 46, 52, 68, 71, 72, 95, 109; writes Louisiana governor, 39
Houmas Indians, treaty of, with French, 13-14; characteristics of, 14-15

Iberville, Pierre Le Moyne, Sieur de, arrives in Louisiana, 1, 26; expedition up Mississippi, 5-18; returns to France, 26

India Company, 113, 148-49, 163, 170, 173, 182, 203, 211, 245-59, 263; is bankrupt, 194
Indians, contest for religious and political control of, 236-43; see also tribal names

Jalot, Medar, 106; accompanies St. Denis to Mexico, 46, 48, 49, 56, 57
Jesuit missionaries, 243, 245, 246, 247, 261
Juchereau, Jean, Sieur de la Ferte, uncle of St. Denis, 58
Juchereau, Jean, Sieur de Maur, grandfather of St. Denis, 57, 58
Juchereau, Noel, Sieur des Chatelets, uncle of St. Denis, 58

King William's War, 4
Koroas Indians, 33

La Chesnaye, Mme. Aubert de, 260-61
La Freniere, M. de, 262
La Harpe, Bernard de, 150-51, 163; sent to take possession of Matagorda Bay, 174-75
La Riola, Andres de, Spanish governor of Pensacola, and French at Biloxi, 23-26
Largen, Pierre, 46, 53
La Salle, Robert Cavelier, Sieur de, 7, 8, 9, 40, 174
Lavaca River, 174
Law, John, 147-50, 166
Legros, Jean, trader, 231-34
L'Epinay, 146
Linares, Duke of, Fernando de Alencastre, Noroña y Silva, 68, 76, 77
Little Sun, chief of the Natchez, 196-97
Los Adaes, Presidio Nuestra Señora del Pilar and Mission San Miguel de, 160-62, 178, 179, 183, 186-87, 189-93, 217, 218, 219; poverty at, 219-21
Louis XIV, of France, 59; grants commercial monopoly in Louisiana to Crozat, 35-37
Louisiana, early description of, 7; becomes commercial colony, 36-37; economic depression in, 145-47

INDEX

Manchac, Bayou, 5
Mandella, Antonio de la, 154, 156
Mercado, Lorenzo, 103
Mexico City, 66, 79, 119-20, 124, 142-43
Miranda, Ignacio José de, 82
Missions, in East Texas, 108 n., 113-14
Mississippi River, 3, 216; English on, 4; ascended by French party, 5-18
Mississippi River Valley, 7, 8
Mobile, 27, 41, 42, 111, 113, 133, 153, 155, 160, 164-69
Mobile Indians, in campaign with French against Alabamas, 29-30
Mobile River, 165, 166
Monclova, 65
Montmagny, Governor de, 58
Moscoso, Luis de, 184
Muñoz, Father, 125-28

Nacogdoches, Tex., 113; tradition concerning, 184
Nacogdoches County, 109
Nakasas Indians, visited by Bienville and St. Denis, 20-21
Natchez, Miss., 214; see also, Fort Rosalie
Natchez Indians, 15, 144; description of, 15-17; war of, against French, 194-98, 200-14; social customs of, 198-200
Natchitoches, La., 161, 190, 226; St. Denis in, 44, 113, 114, 144, 149-51, 176, 182, 183-86; religious controversy in, 246-47; prosperity of, 249-56
Natchitoches Indians, 43, 135; visited by Bienville and St. Denis, 20-21; removed to Bayou St. John, 34; and defense of Natchitoches, 208
Neches River, 101, 177
New Orleans, 204, 209, 216, 258, 260, 263
Nueces River, 101-102

Old Hair, Natchez chief, 200
Olivan, Don Juan de, investigates St. Denis, 131-41
Olivares, Father Antonio de San Buenaventura, 71, 120-24, 128-31, 138

Onion Creek, 115
Ouachita Indians, 20

Pelican (ship), brings women to colony, 32
Penicault, 45, 53, 93
Pensacola, Fla., 120, 152-58, 161
Perdido Bay, 157
Philip V, of Spain, 115, 146
Philippe, Duke of Orleans, 148
Philippe (ship), 155, 156
Phipps, Sir William, 59
Pontchartrain, Lake, 34
Presidio del Norte, see San Juan Bautista
Prouville de Tracy, Governor Alexandre de, 58

Quebec, 58, 132

Ramón, Captain Diego, commandant of San Juan Bautista, 50, 61, 85, 94, 117-18, 119, 122; investigated by Alarcón, 125-28
Ramón, Diego, son of Captain Diego Ramón, 54, 96, 111
Ramón, Diego, son of Domingo Ramón, 54, 107
Ramón, Domingo, son of Captain Diego Ramón, 54, 66, 114, 122, 162, 169, 228; leads expedition to Texas, 80, 81-84, 92-110
Red River, 14, 20, 22, 144, 150, 151, 185, 210, 211, 215, 226; log raft blocks, 15
Red River valley, 27, 185; description of, 43
Renaud, commandant of Natchitoches, 179-81
Renommée (ship), brings colonists to Louisiana, 1
Rio Grande River, 48, 49, 50, 68, 78, 95, 103, 161
Robeline, La., 190

Sabine River, 44, 184
St. Denis, Emanuelle, wife of St. Denis, 115-16, 247, 259-60, 264; at Mobile, 164-69; see also, Sanche de Navarro, Emanuelle
St. Denis, Louis Juchereau de, arrives in Louisiana, 1-3, 5-18; expedition of, to

St. Denis, Louis Juchereau de (*Cont.*) Caddodaquois nation, 18-22; and Natchitoches Indians, 21, 34; as explorer-ambassador among Indians, 27, 188, 252-53; in Red River country and beyond, 27; in Alabama campaign, 29-31; at Fort St. John, 31; refuses to fight against Koroas and Yazoos, 33; among Tejas Indians, 33-34; as commandant of Biloxi, 34; resigns commission, 34; expedition of, to Mexico, 41-57; early life of, 59-60; courtship of, 55, 56, 60, 62, 84-90; letter of, to Cadillac, 62-63; as prisoner, 65, 66-73; after release, 73-88; and Spanish expedition to Texas, 81, 97-109; in Mexico, 114-43; returns to Louisiana, 143; controversy about, 143; and War of 1719, pp. 152-60; made commandant of Upper Cane River, 170-71; reported organizing army against Spanish, 171-73; concerned with Aguayo expedition, 175-81; honors of, 182; made commandant of Natchitoches, 182-84; home of, 185-86; enterprises at Natchitoches, 187; dress of, 188-89; war against Natchez, 204-14; moves Natchitoches fort, 217-23; in boundary disputes, 221-23, 228-35; last days of, 257-65

St. Denis, Luisa Margarita, daughter of St. Denis, 116

St. Denis, Marie-Thérèse Giffard, mother of St. Denis, 58

St. Denis, Nicolas Juchereau de, father of St. Denis, 58, 59

St. John, Bayou, 34

Saltillo, 83, 92

San Antonio River, 48, 103, 189

San Antonio Road; *see* Camino Real, El

San Juan Bautista, 48, 52-54, 69, 84, 92, 115, 116, 125-28, 176

Sanche de Navarro, Emanuelle, 54, 55, 56, 60, 62; writes letter to high authorities on St. Denis' behalf, 66; marriage to St. Denis, 83; *see also*, St. Denis, Emanuelle

Sandoval, Manuel de, governor of Texas, 217, 228-30, 235

Sang pour Sang, Lake, 213

Santa Cruz, La, College of, 82, 118

Sauvole, M., 23; in command at Biloxi, 27

Seminary of Quebec, 243

Spanish Lake, 225-26

Tejas Indians, 39, 40, 45, 46, 68, 104, 114, 133, 135

Tejas, region of, 47, 70, 71, 76, 98, 172

Tensas Indians, 32, 185; temple struck by lightning, 17-18

Tensas River, 15

Tonikan Indians, 33

Tonti, Henry de, 33, 184-85; on lower Mississippi, 7; in Alabama campaign, 29-31; as peacemaker, 185

Trinity River, 177

Urrutia, Captain Joseph, 124

Vallejo, Father, 217, 226, 234, 264

Varona, Captain Gregorio Salinas, 116

Vitry, Pierre, 217, 226, 247

War of 1719, between France and Spain, 152-64, 169

War of Spanish Succession, 28

White Apple (village), 200, 201

White Earth, Natchez chief, 197

Yataches Indians, visited by St. Denis and Bienville, 21

Yazoo Indians, 33

Ybiricu, Fermin de, 231-34

Zúñiga, Baltasar de, the Marquis of Valero, 119

www.ingramcontent.com/pod-product-compliance
Lightning Source LLC
Chambersburg PA
CBHW031309150426
4319ICB00005B/146